iPod + iTunes Starter Kit

Brad Miser
Tim Robertson

800 East 96th Street,
Indianapolis, Indiana 46240

iPod + iTunes Starter Kit
Copyright © 2006 by Que Publishing

International Standard Book Number: 0-7897-3463-X

Non-U.S. International Standard Book Number: 0-7897-3464-8

Library of Congress Catalog Card Number: 2005929929

Printed in the United States of America

First Printing: September 2005

08   07   06   05   4   3   2   1

Trademarks

Warning and Disclaimer

Bulk Sales

Que Publishing offers excellent discounts on this book when ordered in quantity for bulk purchases or special sales. For more information, please contact

U.S. Corporate and Government Sales
1-800-382-3419
corpsales@pearsontechgroup.com

For sales outside of the U.S., please contact

International Sales
international@pearsoned.com

Associate Publisher
Greg Wiegand

Acquisitions Editor
Stephanie J. McComb

Development Editor
Kevin Howard

Managing Editor
Charlotte Clapp

Project Editor
Dan Knott

Production Editor
Heather Wilkins

Indexer
Ken Johnson

Technical Editor
Brian Hubbard

User Reviewer
Rick Ehrhardt

Publishing Coordinator
Sharry Lee Gregory

Multimedia Developer
Dan Scherf

Interior Designer
Anne Jones

Cover Designer
Dan Armstrong

Page Layout
Eric S. Miller

Contents at a Glance

Introduction 1
1 Touring the iPod 7
2 Getting Started with an iPod 17
3 Touring iTunes 35
4 Building, Browsing, Searching, and Playing Your iTunes Music Library .45
5 Labeling, Categorizing, and Configuring Your Music 79
6 Creating, Configuring, and Using Playlists 99
7 Building an iPod's Music Library 119
8 Listening to Music on an iPod, iPod Mini, or iPod Photo 141
9 Listening to Music on an iPod Shuffle 153
10 Configuring an iPod to Suit Your Preferences 159
11 Using an iPod with a Home Stereo or Car Stereo 171
12 Using the iPod for Images 183
13 Maintaining an iPod and Solving Problems 199
14 Maintaining iTunes and Solving Problems 213
15 Toys for Your iPod 221
16 Hacking the iPod 271
Index 277

Table of Contents

Introduction 1

1 Touring the iPod 7

The Apple iPod: A Lot of Hype or Really Hip? 8

So What Is an iPod Anyway? 8

All iPod Models Aren't Equal, But They Are All Cool 9
    The iPod 9
    The iPod mini 11
    The iPod shuffle 11
    Which iPod Is Right for You? 13

What You Can Do with an iPod 14

2 Getting Started with an iPod 17

Exploring the iPod's Box 18

Charging the iPod's Battery 19

Installing the iPod's Software (Including iTunes) 20
    Installing the iPod's Software on a Windows PC 20
    Installing the iPod's Software on a Macintosh 23

Connecting and Configuring an iPod on Your Computer 25
    Preparing an iPod to Connect to a Computer 25
    Connecting an iPod to a Computer 26
    Configuring an iPod on Your Computer 29

Connecting an iPod to a Computer with a Dock 32

3 Touring iTunes 35

What You Can Do with iTunes 36

Audio File Formats You Might Encounter When You Use iTunes 36
    CD Audio 37
    MP3 38
    AAC 38
    WAV 39
    AIFF 39
    Apple Lossless 39

The iTunes Music Library 40

Where Does All That Music Come From? 41

Playlists: Customizing Your Music Experience 41

The Other Members of the Band: The iPod and the iTunes
Music Store 42

4 Building, Browsing, Searching, and Playing Your iTunes
Music Library 45

Gathering Your Music from All the Right Places 46

Determining Where and How the Music Library Music Is Stored 47
    Working with the iTunes Music Folder 47
    Configuring the Location of the Music Folder 49
    Setting Other Organization Preferences 50

Understanding Encoding and Other Important Format Options 51
    Choosing a Format Option 52
    Picking Quality Levels 52
    Configuring iTunes to Import Music 53

Adding Music from Audio CDs to Your iTunes Music Library 54
    Adding Audio CDs to Your Library 55
    Building Your iTunes Music Library in a Hurry 57

Importing Audio Files into Your Library 58

Browsing and Searching Your Music Library 59
    Browsing in the Library 59
    Searching Your Music Library 62

Playing Music in Your Music Library 64

Removing Tunes from the Music Library 64

Subscribing and Listening to Podcasts 66
    Setting Your Podcast Preferences 66
    Subscribing to Podcasts 68
    Listening to and Managing Podcasts 74

5   Labeling, Categorizing, and Configuring Your Music **79**

**Understanding Song Tags and Knowing Why You Should Care
About Them** **80**

Viewing Song Information **82**
   Viewing Tags in the Browser 82
   Viewing Tags in the Content Pane 82
   Viewing Tags in the Info Window 83

Labeling Your Music **85**
   Labeling a Song in the Info Window 85
   Labeling Multiple Songs at the Same Time 85
   Labeling a Song in the Content Pane 87

Configuring a Song's Options **87**
   Configuring Song Options in the Info Window 88
   Rating Songs in the Content Pane 89

Adding and Viewing Album Artwork **90**
   Viewing Album Artwork 90
   Adding Artwork for Songs 92

Customizing the Content Pane **95**

6   Creating, Configuring, and Using Playlists **99**

Understanding Playlists **100**
   The Standard-But-Very-Useful Playlist 100
   The Extra-Special Smart Playlist 101

Building and Listening to Standard Playlists **102**
   Creating a Standard Playlist 102
   Adding Songs to a Playlist 105
   Removing Songs from a Playlist 106
   Setting the Order in Which a Playlist's Songs Play 106
   Listening to a Standard Playlist 107
   Deleting a Standard Playlist 107

Becoming a Musical Genius with Smart Playlists **107**
   Understanding Why Smart Playlists Are Called Smart 108
   Creating a Smart Playlist 108
   Listening to a Smart Playlist 114
   Changing a Smart Playlist 114

Doing the Party Shuffle **115**

7   Building an iPod's Music Library..............................**119**

Creating an iTunes Music Library **120**
Building an iTunes Music Library 120
Creating iTunes Playlists...................................120

Assessing the Size of Your iTunes Library and How Much Disk Space Your iPod Has..**121**
Determining the Size of Your iTunes Library 121
Determining How Much Storage Space You Have on an iPod 121

Understanding and Configuring iPod Synchronization Options **123**
Understanding Your Synchronization Options...................123
Understanding How iTunes Updates Playlists on the iPod.............125
Configuring iTunes to Automatically Update All Songs and Playlists 126
Configuring iTunes to Automatically Update Selected Playlists 128
Configuring iTunes So You Can Manually Manage Songs and Playlists 130

Updating Specific Songs and Playlists Automatically **131**

Manually Updating an iPod **131**

Adding Music to an iPod shuffle **134**
Configuring an iPod shuffle................................134
Using Autofill to Put Music on an iPod shuffle 136
Manually Adding Songs to an iPod shuffle 138
Removing Songs from an iPod shuffle 139

8   Listening to Music on an iPod or iPod mini **141**

Selecting Music You Want to Listen To **142**
Selecting Music with Playlists...............................142
Browsing Your iPod's Music.................................143

Controlling Your Music...................................**146**
Playing the Basic Way 146
Playing the iPod Way......................................147

Creating and Using an iPod On-The-Go Playlist...................**150**

Monitoring an iPod's Battery **151**

9   Listening to Music on an iPod shuffle **153**

Getting Ready to Play......................................**154**

Turning On, Controlling, and Turning Off an iPod shuffle............**155**
Turning On a shuffle and Choosing How Music Will Play.............155
Using the iPod shuffle's Playback Controls 155
Turning Off an iPod shuffle 156

Putting an iPod shuffle on Hold. 157

Monitoring an iPod shuffle's Battery 157

10 Configuring an iPod to Suit Your Preferences 159

Configuring Music Playback. 160
Shuffling Music. 160
Repeating Music 162
Using Sound Check. 163
Using the iPod's Equalizer 164

Setting Up Your Main Menu Preferences. 165

Setting the Screen's Contrast 166

Setting the Sleep Timer 167

Configuring the Clicker. 168

Working with the iPod's Language 168

Returning an iPod to That Factory-Fresh Feeling. 169

11 Using an iPod with a Home Stereo or Car Stereo 171

Using an iPod with a Home Stereo 172
Hard-Wiring an iPod to a Home Stereo 172
Broadcasting iPod Music over FM. 175
Playing an iPod over a Home Stereo System 175

Using an iPod As a Portable Home Stereo or Boombox 176

Using an iPod with a Car Stereo 177
Getting Sound from an iPod to a Car Stereo. 177
Powering and Charging an iPod While You Are on the Road 179
Mounting an iPod in Your Car. 179
Controlling an iPod While You Are on the Road 180

12 Using the iPod for Images 183

iPods and Photos 184

Moving Pictures onto an iPod 184
Using an Application to Move Pictures from a Computer onto an iPod. . . . 184
Moving Image Files from a Computer onto an iPod. 186
Moving Photos from a Digital Camera onto an iPod 187

Viewing Photos on an iPod 189

Viewing Slideshows on an iPod. **191**
   Setting Up an iPod Slideshow 191
   Playing an iPod Slideshow 192

Using an iPod to Display Slideshows on a TV **193**

Moving Photos from an iPod onto a Computer. **195**
   Using an Application to Move Photos from an iPod onto a Computer 195
   Manually Moving Files from an iPod to a Computer 196

13   Maintaining an iPod and Solving Problems. **199**

Maintaining Your iPod's Power **200**
   Monitoring and Maximizing Battery Life. 200
   Charging an iPod's Battery. 202
   Getting More Life Out of an iPod's Battery 203
   Solving Battery Problems 204

Updating or Restoring an iPod's Software. **205**

Identifying and Solving iPod Problems **207**
   Solving iPod Problems 208
   Getting Help with iPod Problems 210

14   Maintaining iTunes and Solving Problems. **213**

Keeping iTunes Up-to-date. **214**
   Keeping iTunes Up-to-date on Any Computer Automatically 214
   Keeping iTunes Up-to-date on a Windows PC Manually 215
   Keeping iTunes Up-to-date on a Macintosh 215

Backing Up Your iTunes Music Library **216**

Solving iTunes Problems. **216**
   Solving the Missing Song File Problem 216
   Getting Help with iTunes Problems. 218

15   Toys for Your iPod **221**

Headphones **222**
   Apple Headphones 222
   Shure—www.shure.com 222
   Bose—www.bose.com 223
   Sennheiser—www.sennheiserusa.com 224
   Sony—www.sony.com. 224
   Koss—www.koss.com 225
   Ultimate Ears—www.ultimateears.com 226
   Nike Phillips—www.nike-philips.com 226
   Bang & Olufsen—www.bang-olufsen.com 226

Wireless Headphones **227**
   BlueTake i-Phono BT420—www.bluetake.com 227
   Macally Bluewave Headphone—www.macally.com 227

iPod Speakers **228**
   inMotion Portable iPod Speakers 228
   Ezison Personal Speakers for iPod 229
   Sony SRS-T55 Folding Travel Speaker 229
   iPod Groove Bag Triplet and Tote 229
   iPal Portable Speaker with Tuner 230
   Cube Travel Speakers 230
   Bose SoundDock 230
   JBL On Stage 231
   JBL On Tour Portable Speakers 231
   Monster iSpeaker Portable 232
   Macally IceTune Speakers 232
   Macally PodWave 233
   DLO iBoom Speakers 233
   PocketParty shuffle 234

iPod in Your Car **235**
   Sony CPA-9C Car Cassette Adapter 235
   The Belkin TuneCast II Mobile FM Transmitter 235
   Griffin iTrip 236
   Monster iCarPlay Wireless 236
   AirPlay for iPod shuffle 237
   Auto Chargers 237
   iPod Automobile Mounting Kits 238

Voice Recorders **239**
   Belkin Voice Recorder for iPod 239
   Griffin Technology iTalk 240
   Belkin Universal Microphone Adapter 240
   DLO VoiceNote Voice Recorder 240

Digital Camera Adapters **241**
   Belkin iPod Media Reader 241
   Belkin Digital Camera Link 241
   Apple iPod Camera Connector 242

Apple World Travel Adapter Kit **242**

iPod Remote Controls **243**
   ABT iJet Wireless RF Remote 243
   Griffin AirClick 244
   DLO iDirect Wireless Remote 244
   Nyko iTop Button Relocator 244

iPod Polishing Kits **245**
   iCleaner Ultra Pro Kit 245
   Ice Crème. 245

iPod Stands, Docks, and Cradles **246**
   Habitat. 246
   ModPod. 247
   PodHolder 247
   PodBoard 247
   Apple iPod shuffle Dock 248
   Belkin USB 2.0 4-Port Hub for iPod shuffle 248
   Apple iPod Dock (iPod and iPod mini) 248
   Westshore Craftworks iDockCover. 249
   Solio Solar Charger. 249

iPod Cases. **250**
   Sheldon iPod Case 250
   Speck iPod Skins. 250
   Speck iStyle 250
   Belkin Leather Flip Case. 251
   MARWARE Sportsuit Convertible Case 251
   MARWARE SportSuit Safari 251
   MARWARE 3G SportSuit Convertible 251
   PodSleevz/mini Sleevz 252
   Gucci iPod Case 252
   TimBuk2 iPod Case. 252
   Anetagenova iPod Case 252
   PodPaqnappa. 253
   Apple iPod Socks 253
   Bumperz for iPod shuffle. 253
   TuffWrapz 254
   Apple iPod shuffle Sports Case 254
   Burton Shield iPod Jacket 254

iPod Stickers and Film. **254**
   Skin EFX iPod Stickers 255
   HP Printable Tattoos 255
   Mobile Juice shuffle Art. 255

CD-ROM Contents. **255**
   Freeware 256
   Shareware 256
   Commercial Software 256

16 Hacking the iPod **271**

Replacing Your iPod Battery **272**

Battery Replacement—First and Second Generation iPod **272**
   Tools Required 272

Battery Replacement—Third and Fourth Generation iPod **273**
   Tools Required 273

Battery Replacement—iPod Mini **275**
   Tools Required 275
   iPod Shuffle 276

Index **277**

About the Author

Brad Miser has written many books about computers and related technology, with his favorite topics being anything that starts with a lower case *i*, such as the iPod and iTunes. In addition to *Absolute Beginner's Guide to iPod and iTunes, Second Edition*, Brad has written *Special Edition Using Mac OS X, Tiger*; *Special Edition Using Mac OS X, v10.3 Panther*; *Absolute Beginner's Guide to iPod and iTunes*; *Absolute Beginner's Guide to Homeschooling*; *Mac OS X and iLife: Using iTunes, iPhoto, iMovie, and iDVD*; *iDVD 3 Fast & Easy*; *Special Edition Using Mac OS X v10.2*; and *Using Mac OS 8.5*. He has also been an author, a development editor, or a technical editor on more than 50 other titles. He has been a featured speaker on various topics at Macworld Expo, at user group meetings, and in other venues.

Brad is the senior technical communicator for an Indianapolis-based software development company. Brad is responsible for all product documentation, training materials, online help, and other communication materials. He also manages the customer support operations for the company and provides training and account management services to its customers. Previously, he was the lead engineering proposal specialist for an aircraft engine manufacturer, a development editor for a computer book publisher, and a civilian aviation test officer/engineer for the U.S. Army. Brad holds a Bachelor of Science degree in mechanical engineering from California Polytechnic State University at San Luis Obispo (1986) and has received advanced education in maintainability engineering, business, and other topics.

In addition to his passion for technology, Brad likes to ride his motorcycle, run, and play racquetball; playing with home theater technology is also a favorite pastime.

Once a native of California, Brad now lives in Brownsburg, Indiana, with his wife Amy; their three daughters, Jill, Emily, and Grace; a guinea pig named Buddy; and a rabbit named Bun-Bun.

Brad would love to hear about your experiences with this book (the good, the bad, and the ugly). You can write to him at bradmacosx@mac.com.

Tim Robertson has been publishing MyMac.com for a decade. He spends much of his time at MyMac.com looking for new writers and other talent, as well as editing all site content before publication. He also evaluates new programs and hardware for product review. Married and the father of three daughters, Tim spends most of his working hours in front of the Mac, pretending to write articles, reviews, or editing others, when in actuality he is probably surfing eBay or playing with iTunes. He has also been the focus and guest of computer-related radio talk shows in New York, Boston, San Francisco, and Los Angeles, as well as being part of Internet-based broadcasts. He has been interviewed for his opinion on Apple and the computer world in general. He is also the host of the weekly MyMac.com Podcast with Chad Perry, found both at the MyMac.com website as well as the iTunes Music Store Podcasting section.

Dedication

From Brad:

I leave you, hoping that the lamp of liberty will burn in your bosoms until there shall no longer be a doubt that all men are created free and equal.

—Abraham Lincoln

From Tim:

My contribution to this book is dedicated to my wife, Julie, and our three kids, Raechel, Brooke, and Brittaney. Also thanks to my parents, Tom and Diane, for believing in me.

Acknowledgments

To the following people on the *iPod + iTunes Starter Kit* project team, my sincere appreciation for your hard work on this book:

Stephanie McComb, my acquisitions editor, who made this project possible and convinced the right people that this was a good idea and that I was the right one to write it. **Marta Justak** of Justak Literary Services, my agent, for getting me signed up for this project and providing advice and encouragement along the way. **Kevin Howard**, my development editor, who helped make the contents and organization of this book much better. **Rick Ehrhardt**, my user reviewer, who made the jump to an iPod and iTunes at just the right time and provided lots of invaluable feedback that made this book much better.

Brian Hubbard, my technical editor, who did a great job ensuring that the information in this book is both accurate and useful. **Heather Wilkins**, my production editor, who corrected my many misspellings, poor grammar, and other problems. **Dan Knott**, my project editor, who skillfully managed the hundreds of files that it took to make this book into something real. **Que's production and sales team** for printing the book and getting it into your hands.

And now for some people who weren't on the project team but who were essential to me personally. **Amy Miser**, my wonderful wife, for supporting me while I wrote this book; living with an author under tight deadlines isn't always lots of fun, but Amy does so with grace, understanding, and acceptance of my need to write. **Jill, Emily**, and **Grace Miser**, my delightful daughters, for helping me stay focused on what is important in life. While an iPod can play beautiful music, these precious people are beautiful music given form! (And, a special thanks to **Buddy** the guinea pig and **Bun-Bun** the rabbit for their early-morning visits to cheer me up while I was working!)

From Tim:

I want to thank the great folks at Que publishing, particularly **Stephanie McComb** and **Kevin Howard**, for their understanding and patience, as well as guiding me in this endeavor.

We Want to Hear from You!

As the reader of this book, *you* are our most important critic and commentator. We value your opinion and want to know what we're doing right, what we could do better, what areas you'd like to see us publish in, and any other words of wisdom you're willing to pass our way.

As an associate publisher for Que Publishing, I welcome your comments. You can email or write me directly to let me know what you did or didn't like about this book—as well as what we can do to make our books better.

Please note that I cannot help you with technical problems related to the topic of this book. We do have a User Services group, however, where I will forward specific technical questions related to the book.

When you write, please be sure to include this book's title and author as well as your name, email address, and phone number. I will carefully review your comments and share them with the author and editors who worked on the book.

Email: feedback@quepublishing.com

Mail: Greg Wiegand
            Associate Publisher
            Que Publishing
            800 East 96th Street
            Indianapolis, IN 46240 USA

For more information about this book or another Que Publishing title, visit our website at www.quepublishing.com. Type the ISBN (excluding hyphens) or the title of a book in the Search field to find the page you're looking for.

Introduction

If you have been toying with the idea of getting into digital music.... If you have an iPod and aren't sure what to do with it.... If you wish you had a good way to stop messing around with a bunch of CDs when you want to listen to music.... If you've heard great things about iPods, have seen the commercials for the iTunes Music Store, and want to know what all the fuss is about, then welcome to the *iPod + iTunes Starter Kit*!

Meet the Digital Music Triumvirate

In this book, you'll learn about three of the most amazing things to happen to music and digital photos since the first time someone decided that banging a stick on a rock had an appealing sound. These are the iPod, iTunes, and the iTunes Music Store.

The iPod Rocks

Apple's iPod has taken the portable digital device market by storm—and for good reason. Because three of the iPods include a hard drive with up to 60GB of space, it is possible for you to take your music collection wherever you go. The iPod's tools enable you to organize, customize, and listen to your music in many ways while you are on the move—in your car, at home, or working at your computer. With its tight integration with iTunes and the iTunes Music Store, managing your music is both fun and easy. Your trusty iPod can also be used as a portable drive (for example, you can use it to carry files from your home to your office), to capture sound, and to store pictures; there are numerous peripheral devices that expand its amazing capabilities even further. And, iPods are just plain cool (see Figure I.1).

If you have never used an iPod before, this book is perfect for you and will help you learn everything you need to know. If you have some experience with an iPod, this book will still help you take your iPod skills to the next level.

iTunes Jams

With iTunes, you can create, organize, and listen to your entire music library from your computer (see Figure I.2). iTunes enables you to build as large a Library as you have space on your computer's hard drive to store it. Then, you can customize music playback through playlists and smart playlists as well as create custom audio CDs in a variety of formats. It also provides other useful features, such as custom labeling and information tools, the ability to share your music on a local network, an Equalizer, and more. Because Apple's iTunes Music Store is integrated into iTunes, you can easily purchase and add music to your Library from within the application. Moreover, iTunes is the best software tool available to manage music on your iPod.

FIGURE I.1
Whatever iPod
model you
choose will rock
your world.

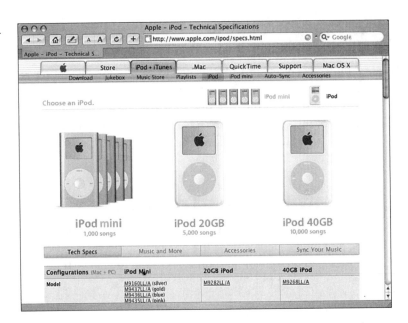

FIGURE I.2
iTunes will
change the way
you listen to
music.

Just as with the iPod, if you have never used iTunes before, this book is perfect for
you and will help you learn everything you need to know. If you have some experience, my hope is that you will learn how to get even more out of this outstanding
program. Even if you have used iTunes quite a bit, you might manage to find some
tidbits that will help your iTunes expertise grow.

iTunes Music Store

Using the iTunes Music Store, you can find, preview, and purchase music from a collection of hundreds of thousands of songs and download that music into your iTunes Music Library. Songs can be purchased individually or in albums, for $.99 per song (less when purchasing an entire album). Music you buy can be listened to, placed on a CD, and moved onto your iPod. Since its inception, the iTunes Music Store has rapidly become the most popular source of legal digital music on the Internet. After you have used it a time or two, you'll understand why.

Quick Guide to *iPod + iTunes Starter Kit*

iPod + iTunes Starter Kit provides all the information you need to get the most out of these amazing digital music tools. From the basics of listening to audio CDs with iTunes to the advanced customizing of music on an iPod and purchasing music online, this book equips you with the information you need.

This book contains many step-by-step instructions—I hope your motto will be "learn by doing." You should be able to learn how to do a task fairly quickly and relatively painlessly by following the steps using your own music and your own tools. Although my writing is so utterly fascinating that you will likely want to read this book like a good novel, try to resist that urge because you will probably get better results if you actually work with the tools while you read this book.

Going Both Ways

Because the iPod, iTunes, and the iTunes Music Store all work equally well on both Windows and Macintosh computers, this book covers these topics from both perspectives. So, you'll notice that some of the figures are screenshots taken on a Windows computer whereas others are taken on a Macintosh. Although the screens on these two computers look slightly different, they work very similarly, so seeing a screen on the Mac shouldn't cause a problem for you if you use a Windows computer, and vice versa. When there are significant differences between the two platforms, I explain them in the text.

Special Elements

As you read, you will see three special elements: Notes, Tips, and, only rarely, Cautions. Also, each chapter ends with a section titled "The Absolute Minimum." Explanations of each of these are provided for you here.

note

Notes look like this. They are designed to provide you with information that is related to the topic at hand but not absolutely essential to it. I hope you will find the Notes interesting, even if you don't find them immediately useful.

caution

If something you can do (and probably shouldn't) might end in a bad result, I warn you in a Caution. Fortunately, you won't find many of these throughout the book, but when you do see one, you might want to take a close look at it.

tip

Tips help you get something done more quickly and easily, or they tell you how to do a task that is related to what's being described at the moment. You might also find an explanation of an alternate way to get something done.

The Absolute Minimum

Finally, each chapter ends with "The Absolute Minimum" section. The contents of this section vary a bit from chapter to chapter. Examples of this content include the following:

- A summary of the key points of the chapter.
- Additional tips related to the chapter's topic.
- References to sources of additional information.

So, now that you know all you need to about this book, it's time to strike up the band....

In THIS CHAPTER

- Understand why the iPod is more hip than hype.
- Get an overview of what makes an iPod an iPod.
- Meet the iPods.
- Learn what you can do with an iPod.

Touring the iPod

Apple's iPod has become one of the most popular personal digital devices ever created. When initially released, the iPod's critics said it was too expensive when compared to other digital music players and that people would never spend the additional money to get the iPod's much superior functionality and style (even the critics couldn't deny the iPod's amazing attributes). As they often are, the critics were very much mistaken. People who love music love the iPod. Its combination of features and style, and because it's simply very, very cool, led it to quickly dominate sales in its category. And with continuous improvements in features and a variety of models from which to choose, the iPod won't be slowing down any time soon.

The Apple iPod: A Lot of Hype or Really Hip?

So, what's the iPod all about?

It's about being able to take your entire music collection with you and listen to anything you want when you want to listen to it. And, using iPod's companion iTunes software, you can create and carry customized collections of your music to make getting to the specific music you want to hear even easier and more fun.

The way your music sounds on an iPod is just amazing, too. You definitely don't have to compromise music quality for portability. With the iPod, you get the best of both. If you have never heard music on an iPod before, prepare to be amazed.

That's the bottom line, but it isn't the whole story. With the iPod, you can do much more, as you will learn through the rest of this part of this book. And because of the iPod's stylish design and ease of use, you will likely want to take it with you wherever you go.

So What Is an iPod Anyway?

The iPod is a small digital device that includes memory (most models include a hard drive just like the one in your computer, only smaller), an operating system, a processor and other computer components, as well as an LCD screen (all models except the iPod shuffle), controls, and other system elements needed to deliver its amazing functionality. It also includes a rechargeable lithium battery to give you plenty of listening time, a Headphones port to which you attach audio devices (including headphones, powered speakers, and so on), and a Dock port or USB connector to enable you to move music from a computer onto the iPod and recharge its battery.

The iPod's software enables you to manage and play digital audio files. You can also use its software to set a variety of preferences, in addition to using the iPod's other built-in tools.

Even with all this, iPods are quite small. The largest iPod is only 2.4 inches wide, is 4.1 inches tall, is .75 inches thick, and weighs a mere 6.4 ounces. This is roughly the size of a deck of playing cards. The smallest model, the iPod shuffle, comes in at a svelte 0.98 inches

> **note**
>
> iPods can work with a variety of audio file formats, including AAC, MP3, Audible books, AIFF (Mac only), and WAV. Because you just listen to these formats on an iPod, you don't need to know that much about them to use one. However, you will want to understand these formats when you prepare music for an iPod using iTunes. If you can't wait to learn what these formats are all about, see "Audio File Formats You Might Encounter When You Use iTunes" on page **36**.

wide, 3.3 inches tall, 0.33 inches thick, and a mere 0.78 ounces, which is about the size of a pack of chewing gum.

All iPod Models Aren't Equal, But They Are All Cool

iPods come in four basic models: iPod, iPod U2, iPod mini, and iPod shuffle. All these models are definitely cool, and all perform the same basic function, which is to enable you to listen to music whenever and wherever. However, each offers specific features and options, as you will see in the following sections.

Before we get into the details of each model, let me warn you that just like the times, the iPod is a changin'. The models listed and described in this chapter are the ones available at press time. Apple regularly makes changes to existing models and introduces new models. The good news is that, even if you use a model that isn't specifically described in this chapter, the information in this book will still help you because in many ways, to know one iPod is to know them all. The controls and options might vary a bit, but most functionality is quite similar, regardless of model.

note

To get the scoop on the iPod models available right now, go to http://www. apple.com/ipod.

The iPod

The iPod is the "standard" iPod, although that word seems to imply that it is less than it really is (see Figure 1.1). The iPod offers many great features in a cool package that you will be proud to carry with you anywhere you go. In addition to your music, you can use an iPod to store your digital images and then display them on its screen or on a TV through its AV port. Because it's designed for more data, this model offers the largest hard drives.

note

With the optional iPod Camera Connector, you can connect a digital camera to your iPod and download images from the camera to the iPod.

FIGURE 1.1
The iPod will definitely rock your world.

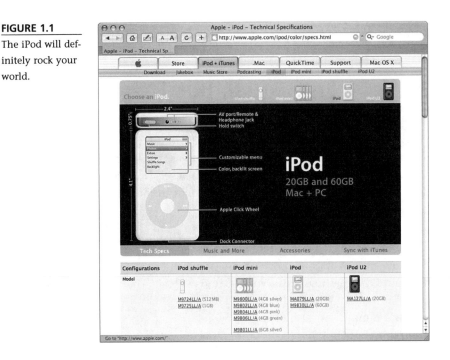

At press time, the iPod's specifications were the following:

- A 20GB hard rated for 5,000 songs or a 60GB drive rated for 15,000 songs

- A battery rated for up to 15 hours of music playing time or up to 5 hours of slideshows with music

- A 2-inch color LCD screen

- Dock Connector, Remote Connector, and Headphone/Composite AV ports

- Dimensions of 4.1 inches by 2.4 inches by 0.63 inches and a weight of 5.9 ounces for the 20GB model or 4.1 inches by 2.4 inches by 0.75 inches and a weight of 6.4 ounces for the 60GB model

- Accessories including earbud headphones, an AC adapter, and a USB 2 cable

- A price of $299 for the 20GB model or $399 for the 60GB model

note

There is also the iPod U2 Special Edition, which is the same as the 20GB iPod in features but has a black and red case and features the signatures of U2 band members engraved on the back; it costs $329. Because it is functionally the same as the 20GB iPod, I won't mention it as a distinct model again in this book outside of this chapter.

The iPod mini

The iPod mini is smaller than an iPod (which you can probably guess from its name). Its other major characteristic is that it comes in a variety of colors (see Figure 1.2).

FIGURE 1.2

With an iPod mini, you can listen to music and make a fashion statement at the same time.

At press time, the iPod's mini offered the following:

- A 4GB hard rated for 1,000 songs or a 6GB drive rated for 1,500 songs
- A battery rated for up to 18 hours of playing time
- A choice of colors including silver, blue, pink, and green
- A 1.67-inch grayscale LCD screen
- Dock Connector, Remote Connector, and Headphone ports
- Dimensions of 3.6 inches by 2.0 inches by 0.5 inches and a weight of 3.6 ounces
- Accessories including earbud headphones, a belt clip, and a USB 2 cable
- A price of $199 for the 4GB model or $249 for the 6GB model

The iPod shuffle

Of all the iPod models and variants, the iPod shuffle is the "most" in many ways (see Figure 1.3). It is the most different from the technical point of view because it does not have a hard drive but instead uses a flash drive to store your music. The benefit to this is that it has no moving parts and will never skip, along with being even more resistant to damage. This also means it uses much less power and so can play the same amount of time with a smaller battery. The downside is that it can store much less music than any of the other models. The shuffle is the most "small" model and is less than half the size of even the iPod mini. The flipside to this is that the shuffle has no screen so you can't see information about the music you are playing or even select what you want to hear. The shuffle also uses the most different interface with your computer in that you plug it directly into a USB port. Finally, the shuffle is the most cost-efficient model.

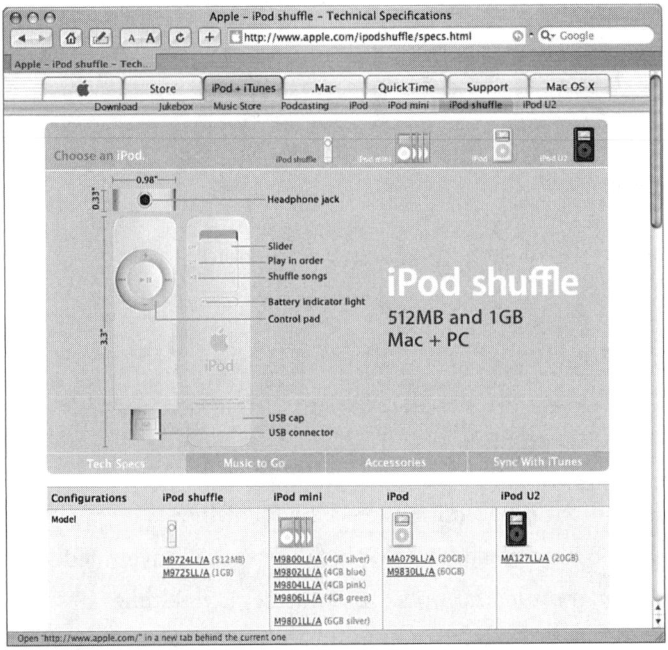

FIGURE 1.3

The iPod shuffle looks quite different from the other iPod models because it is very different from them.

The following is the skinny on this skinniest of iPod models:

- 512MB of memory rated for 120 songs or 1GB of memory rated for 240 songs
- A battery rated for up to 12 hours of music playing time
- USB connector and Headphone port
- Dimensions of 3.3 inches by 0.98 inches by 0.33 inches and a weight of 0.78 ounces
- Accessories including earbud headphones, a lanyard, and a cap for the USB connector
- A price of $99 for the 512MB model or $149 for the 1GB model

Which iPod Is Right for You?

If you already have an iPod and don't envision buying another one, you can skip to the next section. Otherwise, read on for some general guidance on choosing an iPod model.

One of the most frequent questions I get asked is, "Which iPod should I buy?" Unfortunately for me, this is also one of the hardest questions I get asked. That's because each model offers features and benefits that the others don't. And, of course, each costs a different price. There is never a clear-cut answer to this question, unless you can afford to spend only $99, in which case your only choice is the 512MB iPod shuffle (which isn't a bad choice, by the way).

Like all electronic devices, choosing an iPod is a matter of balancing features and options against cost. While I can't address your individual choice, I can provide some general guidance because each model does offer some distinct benefits.

note

Throughout this book, when I write about a specific model, such as an iPod mini, I will mention the model name. Otherwise, I use the term *iPod* to refer to all models. Because the shuffle is an iPod of a different feather altogether, you'll often see it excepted in generic iPod references (as in, *except the shuffle*). Confused? Hopefully you won't be as you get further into this.

If you have a digital camera and often find yourself running out of room for your photos on its memory card, an iPod can be a perfect companion for you. With an adapter, you can move photos from the camera onto the iPod and then erase your camera's card so you can take more pictures. Later, you can move the photos from the iPod onto your computer. Plus, you can view your pictures on the iPod and display them on a TV. And, the iPod offers larger disk drives, which benefits both music and photo storage. The only downside to the iPod is its price, although the 20GB model is only $50 more than the 6GB iPod mini and you get 14GB of additional disk space plus the color screen. The 60GB iPod is only $100 more than the 20GB model; you'll find that additional 40GB of space useful if you have lots of music and photos.

If the iPod's color is important to you or if you want a smaller iPod without the significant storage limitations of the shuffle, the iPod mini is your choice. The color and smaller size do come with a price, though. After a time, you'll probably find the 4GB or 6GB drive size to be a bit limiting unless you don't have a very large music collection. For $100 more than the 4GB mini or $50 more than the 6GB mini, you can get an iPod that offers 14GB more room plus a larger screen.

If you are going to be using an iPod under "extreme" conditions, such as during heavy exercise, sporting activities, or work situations, an iPod shuffle is a good choice because this model is much more resistant to damage than the other models and, with its lower cost, you are risking less by using it in these situations. Plus, it is very small so carrying it is definitely the easiest.

So, what is the bottom line? There isn't one. All iPods are a good choice. Some will fit your needs and budget better than others, but you really can't go wrong with any of them. Pick the most you can afford to spend and then get the model that fits your budget and specific needs.

What You Can Do with an iPod

The iPod is definitely a great music player, but it is much more than that, as you will learn throughout this part of the book. For now, here are just some of the great things you can do with an iPod:

- Take your entire music collection, or at least part of it, with you wherever you go.

- Play your music in many different ways, such as by album, artist, genre, song, playlist, and so on.

- Eliminate the need to carry CDs with you anywhere; using an adapter or an FM transmitter, your iPod can provide music in your home, car, or any other place you happen to be.

- View your calendar.

- Access contact information for your favorite people and companies for quick and easy reference.

- Keep track of the time and date and have a portable alarm clock.

- Listen to your favorite audio book.

- Listen to podcasts.

- Transfer information between computers or back up your important files.

- Record sound.

- Store pictures from a digital camera.

- View pictures and slideshows and play the same on a TV (iPod or iPod U2 Special Edition).

note

When choosing an iPod, consider buying more than one if your budget can support it. For example, if you have a $500 budget, you could get the 60GB iPod for general listening and photos and the 512MB iPod shuffle for exercising. This would be a great combination for most people.

note

Additional accessories are required to perform some of the tasks on this list. And not all models (most notably the shuffle) can do all of them. The shuffle is limited to only playing music (which is, of course, the primary reason to have an iPod in the first place).

The Absolute Minimum

The iPod just might be the neatest gadget ever. After you have tried one, you will likely find it to be indispensable, and you might wonder how you ever got along without it. Before we jump into configuring and using an iPod, consider the following points:

- An iPod enables you to take your music with you and listen to it any time, anywhere.

- The iPod is actually a mini computer and includes a hard drive or flash memory, an operating system, and other computer components.

- There were four types of iPods in production at press time: iPod, iPod U2 Special Edition, iPod mini, and iPod shuffle. There are also variants of all models except the iPod U2 Special Edition, such as the 512MB or 1GB iPod shuffle.

- No matter which iPod you have, you'll be amazed at all the cool things it can do from listening to music to being your own personal portable hard drive (all models except shuffle) or flash drive (shuffle).

- Current iPod models work just as well for Windows and Macintosh computers. Whether you use a Windows computer, a Mac, or both, your iPod will work great.

- Like potato chips, I'll bet you can't get by with just one iPod. After you use one model, you'll probably want to get at least one more for yourself. For example, if you have an iPod, you might want to get a shuffle for those times when device size is important. Or, if you have a mini, you might want to a get an iPod so you can download photos from a digital camera to it. And if you have a family, expect to also need a family of iPods!

IN THIS CHAPTER

- Find out what good stuff came with your iPod.
- Charge the iPod's battery.
- Install the iPod's software on your computer.
- Connect the iPod to your computer and transfer music from your computer to it.
- Use a Dock to connect an iPod to your computer.

Getting Started with an iPod

Getting started with an iPod involves the following general steps:

1. Understand what is included with your iPod.
2. Charge the iPod's battery.
3. Install the iPod's software on your computer.
4. Connect the iPod to your computer and transfer music from your iTunes Library to the iPod.
5. Disconnect the iPod from your computer.

After you have performed these steps, you will be ready to learn how to use the iPod, which you'll start doing in the next chapter.

As you learned in the last chapter, there are three basic models of iPod. Considering iPods work with both Windows and Macintosh computers and how many models and variations of those there are, covering all possible combinations of iPod and computer just isn't possible. So, what I have done instead is to provide general guidelines to help you accomplish the basic tasks you need to do to get your iPod rolling (and rocking). You probably won't need to read every section in this chapter unless you use several kinds of iPods on both types of computers. Use the headings to determine which circumstances apply to you, and skip those sections that don't apply.

Exploring the iPod's Box

The iPod is so cool that even its box is stylish! In this section, you'll learn about the items included in that stylish box and how and where you use them. What you get with an iPod depends on the type and model of iPod you purchased. The following list gives you a general idea of what comes with each type of iPod:

- **The iPod**—You probably didn't need this item listed, but I like to be thorough!

- **Installation CD**—This CD contains the installer applications you will use to install the iPod's software on your computer.

- **Earbud headphones**—You can use these to listen to your iPod's music. The sound quality of the earbuds included with your iPod is remarkably good.

- **USB 2 cable**—All models except the shuffle include the cable you use to connect the iPod to a computer.

- **AC adapter**—Some models include an AC adapter you can use to power the iPod and charge its battery from a wall outlet.

- **Information pamphlets**—These provide basic information you can use to get started with your iPod. (Because you have

tip

As you are handling the iPod, it will turn on if you press any control. For now, turn it off again by pressing and the holding down the **Play/Pause** button until the iPod shuts off again. If you have a shuffle, ignore this because it doesn't apply.

tip

If you use an older Macintosh that doesn't support USB 2 devices, you'll need to purchase the Apple iPod Dock Connector to FireWire Cable. You can obtain this cable at the online Apple Store for $19. Even if your Mac does support USB 2, you might want to use FireWire instead because you probably have more USB peripherals than you have available USB ports.

this book already, you might not find these to be very useful.)

■ **Accessories**—Different iPod models purchased at different times will have different accessories included (did I use *different* in this sentence enough?). For example, the shuffle comes with a lanyard so you can wear it around your neck, while a mini includes a belt clip.

Charging the iPod's Battery

Like all portable electronic devices, the iPod has an internal battery. If your iPod came with an AC adapter, you should charge its battery before you start using it.

note

No matter which iPod you have, it is likely you'll want to get some accessories for it, such as a case, an FM transmitter, and so on. You'll learn about some of the more useful accessories later in this part of the book.

If your iPod didn't include an AC adapter, such as the iPod shuffle, skip to the next section. You'll charge its battery when you connect it to your computer.

To charge an iPod using its AC adapter, connect the USB 2 to iPod Dock connector cable to the AC adapter (USB end) and to the iPod (the larger end with the Dock connector). Then plug the power adapter into a power outlet.

When you plug the AC adapter into a wall outlet, the iPod will start up; you can tell this because an Apple logo will appear on its screen. The first time you start an iPod, a language menu will appear. Ignore this for now and just let the iPod start charging. After a moment or two, this menu will go away.

While the iPod is charging, a battery icon will appear on its display and the word "Charging" will appear at the top of the screen. According to Apple, the iPod's battery is charged to the 80% level in 3 hours and fully charged in 5 hours. While the iPod is charging, you can proceed with installing its software on your computer.

note

When you connect the Dock connector end of the cable to the iPod, the side of the connector with the icon on it should be toward you when you are looking at the iPod's face.

When the iPod is fully charged, the display will contain a "full" battery icon and the status message will be "Charged." Unplug the AC adapter and then disconnect the cable from the power adapter and from the iPod.

Installing the iPod's Software (Including iTunes)

Included in the iPod's box is a software installation CD. On this CD is the software your computer needs to be able to communicate with your iPod, along with the iTunes application you will use to manage the music you place on the iPod. You'll learn all about iTunes in Part II, "iTunes." But for now, install the software by using the steps in the section that is appropriate for the type of computer you are using (a Windows PC or a Mac).

note

If you'd rather, you can download and install a "fresh" copy of iTunes from the Internet. This is usually a good idea so you get the latest version.

Installing the iPod's Software on a Windows PC

If you have installed even one application from a CD, you won't have any trouble with the iPod CD, as the following steps will confirm:

1. Insert the Installation CD in your computer. The disc will be mounted on your computer, the software will begin to run, and the Choose Setup Language dialog box will appear.

2. Choose the **Language** you want to use on the drop-down list and click **OK**. Because I am linguistically challenged and can only read English, that is the language I use throughout this book. You can choose the language that works best for you.

   After you click OK, the InstallShield Wizard window will appear, and you can watch the initial installation process. When that is complete, you will see the iPod for Windows dialog box (see Figure 2.1). This dialog box might have a slightly different title depending on the iPod model you have, but it will work in the same way.

3. Read the information in the installer window and click **Next**.

4. If you have a lot of time and patience, read the license agreement; when you are done (if you are like me, you will realize it is incomprehensible and will just assume you aren't giving away your firstborn), click **Yes**. You'll see a screen recommending that you connect your iPod to your computer to see whether it needs to be formatted for your computer. You can do so if you'd like, but for now you can skip this by performing the following step.

FIGURE 2.1

You might see a slightly different window depending on the model of iPod you are using, but in any case, the Next button is the same.

5. Check the **Click on This Checkbox If You Wish to Continue Without Connecting Your iPod** check box and click **Next**. The iPod Serial Number dialog box will appear.

6. Enter your iPod's serial number, which can be found on the back of your iPod, and click **Next**. You will see the **Select Country or Region** dialog box.

7. Select the country or region that is most applicable to you and click **Next**. You will see the Registration Information dialog box.

8. Complete your registration information. Most of it is optional; however, you do have to provide at least a name and an email address. When you are done, click **Next**. You will see the second screen in the registration process.

9. Complete the fields about where you will use the iPod and what best describes what you do, if you'd like to. These are both optional. (Speaking of which, given how easily you can carry an iPod around with you, which is the whole point, how much sense does a question about where you will use it make?)

note

If you have trouble reading the serial number, you aren't alone. The text is very small!

tip

If the country or region you want to choose isn't listed, check the **Show All** check box and hopefully it will be then.

10. If you want to receive email from Apple, click the **Yes** radio button, or click **No** if you don't want to receive email.

11. Click **Next**. You'll see the Choose Destination Location dialog box.

12. If you want to accept the default installation location (which is `C:\Program Files\iPod\`), skipto the next step. If you don't want to accept the default installation location, click the **Browse** button and choose the location you do want to use.

13. Click **Next**. As the installer starts to work, you will see the Setup Status window. This window provides information about the installation process.

When the iPod software installation process is complete, you'll move on to the iTunes installation process.

If you already have a later version of iTunes installed on your computer, such as if you downloaded a copy from the Internet, you'll see an error dialog box that explains you already have a newer version of iTunes installed on your computer. Click **OK** to close the dialog box. You'll move to the InstallShield Wizard Complete dialog box, which prompts you to restart your computer.

If you don't have a newer version of iTunes installed already, the iTunes installation software will guide you through the installation of the iTunes software. When iTunes has been successfully installed on your computer, you'll move to the InstallShield Wizard Complete dialog box, which prompts you to restart your computer.

note

A pet peeve of mine is forced registration like Apple requires with the iPod. One shouldn't have to register to make a product they purchased work. Ah well, what can we do?

caution

If you have other open applications with unsaved changes, make sure you save any open documents before you restart your computer.

tip

If you installed iTunes from the iPod CD, you should immediately update the application to ensure you are working with the most current version. For information about updating iTunes, see "Keeping iTunes Up-to-date on a Windows PC Manually" on page **215**.

14. Leave the **Yes** radio button selected and click **Finish**. Your computer will restart and you'll be ready to start working with your iPod.

Installing the iPod's Software on a Macintosh

You can install the iPod's software on a Macintosh using the following steps:

1. Insert the installation CD in your Mac. It will be mounted.

2. Using the Finder, open the installation CD so you can see it folders.

3. Open the **iPod Installer** folder.

4. Double-click the icon you see in the folder, which will be the installation application.

5. Click **Continue** to allow the installer to check for the appropriate software. The install window will appear (see Figure 2.2).

FIGURE 2.2

This is the initial screen of the iPod installer on a Mac.

6. Click **Continue**. The installer will start and you will see the next screen in the process.

7. Read the information on each screen that appears and click **Continue** to move to the next screen.

8. When you get to the license agreement prompt, click **Agree**. You'll see the Select a Destination screen.

9. Click the destination on which you want to install the iPod software. Typically, you should install the software on your active startup drive, which will be selected by default. When you select a drive, it will be marked with a green arrow to show you the drive you have selected. In the lower part of the screen, you will see information about the drive on which you have elected to install the software.

10. Click **Continue**.

11. Click **Install**.

12. If prompted to do so, authenticate yourself as an administrator and click **OK**. The installer will run. When the process is complete, you will see the installation complete screen (see Figure 2.3).

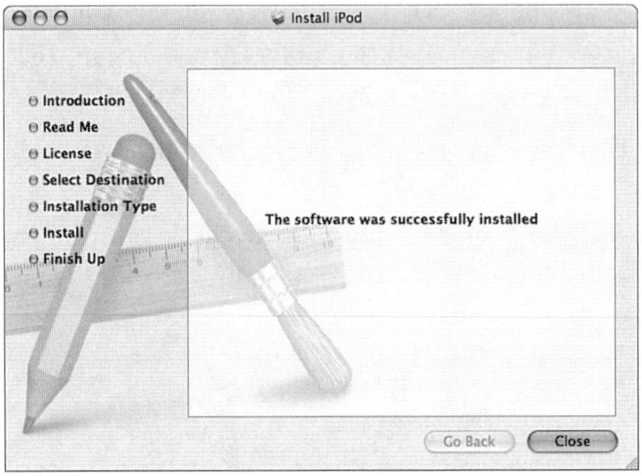

FIGURE 2.3

When you see this screen, you are done installing the iPod software on your Mac.

13. Click **Close**. The installer will quit, and the iPod Updater application will launch. To update the iPod's software, you will need to connect the iPod to your computer. You'll learn how to do that in the next section.

14. For now, quit the iPod Update by selecting **iPod Updater**, **Quit iPod Updater**.

You also need to have iTunes installed on your computer. Because you are using a Mac, you probably already have a copy installed because iTunes is installed on new Macs and as part of the Mac OS X installation. You should update the version you have installed to ensure you are using the most current version of the application. For the steps to do this, see "Keeping iTunes Up-to-date on a Macintosh" on page **215**.

If you don't have a copy of iTunes installed on your Mac already, you can install it from the iPod installation CD or by downloading a copy from the Internet.

Connecting and Configuring an iPod on Your Computer

In order to load music onto an iPod, you must connect the iPod to your computer so the music files can be moved from your iTunes Library onto the iPod. The first time you connect your iPod to your computer you'll need to configure it.

Preparing an iPod to Connect to a Computer

To connect all iPods (except the shuffle) to a computer, you use the USB 2 cable supplied with your iPod or the optional FireWire cable. All iPod cables have the Dock connector connection on one end. Connect this to the iPod's Dock connector port located on the bottom of the iPod (see Figure 2.4).

caution

To connect the Dock connector end of the cable into your iPod's Dock connector port, the icon on the Dock connect end of the cable must be "up," meaning that you see the icon when you are looking at the front face of the iPod (with the controls on it). If you try to insert the connector backwards, you can damage it.

FIGURE 2.4
You use the Dock connector port on the bottom of the iPod to connect it to a computer.

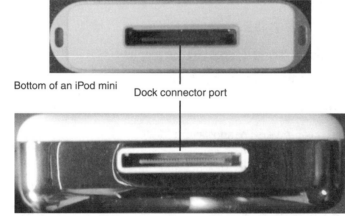

Bottom of an iPod mini   Dock connector port

Bottom of an iPod

You connect the other end of the cable to either a USB 2 or a FireWire port on your computer, depending on which cable you use and which ports your computer has. All current iPod models (except the shuffle) include a USB cable. Some previous models also included a FireWire cable, which you can also purchase separately.

The iPod shuffle has a USB connector built in to one of its ends (see Figure 2.5). To expose the connector, remove the lanyard cap from the end of the shuffle by gently pulling it off the iPod.

FIGURE 2.5

You don't need a cable to connect an iPod shuffle to a computer because it plugs directly into a USB port.

To connect it to your computer, simply plug it into a USB 2 port on the computer itself.

Connecting an iPod to a Computer

Connecting an iPod to a computer requires that you decide on the type of connection you will be using. There are two basic options: USB 2 or FireWire.

All modern computers (Windows and Mac) include USB 2 ports that you can use to connect an iPod to your computer. All Macs and some Windows computers include FireWire ports you can use just as well.

Although these are different connection technologies, you won't really notice any functional difference between them so it doesn't matter

caution

To use USB 2 to connect an iPod to a Mac, you must be running Mac OS X version 10.3.4 or later. If you are running an earlier version of Mac OS X, you'll need to use FireWire instead.

which you use. If you have a choice, the option you choose will likely just depend on if you have more ports available of one kind than the other.

Using USB 2 to Connect an iPod to a Computer

If you have a computer that supports USB 2—and unless you have a very old computer, it probably does—you can use USB 2 to connect your iPod to the computer. If you use a high-power USB 2 port, your iPod's battery will also be charged whenever it is connected to your computer.

A USB 2 port is a rectangular port that is fairly thin (see Figure 2.6). USB is also marked with a trident-like icon. You should use only a USB 2 port that is located on your computer's case so the port will provide enough power to charge your iPod when it is connected.

The slightly confusing thing about USB is that there are two basic kinds of USB ports: USB 1 and USB 2. And, some computers have both kinds.

Locate the USB ports on your computer's case.

caution

Not all USB ports on a computer support high power USB 2, which is what you want to use because, when you connect your iPod to your computer, the iPod's battery is also charged (it is charged when you use FireWire, too). Don't connect an iPod to a USB anywhere except on your computer's case.

FIGURE 2.6

You can use a USB 2 port to connect your iPod to your computer.

Unfortunately, you can't tell by observation whether a USB port supports USB 2 or USB 1 because the ports are identical in appearance. Check the documentation that came with your computer to determine which ports support USB 2. If you can't find that information, contact your computer's manufacturer.

If you still can't determine which ports support USB 2, try one of the USB ports on your computer's case. If the iPod's battery charges when it is connected, you have a USB 2 port. If not, you probably are using an USB 1 port. Try a different one until you locate a USB 2 port.

Plug the USB end of the USB 2 cable into the USB port on your computer. The connector will only fit one way, so if it isn't going in easily, turn the connector over. After it is connected, you'll be ready to configure your iPod. Skip to the section "Configuring an iPod on Your Computer" on page **29**.

If you use a shuffle, plug it directly into the USB 2 port. When it is connected, you'll see its status light (located at the top of the iPod shuffle on the same side as the playback controls) glow amber; this means the battery is charging. When the battery is fully charged, this light will become green. If the light doesn't light up, you need to try a different port. When you find a port that causes the light to come on, you'll be ready to configure your iPod and can skip to the section "Configuring an iPod on Your Computer" on page **29**.

Using FireWire to Connect an iPod to a Computer

All modern Macs and many Windows PCs include FireWire ports that provide high-speed connections and power to devices such as iPods. FireWire ports are shaped like a rectangle with one end being replaced with a sort of semi-circle (see Figure 2.7).

Some previous iPod models included a FireWire cable. If yours didn't and you want to use FireWire to connect, you can purchase an iPod Dock Connector to FireWire Cable from the Apple Store (www.apple.com/store).

Locate the FireWire ports on your computer's case and connect the FireWire end of your iPod cable to it. You'll be ready to configure your iPod.

> **tip**
>
> Diagnostic applications are available that will tell you whether your computer supports USB 2. However, these are beyond the scope of this book. You can do a web search to find to try one.

> **note**
>
> If your computer doesn't have any FireWire ports and does not support USB 2, you'll have to add a PCI FireWire or USB 2 card to your computer before you can connect an iPod to it.

FIGURE 2.7
When you connect an iPod to a computer using FireWire, its battery will be charged.

Configuring an iPod on Your Computer

The first time you connect an iPod to your computer, the iPod will turn on and immediately be mounted on your computer.

Depending on the iPod and computer you are using, you might be prompted that your iPod needs to be reformatted. If so, click **Update**. You'll move into the iPod Updater application, and your iPod will be prepared for use. When that process is complete, you'll see a dialog box that tells you your iPod software is up-to-date (see Figure 2.8). If you are prompted to restart your computer, do so. If not, quit the iPod Updater software on a Windows PC by clicking its **Close** box or on a Mac by selecting **iPod Updater**, **Quit iPod Updater**.

caution

Some older Windows PCs might have a four-pin FireWire port, which is quite different from the modern six-pin version. Even if you can find an adapter to be able to connect to this port, don't do so because your iPod won't charge while it is connected.

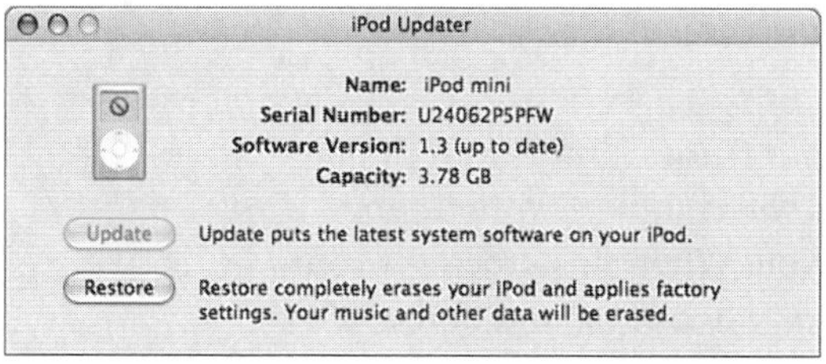

FIGURE 2.8
This updater screen tells you that the iPod's software is up-to-date.

	iPod Updater
	Name: iPod mini
	Serial Number: U24062P5PFW
	Software Version: 1.3 (up to date)
	Capacity: 3.78 GB

Update — Update puts the latest system software on your iPod.

Restore — Restore completely erases your iPod and applies factory settings. Your music and other data will be erased.

After your iPod has been updated, iTunes will open and the iPod Setup Assistant will appear (see Figure 2.9). Type a name for your iPod in the text box. You can use any name you'd like; this will be the name of your iPod when it is shown in the iTunes Source List and on your computer's Desktop. Leave the **Automatically update songs on my iPod** check box checked. Then click **Next**. You'll move to the Registration screen. If you want to register your iPod, click the **Register My iPod** button and follow the onscreen instructions to complete the registration process. When you come back to the Assistant, click **Finish** (Windows) or **Done** (Mac). iTunes will update the iPod and transfer all the music in your iTunes Library onto the iPod—if it can.

tip

If you are using an iPod, the Setup Assistant will also enable you to update your photos when you update your music. For now, leave that option unchecked. You'll learn about working with iPod photos in Chapter 12, "Using the iPod for Images."

FIGURE 2.9

The trusty iPod Setup Assistant is ready to do its work.

While music is being transferred, the iPod icon on the iTunes Source List will flash red (see Figure 2.10). You'll also see information about the transfer in the iTunes Information area at the top of the iTunes window.

If all the music in your iTunes Library will fit on the iPod, the process will complete without any further action from you. When this process is complete, you will hear a "whoosh" sound and you'll

note

If you are playing music while you transfer music to an iPod, you will see information about the music you are playing rather than information about the transfer.

see the `iPod update is complete` message in the information area at the top of the iTunes window. Click the Eject button next to the iPod's icon on the Source List. The iPod will be removed from the Source List and after a moment or two, the `OK to disconnect` message will also be displayed on the iPod's screen. When you see this message, you can disconnect your iPod from your computer. Squeeze the buttons on each side of the Dock connector end of the cable and remove the cable from the iPod; the iPod will be ready to use. You can leave the cable plugged into your computer if you want.

tip

If you haven't charged your iPod's battery already, you should leave your iPod connected to your computer until its battery is fully charged, which will take about 4–5 hours depending on the model you have.

FIGURE 2.10

If this book were printed in color, you would see that the iPod mini icon in the iTunes Source List is flashing red to show that music in the selected playlist is being moved onto the iPod.

iPod mini on Source List   Information area

If there is more music in your iTunes Library than can fit on the iPod, you will see a message telling you that the iPod doesn't have enough room for all your music (see Figure 2.11). You'll be prompted to have iTunes select songs that will fit onto the iPod. Click **Yes** to allow this. In this case, iTunes will create a playlist of music that will fit on the iPod and then transfer this music to your iPod. This is fine for now; in later chapters, you'll learn how to choose which music is transferred onto your iPod.

iTunes will move the playlist it created (whose name will be the name of your iPod plus the word "Selection") onto your iPod. When this process is complete, you will hear a "whoosh" sound and you'll see the iPod update is complete message in the information area at the top of the iTunes window. Click the Eject button next to the iPod's icon on the Source list. The iPod will be removed from the Source list and after a moment or two, the OK to disconnect message will also be displayed on the iPod's screen. When you see this message, you can disconnect your iPod from your computer. Squeeze the buttons on each side of the Dock connector end of the cable and remove the cable from the iPod; the iPod will be ready to use. You can leave the cable plugged into your computer if you want to.

caution

While you have an iPod connected to your computer, you will see the message Do not disconnect on the iPod's screen. You should wait until the file transfer is complete or eject an iPod before you disconnect it. You'll learn more about this in the next chapter.

FIGURE 2.11
Because I had more music than can be stored on an iPod mini, iTunes let me know about it.

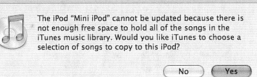

The iPod "Mini iPod" cannot be updated because there is not enough free space to hold all of the songs in the iTunes music library. Would you like iTunes to choose a selection of songs to copy to this iPod?

No   Yes

Connecting an iPod to a Computer with a Dock

Dealing with a cable each time you connect your iPod to your computer is a bit of a pain. An iPod Dock provides a cradle for your iPod so you don't need to use the cable itself. When you want to transfer music to the iPod or charge its battery, you simply set it in the Dock (see Figure 2.12). The connection is made instantly and your iPod is updated while its battery charges.

You can purchase a Dock for any iPod from any retailer that carries iPod accessories or from the online Apple Store located at www.apple.com/store.

note

A *playlist* is a collection of songs. You can use iTunes to create your own playlists and then listen to those playlists on an iPod. There are also a couple of playlists you can create and manage on the iPod itself. You'll learn about these later in this part of the book.

Even though it doesn't use cables, a Dock is available for the shuffle, too. This is useful when the USB port on your computer isn't convenient for you to reach, such as being on the back of a computer that is under a table or desk. You can place the shuffle's Dock in a more convenient location.

FIGURE 2.12

An iPod Dock eliminates the need to mess around with cables every time you connect your iPod to your computer.

In addition to making it easier to connect your iPod to a computer, the Docks for various models also include other ports you might find useful. For example, Docks for iPods (and the older iPod photo models), include AV ports you can connect to a TV to display slideshows on the TV. Additionally, a Dock is the only way to use the better quality S-video connection to display an iPod's slideshows on a TV. Other Docks include an Audio out port you can connect to a home theater to play your iPod's music over a stereo system.

tip

Before you rush out and purchase a Dock, realize that if you use a case on your iPod, you'll have to remove the case to be able to place the iPod into the Dock. Depending on how hard the case is to remove, this might be more trouble than using a cable to connect. Most cases provide access to the Dock port so you can connect the cable directly to the iPod while it is in its case.

To use a Dock, connect the Dock connector end of the cable you use to connect the iPod to your computer into the Dock connector port on the Dock (instead of the port on the iPod). To connect the iPod to the computer, simply set it into the Dock. When the Dock can communicate with the iPod, you'll hear a tone and your iPod will be mounted on your computer.

When you want to disconnect your iPod from the computer, lift it out of the Dock. (You might have to place one hand on the Dock to keep it from lifting up when you lift the iPod out.)

> **caution**
>
> Before you pull an iPod out of a Dock, make sure the OK to disconnect message appears on the iPod's screen.

The Absolute Minimum

Fortunately, a lot of the material in this chapter is useful only the first time you use your iPod. After all, installing software and connecting cables isn't all that thrilling. But it is necessary to do the thrilling stuff that starts in the next chapter. Before we leave this topic, consider the following points:

- You'll need to install the iPod's software on the CD included with it on your computer.

- The CD also contains the iTunes installer. However, you might want to download and install a copy of iTunes from the Internet so you are sure you are working with the latest version.

- To transfer music from your iTunes Library onto your iPod and to charge its battery, you connect the iPod to your computer. You can use a USB 2 or FireWire cable to do this. If you have a shuffle, you plug it directly into a USB 2 port.

- The first time you connect your iPod to your computer you'll need to do some basic setup. Fortunately, the iPod and iTunes software will guide you all the way.

- You can install more than one iPod on the same computer. For example, you might be fortunate enough to have an iPod and an iPod shuffle. If have more than one iPod, use a different name for each so you can keep them straight. You can even connect them to your computer at the same time if you have enough ports and cables available to do so.

- A Dock makes it easier to connect your iPod to your computer. It also includes a Line Out port. You can use this to connect the Dock to speakers or other audio device to play the iPod's music on that device. You'll learn more about this in Chapter 11, "Using an iPod with a Home Stereo or Car Stereo."

- Figure out why iTunes will rock your world.
- Learn to speak in three-letter acronyms (TLAs), such as MP3 and AAC.
- Visit the Library.
- Learn the best three places to get music for your Library.
- Play with playlists.
- Meet the digital music triumvirate.

Touring iTunes

With not-very-sincere apologies to Mr. Edison, Apple's iTunes is the best thing to happen to music since the phonograph. This amazing application enables you to do things with your music you might have never dreamed possible. Of course, you can use iTunes to listen to audio CDs, but that is certainly nothing to write home (or a book) about. Any two-bit boombox can do that. That basic task is barely a warm-up for iTunes. If you have never used iTunes before, prepare to be impressed (and if you have used iTunes before, be impressed anyway).

What You Can Do with iTunes

I could fill a book (or at least Part II of this book) with all the great things you can do with iTunes. Following are some examples just to whet your appetite:

- Listen to audio CDs.

- Listen to Internet radio and podcasts.

- Store all the music you like in a single place so you never need to fuss with individual CDs again.

- Search and organize all this music so listening to exactly the music you want is just a matter of a few mouse clicks (and maybe a few key presses).

- Create custom albums (called *playlists*) containing the specific songs you want to hear.

- Create custom albums (called *smart playlists*) that are based on a set of criteria, such as all the jazz music you have rated at four or five stars.

- Use the iTunes built-in Equalizer to make your music just right.

- Burn your own music CDs to play in those oh-so-limited CD players in your car, a boombox, or in your home.

- Share your music collection with other people over a wired or wireless network; you can listen to music other people share with you as well.

Audio File Formats You Might Encounter When You Use iTunes

As you work with digital music and other audio files, you'll encounter a number of file formats you need to understand. This is important because each of these formats offers specific benefits and limitations that impact what you do with your music. For example, some file formats offer better music quality versus file size than others. You definitely don't need to have all the specifications for each of these formats committed to memory (nor will you find them in this book); instead, all you need is to be able to distinguish between them and to be able to choose the format that is the most appropriate for what you are trying to do.

Most audio file formats are *encoded*. This means specific compression algorithms (because this is a computer book, I am required by contract to use that word at least once) are used to reduce the size of the audio file without—hopefully anyway—lowering the quality of the resulting sound very much. The higher the compression that is used, the lower the quality of the resulting music when it is played back. Note that the words *higher* and *lower* are relative. Often, it takes a musical expert to tell the difference between encoded and unencoded music, but even if it is imperceptible to us mere mortals, it does exist.

When it comes to digital audio files, one trade-off always has to be made. And that is *file size* versus *sound quality*. When you add thousands of songs to your iTunes Library, you can easily consume gigabytes of disk space. Although you might have a humungous hard drive in your computer, you might also have other files you want to store on it, such as photos, Word documents, and so on. Even I realize that computers can be used for more than just music.

To keep the amount of disk space required to store your music to a minimum, you must encode it. When you do, you choose the settings you want to use to encode that music. The more encoding you apply, the less space the music will consume, but the lower quality the playback will be. You will quickly find a happy medium between file size and how the music sounds to you.

You'll learn about encoding music in more detail later in the book, but for now, you should read the following sections so you can become comfortable with the various audio file formats you will encounter.

CD Audio

The CD Audio format was the world's first widely used entry in the digital audio format life cycle. The creation of this format was the start of the CD revolution. Instead of vinyl albums, which were a pain to deal with and included lots of hisses, pops, and other distractions when played, listeners began enjoying digital music. In addition to being easier to handle than LPs, CDs provided a much better listening experience and were—and are—much more durable than records. They also sounded much better than cassettes and could be just as portable.

Eventually, CD Audio made its way to computers, which now can provide all the music-listening enjoyment of a home stereo plus much more, thanks to applications such as iTunes.

Although you can use iTunes to listen to your audio CDs, typically you will just convert those CDs into one of the newer digital formats and store that content on your computer's hard disk so you don't have to bother with a CD when you want to listen to music. You will also use this format when you put your iTunes music on your own audio CD so you can play your iTunes music when you are away from your computer.

caution

Some audio CDs use copyright-protection schemes that prevent you from listening to them on a computer (with the idea being that you won't be able to make copies of the songs for illegal purposes). Unfortunately, not only do these CDs not work in your computer, but they also can actually cause damage. Before playing a CD in your computer, check the CD's label carefully to make sure it doesn't contain any warnings about playing the CD in a computer or state that the CD is copy-protected. If it does have these warnings, don't try to use the CD in your computer.

MP3

Even if this book is your first foray into the wonderful world of digital music, you have no doubt heard of MP3. This audio file format started, literally, an explosion in music technology that is still reverberating and expanding today.

MP3 is the acronym for the audio compression scheme called *Moving Picture Experts Group (MPEG) audio layer 3*. The revolutionary aspect of the MP3 encoding scheme was that music data could be stored in files that are only about 1/12 the size of unencoded digital music without a noticeable degradation in the quality of the music. A typical music CD consumes about 650MB of storage space, but the same music encoded in the MP3 format shrinks down to about 55MB. Put another way, a single 3.5-minute song shrinks from 35MB on audio CD down to a paltry 3MB or so in MP3 format. The small size of MP3 files opened up a world of possibilities.

note

Because MP3 files are relatively small, storing an entire music collection in a small amount of disk space is possible, thus eliminating the need to bother with individual CDs. Using a digital music application such as iTunes, you can easily store, organize, and access an entire music collection on your desktop or laptop computer.

For example, MP3 enabled a new class of portable music devices. Because MP3 files can be stored in small amounts of memory, devices with no moving parts can store and play a fair amount of music; these were the early MP3 players, such as the Rio. Then came other devices containing small hard drives—can you say iPod?—that can store huge amounts of music, enabling you to take your entire music collection with you wherever you go. These devices are extremely small and lightweight, and their contents can be easily managed.

You will encounter many MP3 files on the Internet, and with iTunes, you can convert your audio CDs into the MP3 format so that you can store them in iTunes and put them on an iPod.

AAC

The successor to MP3 is called *Advanced Audio Coding (AAC)*. This format is part of the larger MPEG-4 specification. Its basic purpose is the same as the MP3 format: to deliver excellent sound quality while keeping file sizes small. However, the AAC format is a newer and better format in that it can be used to produce files that have better quality than MP3 at even smaller file sizes.

Also, as with MP3, you can easily convert audio CD files into the AAC format to store them on a computer and add them to an iPod. What's more, you can convert AAC files into the Audio CD or MP3 format when you want to put them on a CD to play on something other than your computer, such as a car stereo.

The AAC format also enables content producers to add some copy-protection schemes to their music. Typically, these schemes won't have any impact on you (unless of course, you are trying to do something you shouldn't).

One of the most important aspects of the AAC format is that all the music in the iTunes Music Store is stored in it; when you purchase music from the store, it is added to your computer in this format.

WAV

The *Windows Waveform (WAV)* audio format is a standard on Windows computers. It has been widely used for various kinds of audio, but because it does not offer the "quality versus file size" benefits of the MP3 or AAC formats, it is mostly used for sound effects or clips people have recorded from various sources. Millions of WAV files are available on the Internet that you can play and download.

You can load WAV files into iTunes, and you can even use iTunes to convert files into the WAV format. However, because MP3 and AAC are much newer and better file formats, you aren't likely to want to do this very often. Occasionally, you might want to add WAV files to your iTunes music collection; this can be easily done, as you will learn later in this book.

tip

If you ever want to find a sound byte from your favorite movie or TV show, you can probably do so at one of the many WAV websites. One example is www.wavcentral.com. Interestingly enough, even the sound clips on these sites have mostly been converted into MP3.

AIFF

The *Audio Interchange File Format (AIFF)* provides relatively high-quality sound, but its file sizes are larger than MP3 or AAC. As you can probably guess from its name, this format was originally used to exchange audio among various platforms.

As with the WAV format, because the MP3 and AAC formats provide a better sound quality versus file size trade-off, you aren't likely to use the AIFF format. The most typical situation in which you might want to use it is when you want to move some music or sound from your iTunes collection into a different application that does not support the MP3 or AAC format.

Apple Lossless

The Apple Lossless format is the only encoding option supported by iTunes that doesn't sport a fancy acronym. The goal of this format is maximum sound quality.

As a result, files in this format will be larger than in AAC or MP3. However, Apple Lossless files will be slightly smaller than AIFF or WAV files.

The Apple Lossless format provides very high-quality music but also larger files sizes. If you have a sophisticated ear, high-quality sound systems, and discriminating taste in music (whatever that means), you might find this format to be the best for you. However, because storing music in this format requires a lot more space on your computer and on an iPod, you will probably use the AAC or MP3 format more.

The iTunes Music Library

Earlier, you read that one of the great things about iTunes is that you can use it to store all your music on your computer. This is done with the iTunes Library (see Figure 3.1). This is the place in which you store all the music and sounds you import into iTunes, such as from audio CDs or other sources. You can then browse or search your Library to find the music you want to listen to or work with.

FIGURE 3.1

The iTunes Library is the one place to go for all the good music in your life.

As you use iTunes, you will frequently be accessing your Library; it will often be your first stop when you do things with your music, such as creating playlists or burning CDs.

Where Does All That Music Come From?

You have three primary sources of the music and sounds from which you will build your iTunes Library:

- **Audio CDs**—You can add music from your audio CDs to the iTunes Library. In iTunes lingo, this process is called *importing*.

- **The Internet**—You can download music, podcasts, and other audio files from the Internet and add those files to your iTunes Library.

- **The iTunes Music Store**—Part III, "The iTunes Music Store," is dedicated to this source, and for good reason. Using the iTunes Music Store, you can search for, preview, and purchase music online and add that music to your Library. You can also choose and subscribe to podcasts from the bewilderingly large selection available.

> **note**
>
> iTunes uses a civilized term (*importing*) for the process of converting an audio CD into a different format and adding the resulting music to your Library. The more traditional term for converting audio CD music into the MP3 format is *ripping*. I kind of like *ripping* myself, but because *importing* is the term iTunes uses, I guess we will go with that.

Playlists: Customizing Your Music Experience

I've saved one of the best features of iTunes for nearly last—*playlists*. Playlists enable you to create custom collections of music from the songs in your iTunes Library. (If you think of a playlist as a custom CD without the disc itself or size limitation of a disc, you will be very close.)

When you create playlists, you can mix and match music to your heart's content. For example, you can build your own "greatest hits" collections that include multiple artists, music genres, and so on. You can repeat the same song multiple times in the same playlist, and you can get rid of songs you don't like by not including them in the playlists you listen to. What's more, you can create a playlist to include a specific amount of music from a single CD or endlessly repeat all the music in your Library.

Basically, you can use playlists to organize a collection of songs in any way you choose. You can then listen to your playlists, put them on a CD, or move them to an iPod.

You'll learn all you need to know about playlists in Chapter 18, "Creating, Configuring, and Using Playlists."

The Other Members of the Band: The iPod and the iTunes Music Store

When it comes to citizenship, iTunes definitely gets an A+ because it plays so well with others.

The iPod might just be the coolest portable electronic device ever to hit the streets. Although the iPod is indeed an awesome piece of technology, it wouldn't get very far without a tool to manage the music it contains. iTunes is that tool. iTunes and the iPod go together like a 1-2 combination punch, peanut butter and jelly, jalapenos on a pizza, Bing Crosby and Bob Hope (well, you get the idea). Using iTunes, you can determine which parts of your music library are on the iPod. iTunes manages moving the music files to the iPod and organizing them, so the process is simple (from your perspective anyway). In fact, iTunes will manage the process for you automatically if you prefer; when you connect your trusty iPod to your computer, iTunes will recognize it and then synchronize the music it has in your Library with that on your iPod.

When you get to Part III, you will learn in detail about the last part of the digital music triumvirate: the iTunes Music Store. With the iTunes Music Store, you can shop for music to add to your Library. When you find songs you'd like to have, you can purchase and download them into your iTunes Library with just a couple of mouse clicks. And you can do all this from within iTunes itself. It feels like the iTunes Music Store is just an extension of iTunes, which, in fact, it is. You access the iTunes Music Store from within iTunes, and the Store uses an interface that looks very similar to the iTunes interface. So, once you know iTunes, you won't have any problems with the iTunes Music Store.

The Absolute Minimum

Now that you have met iTunes, I hope you are jazzed (pun intended) to get into it and start making its musical magic work for you. In the chapters following this one, you'll learn how to do everything from listening to audio CDs and Internet radio to building playlists to sharing your music over a network. Here are the major topics you learned about in this introduction to iTunes:

- You can use iTunes to do just about anything you want to with your music, from listening to CDs to putting your entire music collection on your hard drive to managing the music on an iPod.

- The primary audio file formats you are likely to use with iTunes are AAC and MP3. However, you can also use WAV, AIFF, and the Apple Lossless format when you want to maximize sound quality or for other purposes (such as to export music to another application).

- The iTunes Music Library is where you store and can work with all your iTunes music.

- You can get music for your iTunes Library from audio CDs, the Internet, and the iTunes Music Store.

- You add and listen to podcasts using iTunes and then move those podcasts to an iPod.

- You can use playlists to create and listen to customized collections of music.

- iTunes works seamlessly with the iPod and the iTunes Music Store.

IN THIS CHAPTER

- Know the sources of all iTunes music.
- Find out where your iTunes music will be stored and change the location if it suits your fancy.
- Maximize your music's quality/file size ratio by choosing encoding options and quality levels when you import audio CDs.
- Build your iTunes Library by importing audio CDs into it.
- Browse and search your Library like a master librarian.
- Dump music you don't want cluttering up your digital shelves.
- Add podcasts to your Library so you can enjoy a mind-boggling array of content from the comfort of your computer or iPod.

4

Building, Browsing, Searching, and Playing Your iTunes Music Library

Are you ready for some real iTunes? If the material in the previous chapters covered good features of iTunes, which it did, then this chapter starts the coverage of the amazing, awesome [insert your own superlative here] features that make iTunes something to write a book about. Here is where we start taking your iTunes game to the next level, hitting some home runs, scoring touchdowns, and some other sports clichés that all good books use. It's time to start working with that mysterious Library I have mentioned a number of times but into which until now you have only had glimpses.

The iTunes Library is where you can store all your music, such as that from audio CDs and the Internet, and where any music you purchase from the iTunes Music Store is stored. After you have added music to your Library, you never have to bother with individual CDs again because you can access all your music from the Library. And, you can use the music in your Library in many ways, such as to create playlists, burn CDs, and so on.

Right now, your iTunes Library is probably sort of sad. Like a book library with no books in it, your iTunes Library is just sitting there gathering dust on its digital shelves. You will change that shortly. The first step is to add music to the Library. Then, you'll learn how to browse, search, and listen to the tunes you have added there.

Gathering Your Music from All the Right Places

If you are going to add music to your Library, you have to get it from somewhere, right? The following are the three main sources of tunes for your Library:

- **Audio CDs**—Who wants to bother with audio CDs? Wouldn't it be nice if you could store all the content of your CD collection in one place so you could listen to any music you wanted to at any time just by browsing or doing a quick search? Obviously, that is a loaded question because you already know you can use iTunes to do just that. In this chapter, you'll learn how to copy the music from audio CDs into your Library (as you'll remember from Chapter 3, "Touring iTunes," this is called *importing*) so that you never have to use the original CDs again.

- **MP3 and other audio files**—You can add audio files in just about any format to your Library. For example, there are lots of free and legal MP3 files on the Web that you can add to your own Library. In this chapter, you will learn how to add music to your Library in this way, too.

- **iTunes Music Store**—With the iTunes Music Store, you can browse and search among hundreds of thousands of songs. When you find music you like, you can purchase an entire CD's worth of songs or you can buy individual songs (can you say one-hit wonders!). When you buy a song, it is downloaded and added to your iTunes Library. Instead of ordering a CD or, even

note

Podcasts are a special type of content similar to broadcast radio except that no broadcasting is involved and you have total control over what you hear (so, I guess it isn't all that similar after all). Some podcasts contain music, but there are a lot more including news, talk, and so on. You'll learn about podcasts in detail in the last section of this chapter.

worse, buying one in a physical store, your music is available to you instantly, and you don't even have to import it.

Determining Where and How the Music Library Music Is Stored

It is much easier to organize an empty room, so it is good practice to set up the organization of your iTunes Library before you fill it with music. In this section, you'll learn how iTunes organizes the music in your Library. If its standard practices aren't good enough for you, you can change its ways to suit your own organizational preferences.

Working with the iTunes Music Folder

As you import music into the Library, files are created for each song you add (whether it's from a CD, downloaded from the iTunes Music Store, or imported from an existing file). When you first started the application, iTunes created a folder called iTunes Music in which it stores all the music it manages for you.

The default location of this folder depends on the kind of computer you are using. On Windows computers, the folder will be stored in a folder called iTunes, located within your My Music folder. On Macs, this folder is also called iTunes, but it is located in the Music folder within your Home folder.

To see the current location of the iTunes Music folder on your computer, open the **iTunes Preferences** dialog box and then open the **Advanced** pane (see Figure 4.1). At the top of this dialog box, you will see the iTunes Music Folder Location box. Within this box, you will see the path to your iTunes Music folder.

Just for fun, open your iTunes Music folder so you can see it for yourself. Use the path you see on the Advanced pane to find it. If you haven't added any music to your Library yet, it might be pretty dull. To see what a full folder looks like, check out Figure 4.2.

tip

In case you don't remember from the last chapter, you access the iTunes Preferences dialog box by pressing **Ctrl+,** (Windows) or ⌘**-,** (Macs).

FIGURE 4.1

The current location of your iTunes folder is shown on the Advanced pane of the iTunes Preferences dialog box.

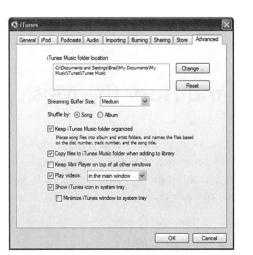

FIGURE 4.2

Don't be envious—soon your iTunes Library will be as full of good tunes as mine is.

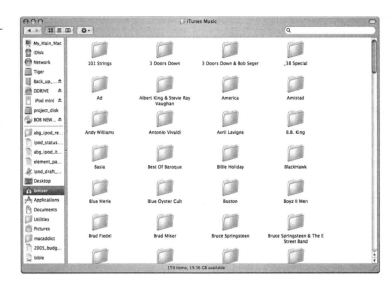

As you can see, within the iTunes Music folder is a folder for each artist. Within the artists' folder, each album from which you have added music is shown. Within each of those album folders, the tracks you have added are individual files (see Figure 4.3). If you take a close look at Figure 4.3, you can see that the files have the extension .mp3, which means the song files for the album *The Best Of BB King* were imported in the MP3 format.

FIGURE 4.3

In this folder, you can see all the songs contained on the album *The Best of BB King* (which is an excellent album by the way, not that I am qualified to be a music critic).

Configuring the Location of the Music Folder

In most cases, the default location of your iTunes Music folder will be fine, and you don't have to do anything about it. However, there are some cases in which you will want to change the location of this folder. For example, suppose you have several hard drives in your computer and the one on which the folder is currently stored doesn't have a lot of room. Even though individual song files are relatively small, you are likely to end up with thousands or tens of thousands of them in your Library. That can add up to a lot of disk space. You might want to change the location of your iTunes Music folder so it is on a drive with more room.

To change the location of this folder, do the following:

1. Open the **Advanced** pane of the iTunes Preferences dialog box.

2. Click the **Change** button. On a Windows PC, you will see the Browse For Folder dialog box (see Figure 4.4). On a Mac, you will see the Change Music Folder Location dialog box (see Figure 4.5).

3. Use the dialog box to move to and select the folder in which you want your iTunes Music folder to be located. For example, if you want to move the folder to another hard drive, move to that drive and click the Make New Folder (Windows) or New Folder (Mac) button to create a new folder for your music.

FIGURE 4.4

You use the Browse For Folder dialog box to move to or select a new home for your iTunes Music folder.

FIGURE 4.5

The Change Music Folder Location dialog box looks a bit different from its Windows counterpart, but the purpose is exactly the same.

4. Click **OK** (Windows) or **Choose** (Mac). You'll return to the Advanced pane, and the folder you selected will be shown in the iTunes Music Folder Location area.

5. Click **OK** to close the iTunes Preferences dialog box.

Setting Other Organization Preferences

The location of the folder in which your music will be stored is likely the most important part of the organization preferences. However, you'll need to understand a couple more preferences that are alsov located on the Advanced pane of the iTunes Preferences dialog box:

note

If you already have music in your Library, changing the location of the iTunes Music folder won't hurt you. When you select a new folder, iTunes will remember the location of any previous music you have added to the Library and will update its database so that music will still be part of your Library.

■ **Keep iTunes music folder organized**—This preference causes iTunes to organize your music as described earlier—that is, by artist, album, and song. Because this is a logical way to organize your music files, I recommend that you leave this option active by making sure this check box is checked.

■ **Copy files to iTunes Music Folder when adding to library**—This preference causes iTunes to make a copy of audio files that already exist on your computer (such as MP3 files you have downloaded from the Internet) and places those copies in your iTunes Music folder, just like files you create by importing them from a CD. If this preference is inactive, iTunes uses a pointer to song files you are adding instead of making a copy of the files; it doesn't actually place the files in your iTunes Music folder. I recommend that you make this preference active by checking its check box. This way, all your music files will be in the same place, no matter where they came from originally.

> **tip**
>
> If you want to go back to the default location of the iTunes Music Folder, open the Advanced pane of the iTunes Preferences dialog box and click the Reset button.

If you don't have iTunes make copies of songs when you add them to your Library and then you delete or move the song files you added, iTunes will lose track of the song and you will experience the "missing song file" problem. To learn how to solve that problem, see "Solving the Missing Song File Problem" on page **216**.

> **caution**
>
> If you do have iTunes copy files to your iTunes Music folder when you add them to your Library, be aware that it does actually make a copy of the file you are adding. This means you will have two files for each song you add to the Library. After you have successfully added songs to your Library, you should delete the song files from their original locations so you aren't wasting disk space.

Understanding Encoding and Other Important Format Options

Back in Chapter 3, you learned about the major music file formats that you need to be aware of as you use iTunes. As you will recall, the two primary formats you use when dealing with music are AAC and MP3, but the Apple Lossless format is useful when you want only the highest quality from your music. When you add music to your Library, you choose the format and then select the specific configuration of that format.

Choosing a Format Option

Although I am sure that going into the specifications for each kind of format would make for fascinating reading, there isn't really any need to get into that detail. Frankly, the benefit of using an application such as iTunes is that it manages all this complexity for you so that you don't have to be concerned with it. If you are like me, you just want to work with the music, not diddle around with complicated settings.

Generally, when you add music to your Library, you should use either the AAC or MP3 format. Because the AAC format is better (with *better* meaning that it provides higher quality music in smaller file sizes), it is usually the best choice.

If you want to have the highest quality music and file size isn't a concern for you, Apple Lossless is the way to go.

Picking Quality Levels

After you select a format, you decide the quality with which the music will be encoded. Higher quality levels mean better-sounding music but larger file sizes. If file size is not a problem, choosing a higher quality setting is the way to go. If you have relatively little disk space, you might want to experiment to see which is the lowest quality setting you can choose that results in music that still sounds good to you. If you demand the absolute best in music quality and have plenty of hard drive space to spare, Apple Lossless is a good option for you.

Your computer's hard disk space isn't the only factor you need to consider when choosing a quality level. iPods also have a hard drive or flash memory, and if you use the higher-quality encoders, such as Apple Lossless, you won't be able to fit as many songs on your iPod as with a format designed for small files, such as the AAC format.

Note that when it comes to music, quality is in the ear of the beholder. Also, it heavily depends on the type of music you listen to as well as how you listen to it. For example, if you listen to heavy metal rock using a low-quality pair of speakers (in other words, cheap speakers), quality will be less of an issue because you likely won't hear any difference anyway. However, if you listen to classical music

note

Nothing against heavy metal rock, of course (I like some of it myself), it's just that it usually includes lots of distortion and constant noise, which means minor flaws in the encoded music won't be as noticeable.

on high-quality speakers, the differences in quality levels might be more noticeable.

The trade-off for quality is always file size. The higher the quality setting you choose, the larger the resulting files will be. If you don't have disk space limitations and have a discriminating ear, you might want to stick with the highest possible quality setting. If disk space is at a premium for you, consider using a lower quality setting if you can't detect the difference or if that difference doesn't bother you.

Configuring iTunes to Import Music

Before you start adding music to your Library, choose the import options (mainly format and quality levels) you want to use. Here are the steps to follow:

1. Open the **Importing** pane of the iTunes Preferences dialog box (see Figure 4.6).

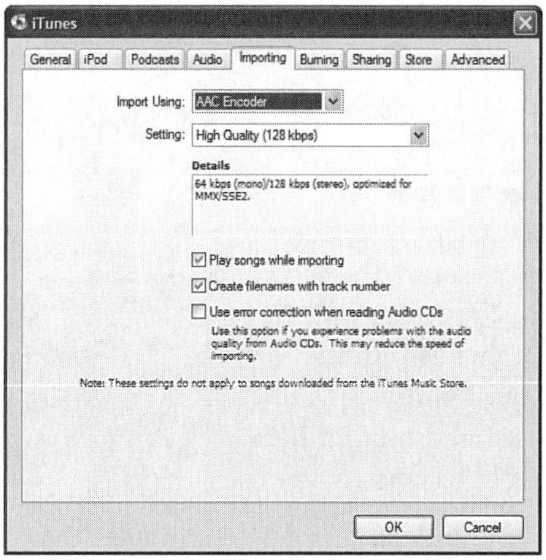

FIGURE 4.6

Here, you can see that the AAC format (the AAC Encoder) is selected.

2. Select the format in which you want to add music to your Library on the **Import Using** menu. For example, to use the AAC format, select **AAC Encoder**. To use the MP3 format, select **MP3 Encoder**. Or, select **Apple Lossless Encoder** to maximize the quality of your music. The other encoder options are WAV and AIFF, but you probably won't use those options except for special circumstances, such as when you are going to use the music you encode in a different application, in which case the AIFF encoder might be a good choice.

3. Select the quality level of the encoder you want to use on the **Setting** menu. The options you see in this list depend on the format you selected in step 1. If you chose AAC Encoder, you have three quality options: High Quality, Podcast, and Custom. If you chose MP3 Encoder, you have four options:

Good Quality, High Quality, Higher Quality, and Custom. If you selected the Apple Lossless Encoder, you have only the Automatic option.

In the Details box, you will see a summary of the settings you have selected. For example, you will see the data rate of the encoder, such as 128Kbps, and the processor for which the encoder has been optimized. (Do you need to worry about these details? Not really.)

If you use the AAC encoder, the High Quality setting will likely be all you ever need.

4. If you want music you add to your Library to play while it is being added, check the **Play songs while importing** check box. This is a personal preference, and it doesn't impact the encoding process significantly.

5. If you want the files that iTunes creates when you import music to include the track number in their filenames, check the **Create filenames with track number** check box. Because this helps you more easily find files for specific songs, I recommend that you keep this preference active.

6. The **Use error correction when reading Audio CDs** check box causes iTunes to more closely control the encoding process. You should use this option only if you notice problems with the music you add to your Library, such as cracking or popping sounds. If that happens, check this check box and try the import process again.

7. Click **OK** to close the dialog box.

Adding Music from Audio CDs to Your iTunes Music Library

Now that you know all you need to about configuring iTunes to build your Library, you are ready to start adding your own audio CDs to your Library.

tip

In most cases, choosing an encoder isn't a difficult decision. If hard drive space is a factor for you, you use an iPod, or you don't have the ears of a music expert, the AAC encoder is the way to go. If you demand perfection, use the Apple Lossless Encoder. Because I don't have musically trained ears, I use the AAC encoder. (Although my music collection does contain a number of MP3 files that I created before the AAC format became available.)

Adding Audio CDs to Your Library

Use these steps to add a CD to your Library:

1. Configure the encoder you want to use for the import session (refer to the section "Configuring iTunes to Import Music" on page **53**).

2. Insert the CD you want to add to your Library. iTunes will attempt to identify it. When it does, the CD will appear in the Source list and will be selected (see Figure 4.7). Notice that the Action button in the upper-right corner of the screen is now the Import button.

tip

You can also select **File**, **Import** or press **Shift+Ctrl+O** (Windows) or **Shift-⌘-O** (Mac) to start the import process. You will see a dialog box that enables you to move to and select the CD you want to import.

FIGURE 4.7

iTunes is ready to add this CD to the Library.

3. If there are songs you don't want to add to the Library, uncheck their check boxes. Only songs with their check boxes checked will be imported. Unless you really hate a song or disk space is at a premium, it is generally better to import all the songs. You can use the check box in another source, such as in your Library, to cause those songs to be skipped when you play that source.

4. Click the **Import** button. It will become highlighted, and the import process will start (see Figure 4.8).

   If you left the Play songs while importing preference active, the music will begin to play as it is imported.

Import information

Imported songs

Stop button

FIGURE 4.8

You can see that the import process is really moving; it is currently moving along at 6.7× speed.

Song currently being imported

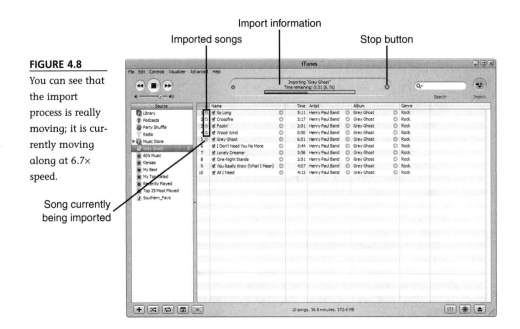

The Information window will show information related to the import process, such as the name of the song currently being imported and the rate at which the import process is happening.

The rate of the import process depends on the hardware you are using and the import settings. In most cases, the import process will occur at a much greater rate than the playing process. For example, with moderate hardware, you can usually achieve import rates exceeding 7×, meaning 7 minutes of music will be imported in 1 minute of time.

An orange circle with a "squiggly" line inside it marks the song currently being imported. When a song has been imported, it is marked with a green circle containing a check mark.

If you want to stop the import process for some reason, click the **Stop** button (the small x within a circle) in the Information window.

When the process is complete, you will hear a tone and all the songs will be marked with the "import complete" icon.

tip

During the import process, you don't have to listen to what you are importing. You can select a different source, such as a playlist, and play it while the CD is being imported. This will slow the import speed slightly, but probably not enough to bother you.

If you have the Play songs while importing preference active, the music will keep playing long after the import process is complete (because importing is much faster than playing is). Listen for the complete tone or keep an eye on the screen to determine when all the music on the CD has been imported.

5. Eject the CD.

Building Your iTunes Music Library in a Hurry

The import process moves along pretty quickly, but you can make it even faster by following these steps:

1. Gather a pile of your CDs in a location close to your computer.

2. Set the import preferences (encoder and quality) for the import session.

3. Open the **General** pane of the iTunes Preferences dialog box.

4. Select **Import Songs and Eject** on the **On CD Insert** menu (see Figure 4.9). This causes iTunes to immediately begin the import process when you insert a CD. When the import process is complete, the CD will be ejected automatically.

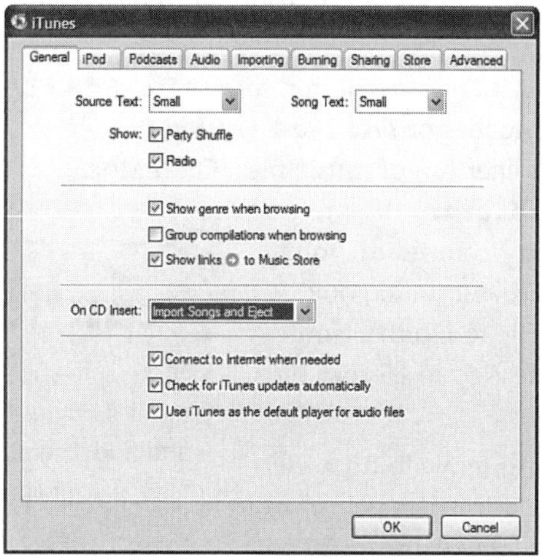

FIGURE 4.9

Choosing the Import Songs and Eject option makes adding lots of CDs to your Library as fast as possible.

5. Click **OK** to close the dialog box.

6. Insert the first CD you want to import. iTunes will start importing it automatically. When the process is complete, the CD will be ejected automatically.

7. Insert the next CD you want to import. Again, iTunes will import the music and eject the disc when it is done.

tip

Consider turning off the Play songs while importing preference on the Importing pane so the import process doesn't impact the music to which you are listening.

8. Repeat step 7 until all the CDs have been imported. You'll be amazed at how quickly you can build a Library, even if you have a large number of CDs.

When you are done batch importing your CDs, you might want to reset the On CD insert menu to **Show Songs** to prevent unintentionally importing a CD more than once.

Importing Audio Files into Your Library

Another potential source of music for your Library is the Internet. There are millions of audio files there, and you can download these files and add them to your Library.

Or, you might have lots of MP3 files on your computer already. You can add all these to your iTunes Library so you can use that music from within iTunes as well.

You can add music stored on your hard drive to your iTunes Library by following these steps:

1. Locate the files you want to add to your Library. For example, find the MP3 files on your hard drive or go to a website that has audio files, such as MP3 files, and download them to your computer.

2. Using iTunes on a Windows computer, select **File**, **Add File to Library** to add individual music files or **File**, **Add Folder to Library** to add a folder full of music files. On a Mac, select **File**, **Add to Library**. If you used the Add Folder to Library command, you'll see the Browse For Folder dialog box. If you used the Add File to Library command, you'll see the Add to Library dialog box.

3. Use the dialog box to move to and select the folder containing the files you want to add or to select the files you want to add to the Library.

4. Click **Open**, **OK**, or **Choose** (the name of the button you see depends on the command you use). The files you selected will be imported into your Library. If you selected a folder, all the songs it contains will be added to your Library.

caution

Make sure you don't download and add illegal files to your Library. In addition to this being the wrong thing to do, you can get prosecuted for downloading files illegally. Make sure any websites from which you get files have those files legally with permission of the files' creators.

Browsing and Searching Your Music Library

It won't be long until you have a large Library with many kinds of music in it. In fact, you are likely to have so much music in the Library that you won't be able to find songs you are interested in just by scrolling up and down the screen. In this section, you'll learn how to find music in your Library, first by browsing and then by searching.

Browsing in the Library

You've already seen the Browser a couple of times. Now it is time to put it to work:

1. Select **Library** on the Source list.

2. If the Browser isn't showing, click the **Action** button, which is now labeled Browse (it looks like an eye). The Browser will appear (see Figure 4.10). The Browser has three columns: Genre, Artist, and Album. The columns start on the left with the most general category, Genre, and end on the right with the most specific category, which is Album.

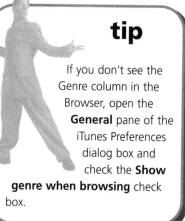

tip

If you don't see the Genre column in the Browser, open the **General** pane of the iTunes Preferences dialog box and check the **Show genre when browsing** check box.

FIGURE 4.10

The Browser offers a good way to find songs in your Library.

The contents of the "path" selected in the Browser are shown in the Content pane that now occupies the bottom part of the right side of the window. At the top of each column is the All option, which shows all the contents of that category. For example, when All is selected in the Genre column, you will see the contents of all the genres for which you have music in the Library. In Figure 4.10, you can see that I have selected All in the Genre column, Phil Keaggy in the Artist column, and Acoustic Sketches in the Albums column. This causes the Content pane to show all the tracks of album titled *Acoustic Sketches* by Phil Keaggy in the Content pane.

At the bottom of the screen, you will see Source Information for the selected source. Again, in Figure 4.10, you can see that the 19 songs shown in the Content pane will play for 1 hour and consume 61.6MB of disk space.

tip

You can also open and close the Browser by selecting **Edit**, **Show Browser** or **Edit**, **Hide Browser**. Pressing **Ctrl+B** (Windows) or ⌘-**B** (Mac) also works.

3. To start browsing your Library, select the genre in which you are interested by clicking it. When you do so, the categories in the other two columns are scoped down to include only the artists and albums that are part of that genre (see Figure 4.11, which shows the Jazz genre in my Library). Similarly, the Content pane now includes only jazz music. Notice in Figure 4.11 that the Source Information has been updated, too. It now shows that I can listen to one day of jazz before I run out of music.

4. To further limit the browse, click an artist in which you are interested in the Artist column. The Album column will be scoped down to show only those albums for the artist selected in the Artist column (see Figure 4.12). Also, the Content pane will show the songs on the albums listed in the Album column.

5. To get down to the most narrow browse possible, select the album in which you are interested in the Album column. The Content pane will now show the songs on the selected album.

6. When you have selected the genre, artist, and album categories in which you are interested, you can scroll in the Content pane to see all the songs included in the group of songs you are browsing.

To make the browse results less narrow again, select **All** in one of the Browser's columns. For example, to browse all your music again, click **All** in the Genre column.

FIGURE 4.11

Because Jazz is selected in the Genre column, the Artist and Album columns and Content pane contain only the jazz that is in my Library.

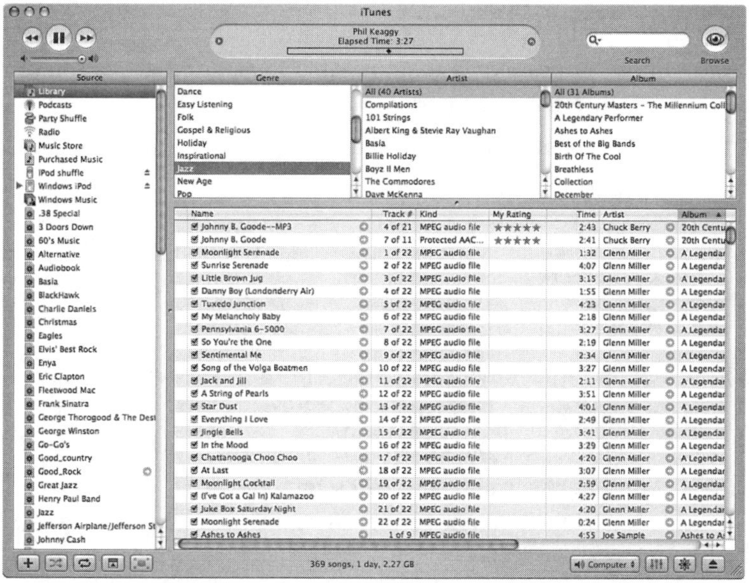

FIGURE 4.12

Now I am browsing all my music in the Jazz genre that is performed by Kenny G.

Hopefully, you can see that you can use the Browser to quickly scan your Library to locate music you want to hear or work with. As you use the Browser more, you will come to rely on it to get you to a group of songs quickly and easily.

Searching Your Music Library

You can use iTunes Search tool to search for specific songs. You can search for songs by any of the following criteria:

- All (searches all possible data)
- Artists
- Albums
- Composers
- Songs

To search for music in your Library, perform the following steps:

1. Select the source you want to search (for example, click the **Library** source). As you might surmise, you can search any source in the Source list—such as a CD, playlist, and so on—by selecting it and then performing a search.

2. Click the **magnifying glass** icon in the **Search** tool (see Figure 4.13). You will see a menu containing the list of data by which you can search. The currently selected search attribute is marked with a check mark.

> **tip**
>
> If you want to search by all data at the same time, you don't need to perform step 2 because All is the default selection.

3. Select the data for which you want to search in the menu. When you release the mouse button, the name of the Search tool will change to reflect your selection on the menu. For example, if you select Artists to search by the Artist field, the Search tool will be labeled Search Artists.

4. Type the data for which you want to search in the field. As you type, iTunes searches the selected source and presents the songs that meet your criterion in the Content pane. It does this on-the-fly so the search narrows with each keystroke. As you type more text or numbers, the search becomes more specific (see Figure 4.14).

5. Keep typing until the search becomes as narrow as you need it to be to find the songs in which you are interested.

After you have found songs, you can play them, add them to playlists, and so on.

To clear your search click the **Clear Search** button that appears in the Search tool after you have typed in it (see Figure 4.14). The songs shown in the Content pane will again be determined by your selections in the Browser.

FIGURE 4.13

By selecting Artists on the menu, you can search the Artist field for all the songs in the selected source (in this case, the Library).

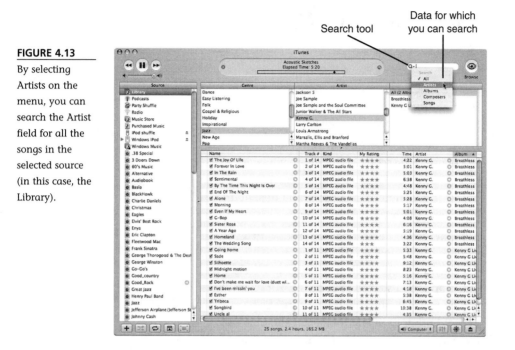

Search tool

Data for which you can search

FIGURE 4.14

Because I selected Artist and typed lyn in the Search tool, the Content pane shows all songs whose artist includes the text *lyn*, as in The Lyndhurst Orchestra, Lynyrd Skynyrd, and so on.

Clear Search

Playing Music in Your Music Library

Remember earlier when I said that you use the same listening techniques to listen to music in your Library as you do when listening to a CD? Now it's time to prove my words.

When you listen to music in your Library, you start by choosing the scope of the music you want to hear. You do this by browsing or searching for music. (If you don't know how to do this, here's a hint: Read the previous two sections.)

After you have the group of songs to which you want to listen showing in the Content pane, use the listening tools you learned about in the previous chapter to listen to your music. For example, you can click Play to play the songs, use the Repeat button to repeat them, sort the Content pane by one of the column headings to change the order in which the songs play, and so on.

note

When you are listening to your Library, I don't recommend that you uncheck a song's check box in the Library or move songs up and down in the list to control how they are played. Use playlists for that kind of customized listening instead (playlists are explained in Chapter 6, "Creating, Configuring, and Using Playlists"). Changes you make to songs in the Library can result in unexpected things happening if you forget to undo a change before making a playlist, burning a CD, and so on.

Removing Tunes from the Music Library

Not all that glitters is gold, nor are all tunes that are digital good. Sometimes, a song is so bad that it just isn't worth the hard disk space it consumes.

To remove songs from your Library, ditch them with the following steps:

1. Find the songs you want to delete by browsing or searching.

2. Select the songs you want to trash. They will become highlighted to show you they are selected (see Figure 4.15).

3. Press the **Delete** or **Backspace** key. You will be prompted to confirm that you really want to delete the song you have selected.

tip

Remember that you can stop a song from playing by unchecking its Song check box in the Content pane. If you aren't sure you want to dump a song permanently, use that method instead so you can always use the song again should you change your mind.

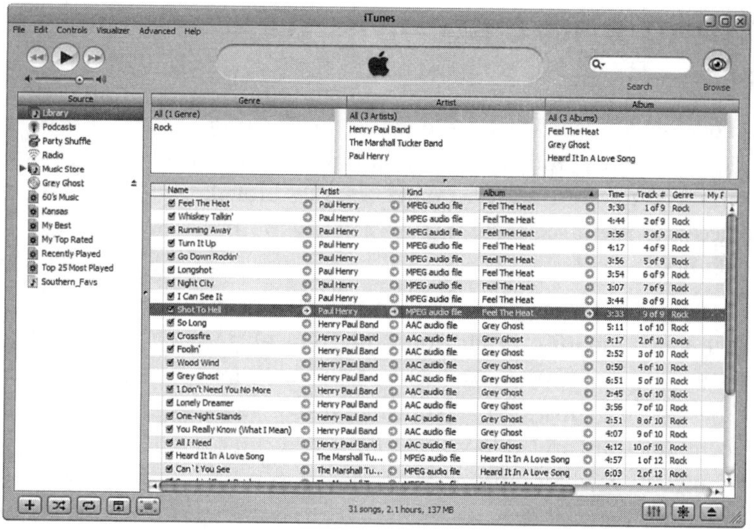

FIGURE 4.15

If I press the Delete key now, "Shot To Hell" will be removed from my Library.

4. If you see the warning prompt, click **Remove** to confirm the deletion. You will see another prompt asking whether you want the selected files to be moved to your Recycle Bin (Windows) or Trash (Mac) or you want to keep the files on your computer. (If you have disabled the warning prompt, you'll move directly to the second dialog box.

5. Click **Move to Recycle Bin** (Windows) or **Move to Trash** (Mac) to move the files so you can get rid of them entirely. The selected songs will be deleted from your Library, and their song files will be moved to the appropriate trash receptacle on your computer. The next time you empty that receptacle, they will be gone forever.

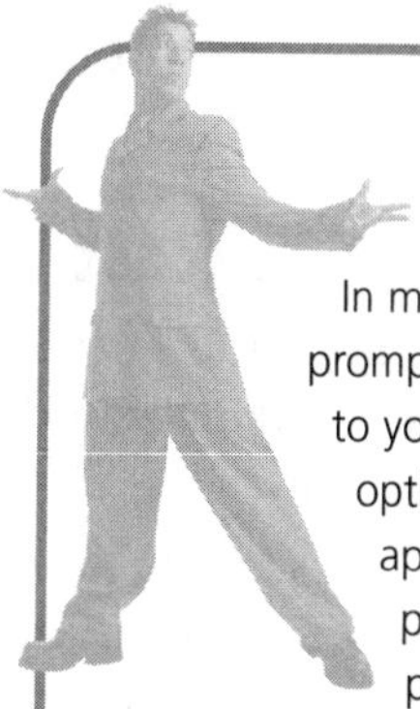

> **tip**
>
> In many of the prompts iTunes presents to you, you have the option of telling the application not to present those prompts again. Just look for the appropriate Do not ask me again check boxes in such prompts and check them to hide those prompts in the future.

If you just want to remove the references to files from the iTunes Library but not delete the song files, click **Keep Files**. The songs will be removed from the Library, but the song files will remain in their current locations.

Subscribing and Listening to Podcasts

Podcasts are radio-like audio you can add to your iTunes Library. You can find thousands of podcasts in the iTunes Music Store. Many websites provide access to podcasts, and some exist solely for that purpose.

Most podcasts are provided in episodes you can listen to individually. When you want to be able to listen to a podcast, you subscribe to it; subscribing to a podcast causes it to be downloaded to your computer and added to your Library. You can also choose to download previous episodes if you want to.

After you have downloaded podcasts, you can listen to them on your computer, move them to an iPod, and so on.

Setting Your Podcast Preferences

Some podcast preferences should be set before you start working with podcasts. Do so with the following steps:

1. Open the iTunes Preferences dialog box and click the **Podcasts** tab (see Figure 4.16).

2. Choose how often you want iTunes to check for new episodes using the **Check for new episodes** drop-down list. The options are Every hour, Every day, Every week, or Manually. iTunes will check for new episodes according to the timeframe you select—unless you select Manually, in which case you must manually check for new episodes.

note

Of course, songs you delete probably aren't really gone forever. You can always add them back to the Library again by repeating the same steps you used to place them in there the first time. This assumes you have a copy somewhere, such as on a CD or stored in some other location. If you imported the music from your hard disk and had iTunes move the songs files to your iTunes Music folder, your only copy will reside in your iTunes Library, so make sure you have such music backed up before you delete it if you might ever want it again.

caution

You should never delete music you purchased from the iTunes Music Store unless you are absolutely sure you will never want it again or you have that music backed up elsewhere. You can download music you purchased from the store only one time. After that, you have to pay for it to download it again.

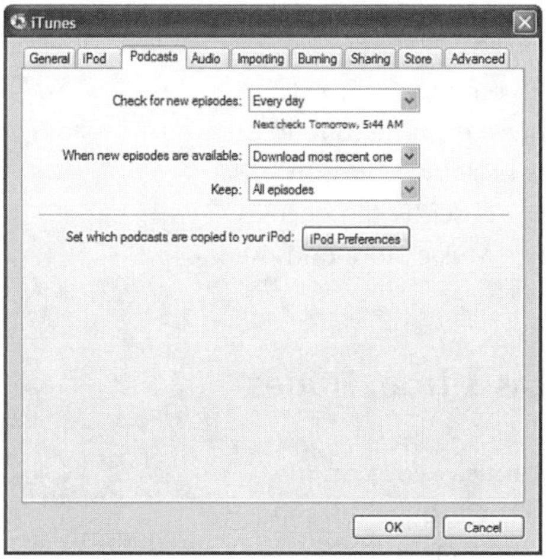

FIGURE 4.16

Use the Podcasts preferences to determine how you want your podcast subscriptions to be managed.

3. Use the **When new episodes are available** drop-down list to determine what iTunes does when it finds new episodes of the podcasts to which you are subscribed. Select **Download most recent one** if you want only the newest episode to be downloaded. Select **Download all** if you want all available episodes downloaded. Select **Do nothing** if you don't any episodes to be downloaded.

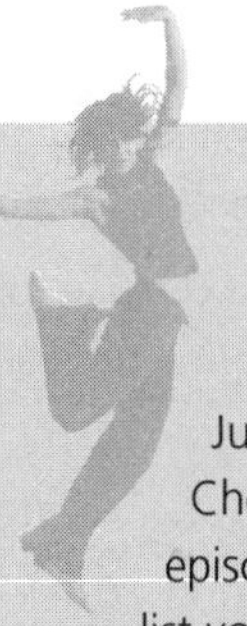

4. Use the **Keep** drop-down list to determine if and when iTunes deletes podcast episodes. Select **All episodes** if you don't want iTunes to automatically remove any episodes. Select **All unplayed episodes** if you want iTunes to remove episodes to which you have listened, and select **Most recent episode** if you want iTunes to keep only the most recent episode even if you haven't listened to all of them. Select **Last _X_ episodes**, where _X_ is 2, 3, 4, 5, or 10, to have iTunes keep the selected number of episodes.

5. Click **OK**. The dialog box will close and your podcast preferences will be set.

note

Just under the Check for new episodes drop-down list you'll see when the next check for new episodes will be performed.

Subscribing to Podcasts

Now that iTunes is ready to manage podcasts according to your preferences, it's time to load up your Library with podcasts of your choice. In this section, you'll learn how to subscribe to podcasts from two sources: the iTunes Music Store and the Internet.

Subscribing to Podcasts from iTunes Music Store

In addition to lots of great music, you can also access thousands of podcasts via the iTunes Music Store. Most of these podcasts are free and you don't even need an iTunes Music Store account to gain access to them.

> **note**
>
> You'll also see the iPod Preferences button. If you click this, you'll move to the Podcasts tab of the iPod preferences tab. You can use the controls on this tab to configure how podcasts are moved into an iPod.

When you access the podcasts section of the iTunes Music Store, you can browse or search for podcasts to which you can then subscribe.

To browse for podcasts in the iTunes Music Store and subscribe to them, perform the following steps:

1. Select **Music Store** on the Source list. The iTunes Music Store will fill the Content pane.

2. Click the **Podcasts** link in the iTunes Music Store. You'll move to the Podcasts home page (see Figure 4.17).

3. Scroll down the window until you see the **Categories** section. Here, you can access podcasts based on various categories, such as Arts & Entertainment, Audio Blogs, Business, Comedy, and so on.

4. Click a category in which you are interested, such as News. The Content pane will be refreshed and will become the Browse window (see Figure 4.18). The podcast Browser works just like the Browser when you browse your Library or other sources.

FIGURE 4.17

Want podcasts?
The iTunes
Music Store has
them!

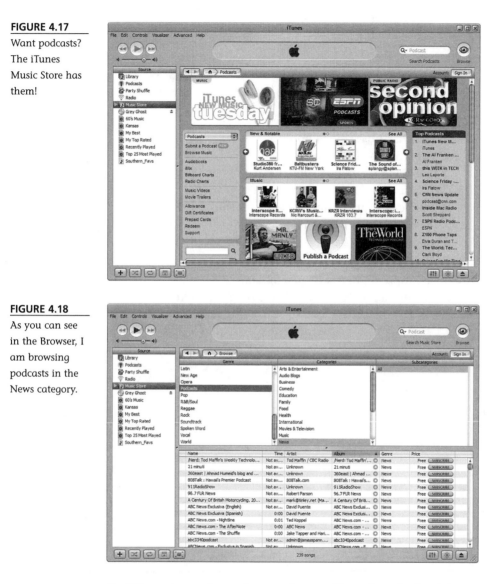

FIGURE 4.18

As you can see
in the Browser, I
am browsing
podcasts in the
News category.

5. If the category has subcategories, you'll see them in the rightmost pane of the Browser; click the subcategory in which you are interested. The Content pane will show all podcasts in the categories selected in the Browser.

6. Use the scrollbar in the Content pane to browse all the podcasts available. For each podcast, you'll see the name, time, artist, album, genre, and price information (which is free for most podcasts).

7. When you find a podcast in which you are interested, you can listen to it by selecting it and clicking the **Play** button. The podcast will begin to play.

8. When you find a podcast that you would like to listen to on a regular basis, click its **Subscribe** button. You'll see a confirmation dialog box; click the **Subscribe** button to subscribe to the podcast. You'll move to the Podcasts source in your Library and episodes will be downloaded according to the preferences you set earlier (see Figure 4.19).

9. Click the **Music Store** source to go back to browse for and subscribe to more podcasts. You'll return to your previous location in the store.

> ## tip
>
> You can click just about any object on the Podcasts home page to move to individual podcasts. The steps in this section are focused on browsing by category, but there are many other ways to browse for podcasts.

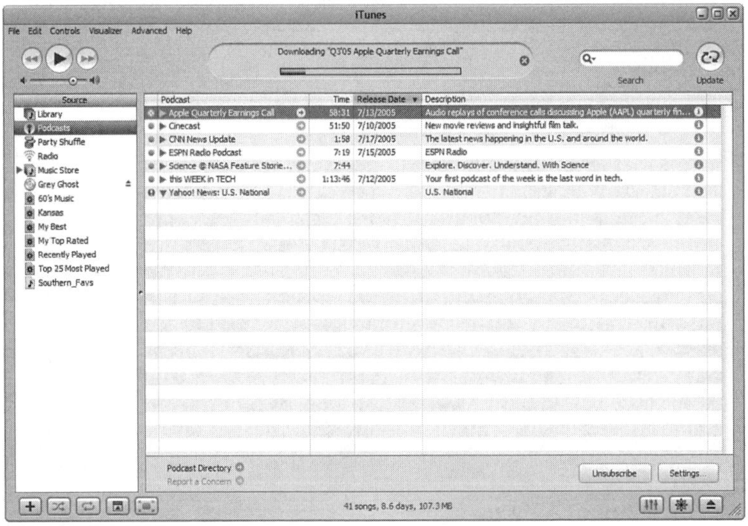

FIGURE 4.19

Here, I've subscribed to the Apple Quarterly Earnings Call podcast and the most recent episode is being downloaded to my computer.

You can also search for specific podcasts in the iTunes Music Store using the following steps:

1. Select the **Music Store** source.

2. Click the **Podcasts** link.

3. Use the **iTunes Search** tool to search for specific podcasts. This works just like it does in other contexts; select the attribute by which you want to search using the magnifying glass icon and then type search text in the box. Press

the **Enter** (Windows) or **Return** (Mac) key to perform the search. The results will appear in the Content pane (see Figure 4.20).

FIGURE 4.20

Here I've searched for podcasts containing "fox;" as you can see, a number of podcasts were found, many of which are from Fox News.

4. Use the scrollbar in the Content pane to browse all the podcasts that were found by your search. For each podcast, you'll see the name, artist, category, description, relevance to your search, and price information (which is free for most podcasts).

5. When you find a podcast in which you are interested, you can listen to it by selecting it and clicking the **Play** button. The podcast will begin to play.

6. When you find a podcast that you would like to listen to on a regular basis, click its **Subscribe** button. You'll see a confirmation dialog box; click the **Subscribe** button to subscribe to the podcast. You'll move to the Podcasts source in your Library and episodes will be downloaded according to the preferences you set earlier.

7. Click the **Music Store** source to go back to search for and subscribe to more podcasts. You'll return to your previous location in the store.

To learn how to work with podcasts to which you have subscribed, see "Listening to and Managing Podcasts" on page **74**.

Subscribing to Podcasts from the Internet

A tremendous amount of podcasts are available on the Internet, and you can subscribe to these to listen to them and download them to an iPod. The most challenging part is finding podcasts that are worth the time to listen to, but that judgment is, of course, in the ear of the beholder.

There are two general sources of podcast websites on the Internet. One includes websites whose sole purpose is to provide access to podcasts. The other includes websites from specific organizations, such as radio shows, that provide podcasts related to those organizations. Subscribing to podcasts from either source is similar.

The following steps show you how to subscribe to a podcast accessed from a specific podcast collection website. You can use similar steps to find other podcast sites.

1. Open a web browser and move to a website that provides podcast information. For example, www.podcastalley.com contains information about thousands of podcasts.

2. Browse or search the website for podcasts that interest you.

3. Click the **Subscribe** link for a podcast in which you are interested. You'll move to an information page that provides a URL for you to subscribe to the podcast (see Figure 4.21).

4. Copy the URL that is displayed.

5. Move into iTunes.

6. Select **Advanced, Subscribe to Podcast**. You'll see the Subscribe to Podcast dialog box (see Figure 4.22).

7. Paste the URL you copied in step 4 into the dialog box and click **OK**. The dialog box will close and you'll move into the Podcasts source. You'll see the podcast to which you subscribed in the Content pane (see Figure 4.23).

To learn how to work with podcasts to which you have subscribed, see "Listening to and Managing Podcasts" on page **74**.

note

Some websites provide access to podcasts only if you are paying subscriber to that site. This is true for some radio shows, for example. Some sites also provide specific tools you must use to access their podcasts. Exploring how to use these kinds of podcasts is beyond the scope of this chapter. Most such sites also provide help information to enable you to use them.

tip

If you want to explore the variety of podcast sites available, perform a Google search on the term "podcast."

FIGURE 4.21

Here I am viewing the URL for a podcast called this WEEK in TECH.

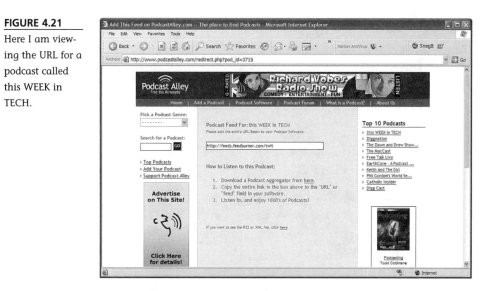

FIGURE 4.22

When you paste a podcast's URL into this dialog box, you can subscribe to it.

FIGURE 4.23

I've subscribed to the this WEEK in TECH podcast.

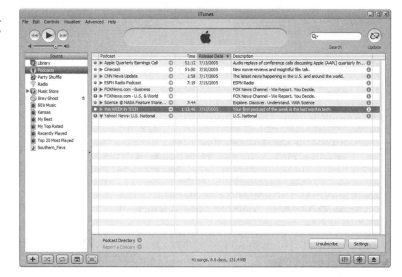

Listening to and Managing Podcasts

After you have subscribed to podcasts, you can listen to them. You can also manage the podcasts to which you have subscribed.

To work with your podcasts, click **Podcasts** on the Source list. You'll see the podcasts to which you have subscribed in the Content pane (see Figure 4.24).

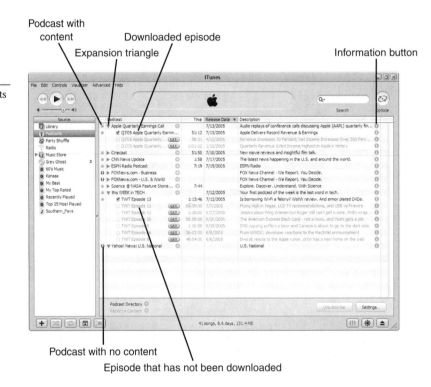

FIGURE 4.24
Use the Podcasts source to work with the podcasts to which you have subscribed.

Podcast with content
Downloaded episode
Expansion triangle
Information button
Podcast with no content
Episode that has not been downloaded

To perform various podcast actions, refer to the following list:

■ To see all the episodes available for a podcast, click its expansion triangle. All the available episodes will be shown. The episodes that have been downloaded to your computer and to which you can listen will have a blue dot next to them. Those that haven't been downloaded yet will be grayed out and the Get button will be shown.

■ To download an episode, click its **Get** button. The episode will be downloaded

tip

Remember that you control how many episodes are downloaded to your computer using the Podcasts preferences you learned about earlier in this section.

to your computer. When that process is complete, it will be marked with a blue dot and you will be able to listen to it. The Information area will present information about the download process.

▓ To play an episode of a podcast, select it and click the **Play** button. The other iTunes playback controls work similarly to how the do for other sources, too.

▓ To get information about an episode, click its **Information** button. You'll see the Podcast Information window that presents a summary of the episode (see Figure 4.25).

FIGURE 4.25

Here I am viewing information for an episode of the World Vision Report podcast.

tip

You can click the Settings button to jump to the Podcasts pane of the iTunes Preferences dialog box.

▓ To move a website associated with a podcast, click the arrow in its **Podcast** column. If the podcast came from the iTunes Music Store, you'll move to its page in the store. If it came from outside the iTunes Music Store, you'll move to the podcast's home page on the Web.

▓ Click the **Podcast Directory** link at the bottom of the Content pane to move to the Podcast home page in the iTunes Music Store.

▓ To unsubscribe from a podcast, select it and click the **Unsubscribe** button. Episodes of the podcast will no longer be downloaded to your computer. You can subscribe again by clicking the Subscribe button that appears next to the podcast.

note

After you have listened to an episode, it might be removed from the Podcasts source, depending on the Keep preference set in the Podcasts pane of the iTunes Preferences dialog box. For example, if you select All unplayed episodes, episodes will be removed after you have played them.

- To remove a podcast, select it and press the **Delete** key. Click the **Move to Recycle Bin** (Windows) or **Move to Trash** (Mac) button to delete the podcasts files from your computer and from the Library or the **Keep Files** button to remove the podcast from your Library but leave its files on your computer.

- You can click the Update button to refresh the list of episodes available for each podcast to which you are subscribed.

- If a podcast has an exclamation point icon next to it, that podcast has a problem, such as no content being available. If you want to report the problem, select the podcast and click the Report a Concern link. This is available only for podcasts that are available in the iTunes Music Store.

tip

You should periodically review your Podcast preferences to ensure they match your current podcast habits, such as how you want episodes to be downloaded.

The Absolute Minimum

Although it might not smell like a book library, your iTunes Library is at least as useful and is a heck of a lot easier to get to. In this chapter, you learned how to build and use your iTunes Library. Before we move on to the next great thing about iTunes, check out some related points of interest (well, my interest anyway; hopefully, they will be yours, too):

- Through the Audible.com service (accessible via the iTunes Music Store), you can also add audio books to your iTunes Library to listen to them on your computer and you can add them to an iPod. Working with audio book content is similar to working with music. Unfortunately, covering the details of doing so is outside the scope of this book.

- You learned that you can choose the import encoder and quality settings when you import music from audio CDs to your Library. You can import the same songs at different quality levels to experiment with various settings or to create different versions of the same song. For example, you might want a high-quality version to play from your computer and a lower-quality version with a smaller file size for a portable device. To create another version of a song, you can change the import settings and import it from a CD again. You can also reimport a song already in the Library by setting the encoding settings and adding its file (which will be located in the iTunes Music folder) to the Library, just like other music files stored on your computer.

continues

■ Although we focused on the AAC and Apple Lossless Encoder formats in this chapter, in some cases you might want to use the WAV or AIFF format. For example, suppose you want to use part of a song as a sound byte in an application that doesn't support either of the primary formats but does support WAV files. You could choose the WAV format and then import the song you want to use in that format. The WAV file, which would be located in your iTunes Music folder, could then be added to the other application you are working with.

■ If you are listening to music while doing something else, such as browsing your Library, you might move away from the song that is currently playing. If you want to move back to it again, select **File**, **Show Current Song** or press **Ctrl+L** (Windows) or ⌘**-L** (Mac).

■ If you like to shuffle while you listen, you can determine whether iTunes shuffles by song or by album. It can be interesting when listening to the Library if you shuffle by album because iTunes will pick an album and play all the songs it contains, then pick another album, play all its songs, and so on. If you choose to shuffle by song, individual songs will be played regardless of the albums of which they are a part. To set this behavior, open the **Advanced** pane of the iTunes Preferences dialog box and click either the **Album** radio button next to the Shuffle by album or the **Song** radio button to shuffle by song.

■ Podcasts are similar to broadcast radio except that you can store episodes in your iTunes Library so you can listen to them from your computer at a time of your choosing or by moving them to an iPod so you can listen on the move. iTunes includes all the tools you need to subscribe to, manage, and listen to any podcasts you can find.

■ You can use the Browser with any source, although it defaults to being closed with CDs and some playlists because it usually isn't that useful in those contexts (especially when the source is a single CD). To open it for any source, just select the source you want to browse and open the Browser.

IN THIS CHAPTER

- Get to know and love tags.
- Get the details for your music.
- Label your music so you can do cool things with it, such as creating playlists based on a music's information.
- Rate your songs, set the relative volume level, and hear only the parts you want to hear.
- Don't miss out on album artwork just because you have gone digital.
- Work the Content pane like a pro.

5

Labeling, Categorizing, and Configuring Your Music

It's confession time. I admit it. This topic might not seem too exciting at first glance. Who wants to spend their time labeling and categorizing music? That is a fair question, but I hope by the time you read through this chapter, you answer that question with an enthusiastic, "I do, that's who!" Of course, I would be almost as happy even if your response is, "It might not be as fun as building my Library, but it will make my iTunes world a lot better." Think of this chapter as learning the nuts and bolts of how iTunes works so you can become an iTunes wizard later.

After you have worked through the labeling content in this chapter, I think you will find the ability to configure the songs in your Library to be pretty exciting because that is where you really start bending iTunes to your will (which isn't as dramatic as it sounds because iTunes is really pretty easy to command).

Understanding Song Tags and Knowing Why You Should Care About Them

In the previous chapter, you saw how you can browse your iTunes music collection by genre, artist, and album. This makes finding music fast and easy, even if you have thousands of songs in your Library. This functionality is enabled because each song in your Library has information—also called a *tag*—that categorizes and identifies that song for you. Genre, artist, and album are just three of the possible tags for each song in iTunes. There are many more items of information that iTunes manages.

These types of data fall into two groups: data that iTunes assigns for you and that you can't change, and data that you or iTunes assigns and that you can change.

Data that iTunes assigns and that you can view but can't change include the following:

> ### note
>
> Not all songs have all the data fields listed. You will only see data that is applicable to a specific song. For example, only music purchased from the iTunes Music Store has information about the purchase.

- **Kind**—This identifies the type of file the song is, such as Protected AAC audio file, AAC audio file, MP3, and so on.
- **Size**—The amount of disk space required to store the song.
- **Bit Rate**—The quality level at which the song was encoded. Larger numbers, such as 128Kbps, are better.
- **Sample Rate**—The rate at which the music was sampled when it was captured.
- **Date Modified**—The date on which the song file was last changed.
- **Play Count**—The number of times the song has been played.
- **Last Played**—The last time the song was played.
- **Profile**—A categorization of the song's complexity.
- **Format**—The format in which the song was encoded, such as MPEG-1, Layer 3.
- **Channels**—Whether the track is stereo or mono.

- **Encoded With**—The tools used to encode the song, such as iTunes, QuickTime, and so on.

- **ID3 Tag**—ID3 tags are data formatted according to a set of specifications. If a song's data has been formatted with this specification, the ID3 version number will be shown.

- **Purchase By, Account Name, and FairPlay Version**—If a song was purchased from the iTunes Music Store, this information identifies who purchased the music and which account was used. The FairPlay version information relates to the means by which the song is protected.

- **Where**—This shows a path to the song's file on your computer along with the filename.

Data collected for songs that you can change includes the following:

- **Name**—This is the name of the song.

- **Artist**—The person who performs the song.

- **Album**—The name of the album from which the song comes.

- **Grouping**—This is a label you can assign to group songs together in some fashion.

- **Composer**—The person who is credited with writing the song.

- **Comments**—This is a free-form text field in which you can make comments about a song.

- **Genre**—This associates a song with its musical genre, such as jazz or classical.

- **Year**—The year the song was created.

- **Track Number**—The song's position on the CD from which it came, such as "2 of 12."

- **Disc Number**—The number of the CD or DVD. This is meaningful only for multiple-disc sets.

- **BPM**—The song's beats per minute.

- **Part of a Compilation**—This indicates whether the song is part of a compilation CD, meaning one that contains music from a variety of artists (you know, like that *Greatest TV Theme Songs from the 1970s* CD you love so much).

> **note**
>
> One "kind" you will see is Protected AAC audio file. This indicates that the song was purchased from the iTunes Music Store.

When you add a song to your Library, iTunes will add as much of this data as it can find for each song. However, you can add or change the data in the previous list.

So, why should you care about all this data? There are a couple of reasons.

The first is that, as you already know because you learned how to browse and search your Library in the previous chapter, this data can be used to find music in which you are interested. That reason alone should be enough to convince you that these types of data are important to you.

The second reason is that when it comes time to create playlists (which you will learn about in Chapter 6, "Creating, Configuring, and Using Playlists"), you can use song tags to determine which songs are included in your playlists. For example, you can configure a playlist to include the last 25 songs you have played from the Jazz genre. This is just a basic example—you can get much more sophisticated than this. In fact, you can include several combinations of these types of data as criteria in playlists to create interesting sets of music to listen to.

note

When you insert a CD, iTunes attempts to get that CD's information from the CDDB (the online CD database), which is why it connects to the Internet. If iTunes finds the CD in this database, the information for that CD is applied to the CD and carried into the Library if you import the songs from that CD into iTunes. If you purchase music from the iTunes Music Store, it also contains many of these tags.

Viewing Song Information

Now that you understand the types of data that can be associated with songs in your Library, it's time to learn how to view that information. You have three basic areas in which to view song information: the Browser, the Content pane, and the Info window.

Viewing Tags in the Browser

If you read through the previous chapter, you have already used this technique. When you view the Browser, you see the genre, artist, and album tags associated with the songs you are browsing (see Figure 5.1).

Viewing Tags in the Content Pane

Even if you don't realize it, you have also seen tags in the Content pane. The column headings you see in the Content pane are actually the tags associated with the songs you are viewing (see Figure 5.2).

FIGURE 5.1

Each column in the Browser is a tag associated with songs in your Library.

FIGURE 5.2

Each column heading in the Content pane is a tag.

You can customize the columns (tags) shown in the Content pane, as you will learn later in this chapter.

Viewing Tags in the Info Window

The Info window is probably the only area in which you haven't seen tags yet. To view the Info window, select a song in your Library and select **File**, **Get Info** or press **Ctrl+I** (Windows) or ⌘-**I** (Mac). The Info window will appear; at the top of the window, you'll see the name of the song whose information you are viewing (see Figure 5.3). This window has four panes that you will be using throughout the rest of this chapter.

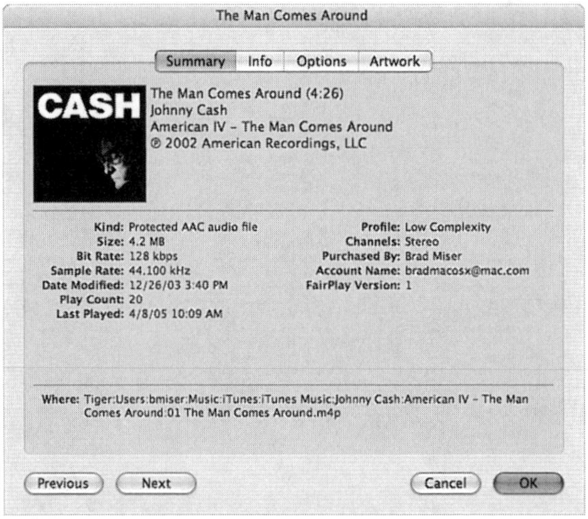

FIGURE 5.3

The Info window enables you to view the tags associated with a song, and you can change many of them.

The Summary pane provides a summary view of the song's information, starting at the top with any album art associated with the song and including its name, length, artist, and album. In the center part of the pane, you see the data iTunes manages (you can view this data, but you can't change it). At the bottom of the pane, you can see the path to the song's file on your computer.

When you click the Info tab, you will see the tags you can change (see Figure 5.4). You'll learn how to change this data in the next section.

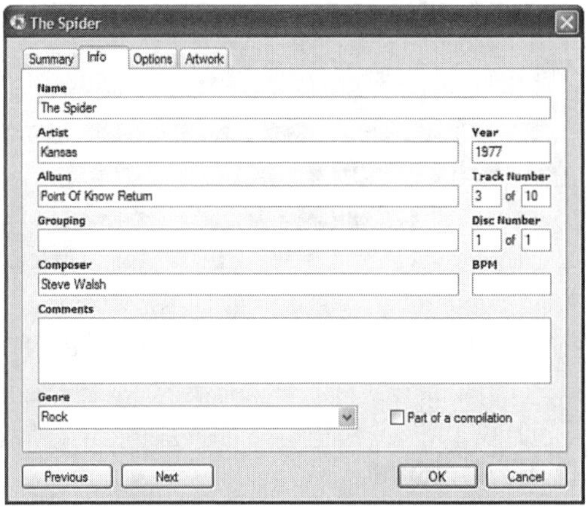

FIGURE 5.4

Although you can't change the tags shown on the Summary pane, you can change the ones on the Info pane.

The other two panes of the window, Options and Artwork, are used to configure specific aspects of a song (again, we'll get to these topics in a few pages).

You can view information for other songs without closing the window. Click **Next** to move to the next song in the source you are viewing (such as your Library) or **Previous** to move to the previous song. When you do, that song's information will be displayed in the Info window.

To close the Info window, click **OK**.

Labeling Your Music

There are a couple of places in which you can change a song's tags.

Labeling a Song in the Info Window

You can use the Info window to change a song's tags, as you can see in the following steps:

1. Open the **Info** window for the song whose information you want to change.

2. Click the **Info** tag, and the Info pane will appear.

3. Enter or change the information shown in the various fields. For example, you can change the song's name or artist. Or you might want to add comments about the song in the Comments box.

4. To change a song's genre, select the new genre from the **Genre** menu.

5. When you are done entering or changing tags, click **OK**. The Info window will close, and any changes you made will be saved.

Labeling Multiple Songs at the Same Time

You can change some tags, such as Genre, for a group of songs at the same time. This can be a faster way to entering data because you can change multiple songs at the same time. Here are the steps to follow:

> **note**
>
> Typically, if you have imported a CD or purchased music from the iTunes Music Store, you shouldn't change the data that came from the source, such as name, artist, album, track number, and so on. Occasionally, a CD's information will come in incorrect (such as a misspelling in the artist's name); you'll probably want to fix such mistakes. You can certainly add data in those fields that are empty.

> **note**
>
> One of the more useful tags is Genre. This can be used for browsing and also in playlists.

1. Select the songs whose data you want to change.
2. Open the **Info** window. You'll be prompted to confirm that you want to change the information for a group of songs.
3. Click **Yes** to clear the prompt. The Multiple Song Information window will appear (see Figure 5.5). The information and tools in this window work in the same way as they do for individual songs. The difference is that the information and settings apply to all the songs you have selected.

tip

If a genre by which you want to classify music isn't listed on the menu, you can add it to the menu by selecting Custom on the menu and then typing the genre you want to add. That genre will be added to the menu and associated with the current song. You can use the genres you create just like the default genres.

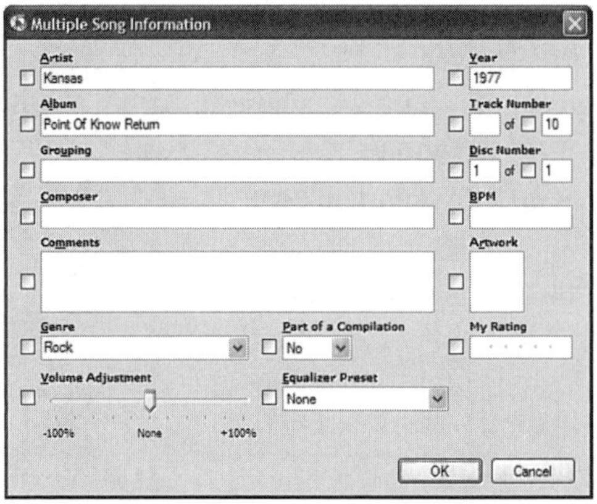

FIGURE 5.5

You can use this window to change the data for multiple songs at the same time.

4. Enter data in the fields, make changes to existing data, or use the other tools to configure the songs you have selected. As you change information, the check box next to the tag will become checked to show that you are changing that data for all the selected songs.
5. When you are done making changes, click **OK**. The window will close and the changes you made will be saved.

tip

To select multiple songs that are next to each other, hold down the **Shift** key while you click songs. To select multiple songs that aren't next to each other, hold down the **Ctrl** (Windows) or ⌘ (Mac) key while you click songs.

Labeling a Song in the Content Pane

You can also edit tags within the Content pane:

1. Click once on a song to select it.

2. Click once on the tag you want to edit. The tag will become highlighted to show that it is ready to be edited (see Figure 5.6).

3. Type the new information.

4. Press **Enter** (Windows) or **Return** (Mac). The changes you made will be saved.

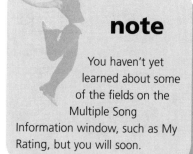

note

You haven't yet learned about some of the fields on the Multiple Song Information window, such as My Rating, but you will soon.

FIGURE 5.6

You can also change tags from the Content pane; in this example the album name is highlighted and can be changed.

Configuring a Song's Options

You can configure a number of options for the songs in your Library, including the following:

■ **Relative Volume**—You can change a song's relative volume so it is either louder or quieter than "normal." This is useful if you like to listen to songs recorded at a variety of volume levels because the volume remains somewhat similar as you move from song to song.

- **Equalizer Preset**—You can use the iTunes Equalizer to configure the relative volume of sound frequencies.

- **My Rating**—You can give tunes a rating from one to five stars. You can use ratings in various ways, such as to create criteria for playlists (such as include only my five-star songs) or to sort the Content pane.

- **Start and Stop Time**—You can set songs to start or stop at certain points in the track. This can be useful if you don't want to hear all of a track, such as when a song has an introduction you don't want to hear each time the song plays.

Configuring Song Options in the Info Window

You can configure a song's options in the Info window by performing the following steps:

1. Select the song whose options you want to set.
2. Open the **Info** window.
3. Click the **Options** tab (see Figure 5.7).

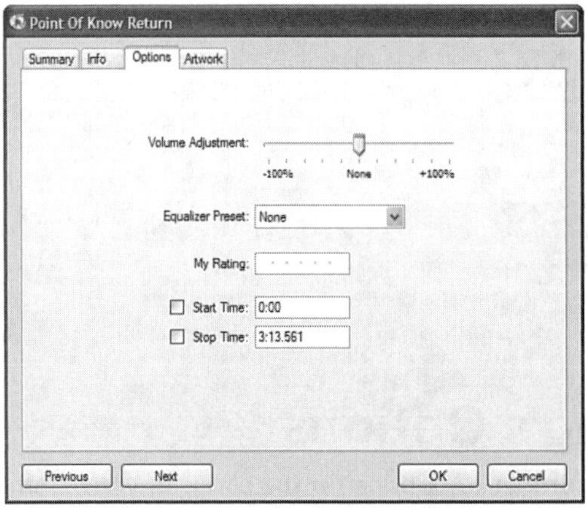

tip

Another way to open the Info window is to point to a song and right-click (or Ctrl-click on a Mac with a single-button mouse). A contextual menu will appear, from which you select Get Info.

FIGURE 5.7

Using the Options tab, you can configure a number of settings for a song.

4. To change the song's relative volume, drag the **Volume Adjustment** slider to the left to make the song quieter or to the right to make it louder.

5. To rate the song, click the dot representing the number of stars you want to give the song in the **My Rating** field. For example, to give the song three

stars, click the center (third) dot. Stars will appear up to the point at which you click. In other words, before you click you'll see a dot. After you click a dot, it becomes a star.

6. To set a start time, check the **Start Time** check box and enter a time in the format *minutes:seconds*. When you play the song, it will start playing at the time you enter.

7. To set a stop time, check the **Stop Time** check box and enter a time in the format *minutes:seconds*. When you play the song, it will stop playing at the time you enter.

8. Click **OK**. The window will close and your changes will be saved.

note

When you set a start or stop time, you don't change the song file in any way. You can play the whole song again by unchecking the Start Time or Stop Time check box.

Rating Songs in the Content Pane

You can also rate songs in the Content pane. To do so, follow these steps:

1. Scroll in the Content pane until you see the **My Rating** column (see Figure 5.8).

FIGURE 5.8

You can also rate songs from the Content pane.

2. Select the song you want to rate. Dots will appear in the My Rating column for that song.

3. Click the dot representing the number of stars you want to give the song. The dots up to and including the one on which you clicked will become stars.

Adding and Viewing Album Artwork

note

The My Rating column might not appear in the Content pane for every source. In a later section, you will learn how to choose the columns shown for a given source.

Many CD and album covers are works of art (though many aren't!), and it would be a shame never to see them just because your music has gone digital. With iTunes, you don't need to miss out because you can associate artwork with songs and display that artwork in the iTunes window.

Most of the music you purchase from the iTunes Music Store will include artwork you can view. You can also add artwork to songs and view that in the same way.

Viewing Album Artwork

To view a song's artwork, do one of the following:

■ Click the **Show/Hide Song Artwork** button located under the Source list. The Artwork pane will appear and display the artwork associated with either the currently playing song or the currently selected song (see Figure 5.9). At the top of the artwork, you will see **Selected Song**, which indicates you are viewing the artwork associated with the selected song, or **Now Playing**, which indicates you are viewing artwork associated with the song currently playing.

tip

Yet another way to rate a song is to open its contextual menu (right-click it with a two-button mouse or Ctrl-click it with a one-button mouse). Select the **My Rating** command and then select the number of stars on the pop-up menu.

■ Double-click the artwork to see a larger version in a separate window (see Figure 5.10). The title of the window will be the name of the song with which the artwork is associated.

FIGURE 5.9

You can view the artwork associated with a song in the Artwork pane.

Show/Hide Song Artwork

FIGURE 5.10

You can view a large version of a song's artwork in a separate window.

To choose between viewing artwork associated with the selected song or the song currently playing, click the arrow button or text at the top of the Artwork pane. The artwork will change to the other option (for example, if you click Now Playing, it will become Selected Song), and you will see the artwork for that song.

- If you select the Now Playing option, the artwork will change in the Artwork pane as the next song begins playing (unless, of course, the songs use the same artwork). When nothing is playing, you'll see a message saying so in the pane.

- If the song has more than one piece of artwork associated with it, click the arrows that appear at the top of the pane to see each piece of art.

Adding Artwork for Songs

You might want to associate artwork with a song. For example, if a song doesn't have album art associated with it (songs you import from a CD won't), you can add the art yourself. Or, you might want to add the artist's picture or some other

meaningful graphic to the song.

If you burn discs for your music, you should add art to your music because you can use iTunes to print jewel case covers that include this art.

You can add one or more pieces of art to songs by using the following steps:

1. Prepare the artwork you are going to associate with a song. You can use graphics in the usual formats, such as JPG, TIFF, GIF, and so on.

2. Select the song with which you want to associate the artwork.

3. Open the **Info** window and then click the **Artwork** tab (see Figure 5.11). If the selected song has artwork with it, you will see it in the Artwork pane.

note

If you view the artwork in a separate window, it does not change with the music. When you open the artwork in a new window, it is static, meaning you can only view the image you double-clicked.

tip

A great source of album covers for your CDs are online CD retailers (such as Amazon.com). Most of these provide the album cover as an image when you view a CD. You can download these images to your computer and then add them to songs in your Library.

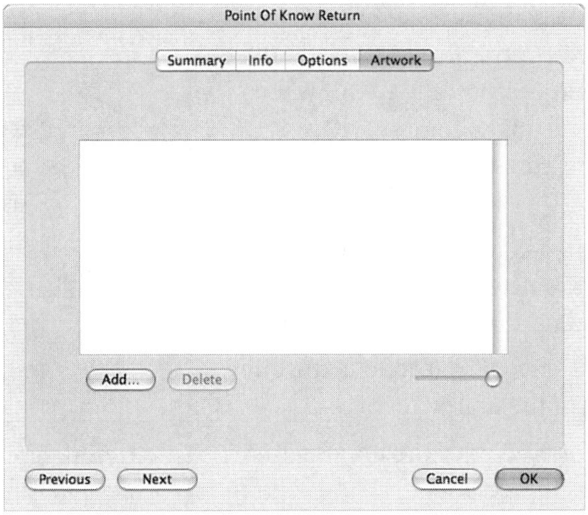

FIGURE 5.11

You use the Artwork pane to add artwork to a song.

4. Click **Add**. A dialog box that enables you to choose an image will appear.

5. Move to and select the image you want to associate with the song.

6. Click **Open** (Windows) or **Choose** (Mac). The image will be added to the Artwork pane of the Info window (see Figure 5.12).

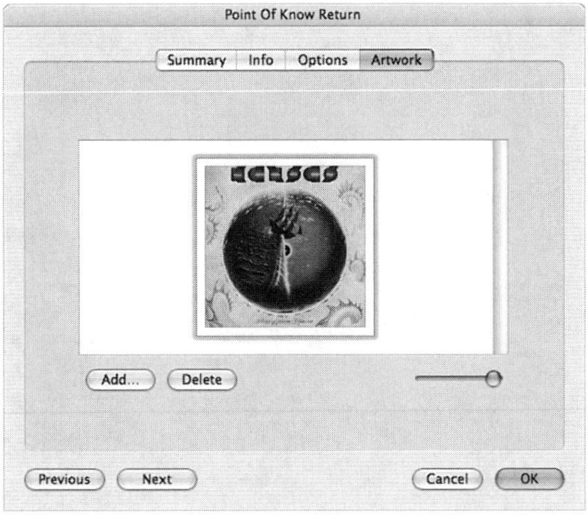

FIGURE 5.12

This song now has album art associated with it.

You can use the slider under the image box to change the size of the previews you see in the window. Drag the slider to the right to make the image larger or to the left to make it smaller. This doesn't change the image;

instead, it only impacts the size of the image as you currently see it in the Info window. This is especially useful when you associate lots of images with a song because you can see them all at the same time.

7. Repeat steps 4–6 to continue adding images to the Artwork pane until you have added all the images for a song.

The default image for a song is the one on the left of the image box.

8. To change the order of the images, drag them in the image box.

9. Click **OK**. The window will close and the images will be saved with the song (see Figure 5.13).

tip

You can associate art with multiple songs at the same time, such as for an entire CD. To do so, select multiple songs and open the **Info** window. Use the **Artwork** box on the Multiple Song Info window to add images. Either drag images onto this box or double-click it to open the image selection dialog box and then select the images you want to add to all the songs at once.

FIGURE 5.13

You can tell this song has multiple images associated with it by the arrows at the top of the Artwork pane. Click an arrow to see its other images.

View previous image

View next image

Customizing the Content Pane

There are a number of ways to customize the columns (tags) that appear in the Content pane. What's more, you can customize the Content pane for each source. The customization you have done for a source (such as a CD or playlist) is remembered and used each time you view that source.

You can select the tags (columns) that are shown for a source by using the following steps:

1. Select the source whose Content pane you want to customize. Its contents will appear in the Content pane.

2. Select **Edit**, **View Options** or press **Ctrl+J** (Windows) or ⌘-**J** (Mac). You will see the View Options dialog box (see Figure 5.14). At the top of the dialog box, you'll see the source for which you are configuring the Content pane. (In Figure 5.4, it is a playlist called Johnny Cash.) You'll also see all the available columns that can be displayed. If a column's check box is checked, that column will be displayed; if not, it won't be shown.

> **note**
>
> If you really get into finding and adding artwork for the CDs you import, tools are available to help you. If you use a Mac, one such tool is called CDCoverTool. While I haven't used it, you can try it for yourself by going to www.hillmanminx.net.

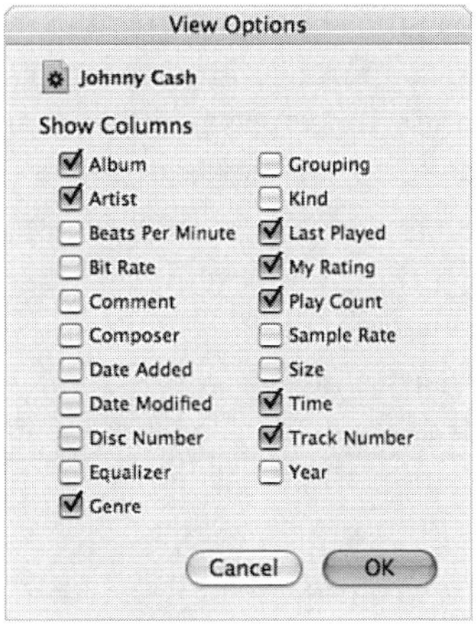

FIGURE 5.14

You can set the columns shown in the Content pane with the View Options dialog box.

3. Check the check boxes next to the columns you want to see.

4. Uncheck the check boxes next to the columns you don't want to see.

5. Click **OK**. When you return to the Content pane, only the columns you selected will be shown (see Figure 5.15).

FIGURE 5.15

If you could view all the columns in this Content pane, you would see that they correspond to the check boxes checked in the previous figure.

If you can't see all the columns being displayed, use the horizontal scrollbar to scroll in the Content pane. You can also use the vertical scrollbar to move up and down in the Content pane.

Following are some other ways to customize the Content pane:

- You can change the width of columns by pointing to the line that marks the boundary of the column in the column heading section. When you do, the cursor will become a vertical line with arrows pointing to the left and right. Drag this to the left to make a column narrower or to the right to make it wider. The rest of the columns will move to accommodate the change.

- You can change the order in which columns appear by dragging a column heading to the left or to the right. When you release the mouse button, the column will assume its new position and the other columns will move to accommodate it.

- As you learned when playing a CD, you can sort the Content pane using any of the columns by clicking the column heading by which you want the pane to be sorted. The songs will be sorted according to that criterion, and the column heading will be

note

The only column you can't change (width or location) is the first one (which usually displays the track if you are viewing a CD or playlist and is empty when you are viewing your Library).

highlighted to show it is the current sort column. To change the direction of the sort, click the sort order triangle, which appears only in the Sort column. When you play a source, the songs will play according to the order in which they are sorted in the Content pane, starting from the top of the pane and playing toward the bottom.

The Absolute Minimum

Hopefully, this chapter turned out to be more exciting than you might have expected based on its title. Although labeling your music might not be fun in itself, it does enable you to do fun things. Setting options for your music enables you to enhance your listening experience, and adding and viewing artwork is fun. Finally, you saw that the Contents pane can be customized to your preferences. As we leave this chapter, here are some nuggets for you to chew on:

- If iTunes can't find information about a CD, you can enter that information yourself by using the Info window you learned about in this chapter.

- If you want to check for information about a CD on command, select **Advanced**, **Get CD Track Names**. (You can also use this command if you turned off the preference that allows iTunes to automatically perform this task.) iTunes will connect to the Internet and attempt to get the CD's information.

- Occasionally, iTunes will find more than one CD that seems to be the one it looked for. When this happens, you will see a dialog box that lists each candidate iTunes found. Select the information you want to apply to the CD by clicking one of the candidates.

- You can submit track names for a CD, label the CD, and select it. Then select **Advanced**, **Submit CD Track Information**. The CD's information will be uploaded into the CDDB and will be provided to other people who use the same CD.

- When adding artwork to songs, you aren't limited to just the related album cover. You can associate any kind of graphics with your songs. For example, you can use pictures of the artists, scenes that relate to the music, pictures you have taken that remind you of the music, and so on.

- If you have looked at the figures in this chapter, you should be able to guess who at least two of my favorite artists are. Can you remember that far back?

- Learn why playlists might just be the best of iTunes' many outstanding features.

- Collect your favorite music in a standard playlist so you hear only the music you want to hear when you want to hear it.

- Change your playlists whenever the spirit moves you.

- Become an iTunes master by creating your own smart playlists to make iTunes choose music for you to listen to based on your criteria.

- Use the Party Shuffle to keep your iTunes experience fresh and interesting.

Creating, Configuring, and Using Playlists

Of all the cool features iTunes offers (and as you have seen, there lots of cool features), this chapter's topic—playlists—just might be the coolest of them all. Playlists enable you to listen to exactly the music you want to hear, when and how you want to hear it. Do you love a CD but hate a song or two on it? Fine, just set up a playlist without the offensive song. Wish you could hear different songs from a variety of albums? No problem. Ever thought it would be neat if you could pick a style of music and hear your favorites tunes in that style? What about if the tunes you hear are selected for you automatically based on your preferences? With iTunes playlists, you can do all this and more.

Understanding Playlists

Simply put, playlists are custom collections of songs that you create or that iTunes creates for you based on criteria you define. After a playlist has been created, you can listen to it, put it on a CD, move it to your iPod, share it over a network, and more.

There are two kinds of playlists: standard playlists and smart playlists.

The Standard-But-Very-Useful Playlist

A *standard playlist* (which I'll sometimes call just a *playlist* from here on) is a set of songs you define manually. You put the specific songs you want in a playlist and do what you will with them. You can include the same song multiple times, mix and match songs from many CDs, put songs in any order you choose, and basically control every aspect of that music collection (see Figure 6.1).

> **note**
>
> In the Source list, the playlist icon is a blue box with a musical note in its center (see Figure 6.1). A smart playlist has a purple box with a gear inside it (see Figure 6.2). Smart playlists are grouped nearer the top of the Source pane, while standard playlists remain toward the bottom.

FIGURE 6.1

Here is a standard playlist that contains a wide variety of tunes from an assortment of artists.

Playlists are useful for creating CDs or making specific music to which you might want to listen available at the click of the mouse. With a playlist, you can determine exactly which songs are included and the order in which those songs play. Playlists are also easy to create and they never change over time—unless you purposefully change them, of course.

The Extra-Special Smart Playlist

A *smart playlist* is smart because you don't put songs in it manually. Instead, you tell iTunes which kind of songs you want included in it by the attributes of that music, such as genre or artist, and iTunes picks those songs for you (see Figure 6.2). For example, you can create a playlist based on a specific genre, such as Jazz, that you have listened to in the past few days. You can also tell iTunes how many songs to include.

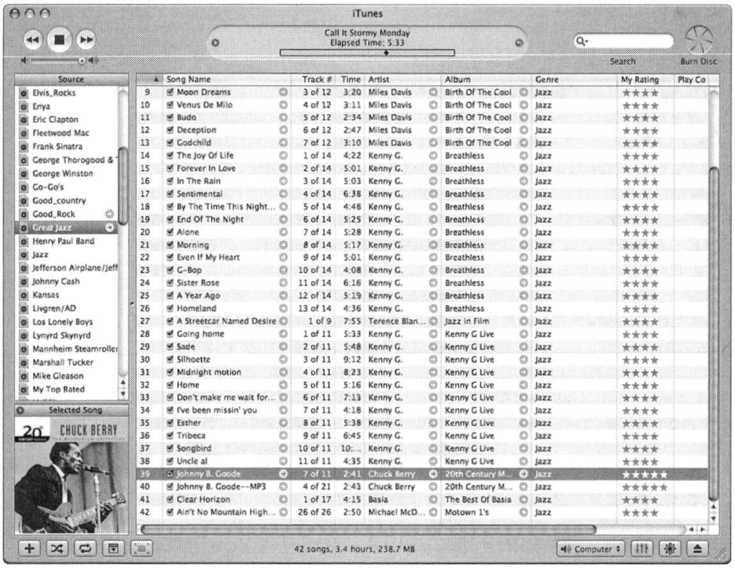

caution

Creating smart playlists depends on your music being properly tagged with information, such as genre, artist, song names, and so on. Sometimes music you add to your Library, such as by MP3 files that are stored on your hard drive, won't have all this information. Before you get going with smart playlists, make sure you have your music properly labeled and categorized. Chapter 5, "Labeling, Categorizing, and Configuring Your Music," explains how you do this.

FIGURE 6.2

On the surface, a smart playlist doesn't look all that different from a playlist, but when you take a closer look, you will see that a smart playlist lives up to its name.

The really cool thing is that smart playlists can be dynamic, meaning the songs they contain are updated over time based on criteria you define. As you add, listen to, or change your music, the contents of a smart playlist can change to match those changes; this happens in real time so the songs included in a smart playlist can change, too. Imagine you have a smart playlist that tells iTunes to include all the music you have in the Jazz genre that is performed by Kenny G, the Pat Metheny Group, Joe Sample, and Larry Carlton. If you make this a "live" smart playlist, iTunes will automatically add any new music from any of the artists to it as you add that music to your Library. The content of a live smart playlist changes over time, depending on the criteria it contains.

> **note**
>
> Whether it's a standard playlist or a smart playlist, the playlist is the starting point for some iTunes activities such as burning a CD. And much of the time, a playlist makes listening to specific music easy and fast.

Building and Listening to Standard Playlists

Although they aren't as smart as their younger siblings, standard playlists are definitely useful because you can choose the exact songs included in them and the order in which those songs will play. In this section, you will learn how to create, manage, and use playlists.

Creating a Standard Playlist

You have two ways to create a playlist. One is to create a playlist that is empty (meaning it doesn't include any songs). The other is to choose songs and then create a playlist that includes those songs.

The place you start depends on what you have in mind. If you want to create a collection of songs but aren't sure which specific songs you want to start with, create an empty playlist. If you know of at least some of the songs you are going to include, choose them and create the playlist. Either way, creating a playlist is simple and you end up in the same place.

Creating an Empty Standard Playlist

You can create an empty playlist from within iTunes by using any of the following techniques:

- Selecting File, New Playlist.
- Pressing Ctrl+N (Windows) or ⌘-N (Mac).
- Clicking the Create Playlist button (see Figure 6.3).

FIGURE 6.3
This playlist has
been created and
is ready to be
renamed.

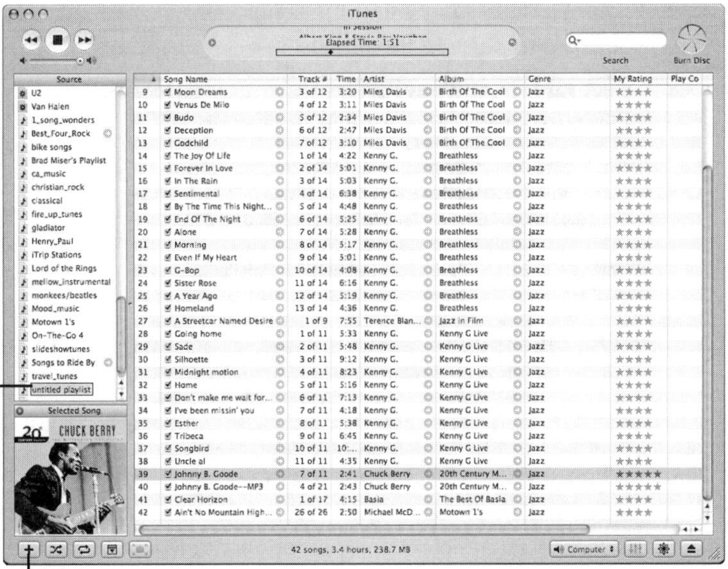

New playlist

Create Playlist

Whichever method you use will result in an
empty playlist whose name will be highlighted
to show you that it is ready for you to edit. Type
a name for the playlist and press **Enter**
(Windows) or **Return** (Mac). The playlist will
be renamed and selected. The Content pane
will be empty because you haven't added any
songs to the playlist yet. You will learn how to
do that in the section "Adding Songs to a
Playlist" on page **105**.

Creating a Standard Playlist with Songs in It

If you know some songs you want to place in a
playlist, you can create the playlist so it includes
those songs as soon as you create it. Here are the
steps to follow:

tip

iTunes keeps playlists
in the Source pane in
alphabetical order
within each group
(standard and smart
playlists). So, when
you rename a
playlist, it will jump to the location in the standard playlist section
on the Source list to where it
belongs.

1. Browse or search the Library to find the songs you want to be included in the
   playlist. For example, you can browse for all the songs in a specific genre or
   search for music by a specific artist.

2. In the Content pane, select the songs you want to place in the playlist.

3. Select **File**, **New Playlist from Selection**. A new playlist will appear on the Source list and will be selected. Its name will be highlighted to indicate that you can edit it, and you will see the songs you selected in the Content pane (see Figure 6.4).

tip

You can create a new playlist containing one or more songs by selecting the songs and pressing Ctrl+Shift+N (Windows) or ⌘-Shift-N (Mac).

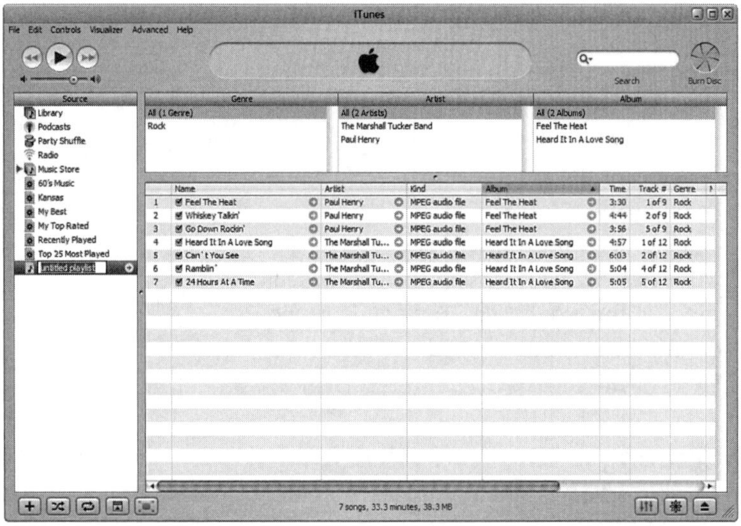

iTunes will attempt to name the playlist by looking for a common denominator in the group of songs you selected. For example, if all the songs are from the same artist, that artist's name will be the playlist's name. Similarly, if the songs are all from the same album, the playlist's name will be the artist's and album's names. Sometimes iTunes picks an appropriate name, and sometimes it doesn't.

FIGURE 6.4

Because I created a playlist from selected songs, the new playlist contains the songs I selected when I created it.

4. While the playlist name is highlighted, edit the name as needed and then press **Enter** (Windows) or **Return** (Mac). The playlist will be ready for more songs.

Adding Songs to a Playlist

The whole point of creating a playlist is to add songs to it. Whether you created an empty playlist or one that already has some songs in it, the steps to add songs are the same:

tip

You can add the same song to a playlist as many times as you'd like to hear it.

1. Select the **Library** as the source.

2. Browse or search the Library so that songs you want to add to the playlist are shown in the Content pane.

3. Select the songs you want to add to the playlist by clicking them (remember the techniques to select multiple songs at the same time). To select all the songs currently shown in the Content pane, press **Ctrl+A** (Windows) or ⌘-**A** (Mac).

4. Drag the selected songs from the Content pane onto the playlist to which you want to add them. As you drag, you'll see the songs you have selected in a "ghost" image attached to the pointer. When the playlist becomes high-lighted and the cursor includes a plus sign (+), release the mouse button (see Figure 6.5). The songs will be added to the playlist.

FIGURE 6.5

You add songs to a playlist by dragging them from the Content pane onto the playlist in the Source pane.

5. Repeat steps 2–4 until you have added all the songs you want to include in the playlist.

6. Select the playlist on the Source list. Its songs will appear in the Content pane (see Figure 6.6). Information about the playlist, such as its playing time, will appear in the Source Information area at the bottom of the iTunes window.

Removing Songs from a Playlist

If you decide you don't want one or more songs included in a playlist, select the songs you want to remove in the playlist's Content pane and press the **Delete** key. A warning prompt will appear. Click **Yes** and the songs will be deleted from the playlist. (If this dialog box annoys you like it does me, check the **Do not ask me again** check box and you won't ever have to see it again.)

> **note**
>
> The Source Information area becomes very important when you are creating a CD because you can use this to make sure a playlist will fit onto a CD.

FIGURE 6.6

This playlist, called "Songs to Ride By," are tunes that are a good companion while traveling on my motorcycle.

Setting the Order in Which a Playlist's Songs Play

Just like an audio CD, the order in which a playlist's songs play is determined by the order in which they appear in the Content pane (the first song will be the one at the top of the window, the second will be the next one down, and so on). You can drag songs up on the list to make them play earlier or down in the list to make them play later.

Listening to a Standard Playlist

After you have created a playlist, you can listen to it by selecting it on the Source list and using the same controls you use to listen to a CD or music in the Library. You can even search in and browse playlists just as you can the Library or CDs. (That's the real beauty of iTunes; it works the same way no matter what the music source is!)

Deleting a Standard Playlist

If you decide you no longer want a playlist, you can delete it by selecting the playlist on the Source list and pressing the **Delete** key. A prompt will appear; click **Yes** and the playlist will be removed from the Source list. (Be sure to check the **Do not ask me again** check box if you don't want to be prompted in the future.) Even though you've deleted the playlist, the songs in the playlist remain in the Library or in other playlists for your listening pleasure.

note

When you delete a song from a playlist, it *isn't* deleted from the Library. It remains there so you can add it to a different playlist or listen to it from the Library. Of course, if it is included in other playlists, it isn't removed from those either.

Becoming a Musical Genius with Smart Playlists

The basic purpose of a smart playlist is the same as a standard playlist—that is, to contain a collection of songs to which you can listen, put on a CD, and so on. However, the path smart playlists take to this end is completely different from standard playlists. Rather than choosing specific songs as you do in a standard playlist, you tell iTunes the kind of songs you want in your smart playlist and it picks out the songs for you and places them in the playlist. For example, suppose you want to create a

tip

You can also change the order in which songs will play by sorting the playlist by its columns. You do this by clicking the column title in the column by which you want the Content pane sorted. You can set the columns that appear for a playlist by selecting Edit, View Options, as you learned to do in the previous chapter.

playlist that contains all your classical music. Rather than picking out all the songs in your Library that have the Classical genre (as you would do to create a standard playlist), you can use a smart playlist to tell iTunes to select all the classical music for you. The application then gathers all the music with the Classical genre and places that music in a smart playlist.

Understanding Why Smart Playlists Are Called Smart

You create a smart playlist by defining a set of criteria based on any number of tags. After you have created these criteria, iTunes chooses songs that match those tags and places them in the playlist. Another example should help clarify this. Suppose you are a big-time Elvis fan and regularly add Elvis music to your Library. You could create a playlist and manually drag your new Elvis tunes to that playlist. But by using a smart playlist instead, you could define the playlist to include all your Elvis music. Anytime you add more Elvis music to your Library, that music would be added to the playlist automatically so it always contains all the Elvis music in your Library.

You can also base a smart playlist on more than one attribute at the same time. Going back to the Elvis example, you could add the condition that you want only those songs you have rated four stars or higher so the smart playlist contains only your favorite Elvis songs.

As the previous example shows, smart playlists can be dynamic; iTunes calls this *live updating*. When a smart playlist is set to be live, iTunes changes its contents over time to match changes to the music in your Library. If this feature isn't set for a smart playlist, that playlist will contain only those songs that met the criteria at the time the playlist was created.

Finally, you can also link a smart playlist's conditions by the logical expression All or Any. If you use an All logical expression, all the conditions must be true for a song to be included in the smart playlist. If you use the Any option, only one of the conditions has to be met for a song to be included in the smart playlist.

Creating a Smart Playlist

You can create a smart playlist by performing the following steps:

1. Select **File**, **New Smart Playlist** or hold down the **Shift** (Windows) or **Option** (Mac) key and click the **New Playlist** button, which becomes the **New Smart Playlist** button when the Shift or Option key is pressed down. You will see the Smart Playlist dialog box (see Figure 6.7).

note

iTunes includes several smart playlists by default. These include 60's Music (music based on the Year attribute being 1960 to 1969), My Top Rated (all the music you have rated three stars or above), Recently Played (songs you have played within the past two weeks), and Top 25 Most Played (the 25 songs you have played most often). To see the songs that meet these conditions, select a smart playlist and you will see its songs in the Content pane.

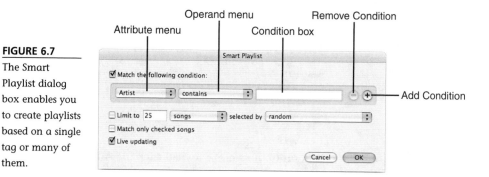

FIGURE 6.7

The Smart Playlist dialog box enables you to create playlists based on a single tag or many of them.

2. Select the first tag on which you want the smart playlist to be based in the **Attribute** menu. For example, you can select Artist, Genre, My Rating, or Year, among many others. The Operand menu will be updated so that it is applicable to the attribute you selected. For example, if you select Artist, the Operand menu will include contains, does not contain, is, is not, starts with, and ends with.

3. Select the operand you want to use on the **Operand** menu. For example, if you want to match data exactly, select **is**. If you want the condition to be more loose, select **contains**.

4. Type the condition you want to match in the **Condition** box. The more you type, the more specific the condition will be. As an example, if you select Artist in step 1, select contains in step 2, and type **Elvis** in this step, the condition would look like the one shown in Figure 6.8 and would find all songs that include Elvis, Elvis Presley, Elvis Costello, Elvisiocity, and so on. If you typed Elvis Presley in the Condition box and left the contains operand, iTunes would include only songs whose artist includes Elvis Presley, such as Elvis Presley, Elvis Presley and His Back-up Band, and so on.

> **tip**
>
> You can also create a new smart playlist by pressing Ctrl+Alt+N (Windows) or Option-⌘-N (Mac).

> **note**
>
> As you make selections on the Attribute menu and type conditions in the Condition box, iTunes will attempt to automatically match what you type to data from the songs in your Library. If your Library includes Elvis music and you use Artist as an attribute, iTunes will enter Elvis Presley in the Condition box for you when you start typing "Elvis."

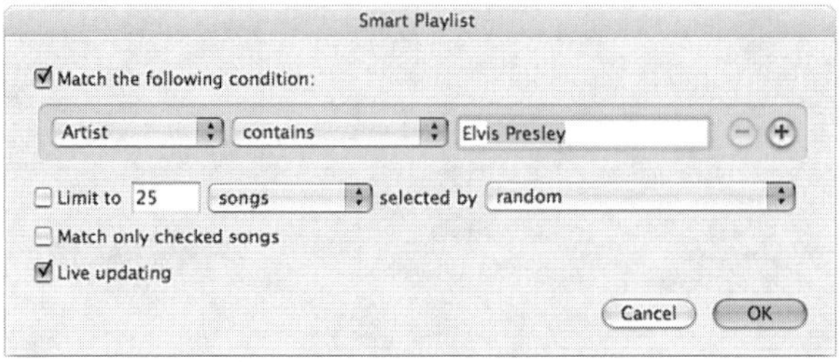

FIGURE 6.8

This smart playlist is getting smarter.

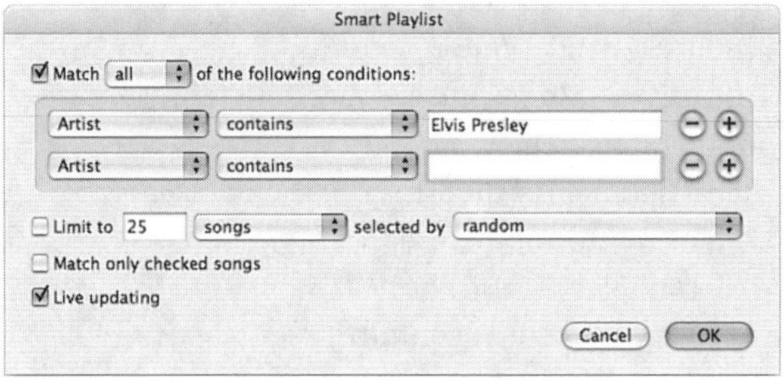

FIGURE 6.9

This smart playlist now contains two conditions; both are currently based on Artist.

5. To add another condition to the smart playlist, click the **Add Condition** button. A new, empty condition will appear (see Figure 6.9). At the top of the dialog box, the all or any menu will also appear.

6. Select the second tag on which you want the smart playlist to be based in the second condition's **Attribute** menu. For example, if you want to include songs from a specific genre, select **Genre** on the menu.

7. Select the operand you want to use in the **Operand** menu, such as contains, is, and so on.

8. Type the condition you want to match in the **Condition** box. If you selected Genre in step 6, type the genre from which the music in the playlist should come. As you type, iTunes will try to match the genre you type with those in your Library.

9. Repeat steps 5–8 to add more conditions to the playlist until you have all the conditions you want to include (see Figure 6.10).

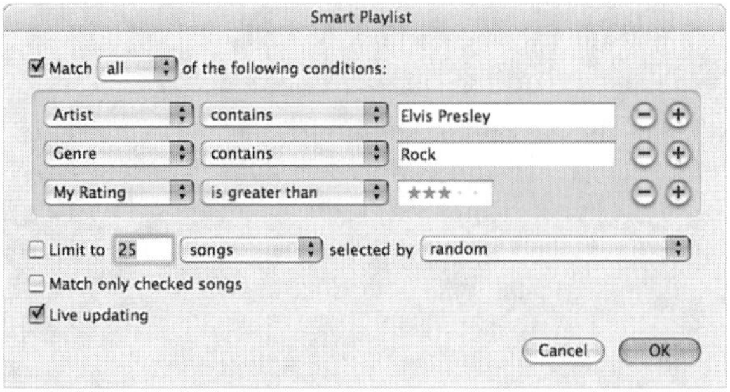

FIGURE 6.10

This smart playlist is approaching the genius level; it now includes three conditions.

10. Select **all** on the menu at the top of the dialog box if all the conditions must be met for a song to be included in the smart playlist, or select **any** if only one of them must be met. For example, you could create a smart playlist based on multiple Artist conditions and the playlist would feature music by those artists. In this case, you would choose any so that if a song is associated with *any* of the artists for which you created a condition, it would be included in the playlist. As a contrasting example, if you want the playlist to include songs you have rated as three stars or better by a specific artist, you would include both of these conditions and then select all in the menu so that both conditions would have to be met for a song to be included (a song is both by the artist and is rated with three or more stars).

    You can limit the length of a smart playlist based on a maximum number of songs, the time it plays, or the size of the files it includes. You set these limits using the Limit to check box and menus.

11. If you want to limit the playlist, check the **Limit to** check box. If you don't want to set a limit on the playlist, leave the check box unchecked and skip to step 15.

12. Select the attribute by which you want to limit the playlist in the first menu; by default, this menu has songs selected (see Figure 6.11). Your choices include the number of songs (just songs on the menu), the time the playlist will play (in minutes or hours), and the size of the files the playlist contains (in MB or GB).

13. Type the data appropriate for the limit you selected in the **Limit to** box. For example, if you selected minutes in the menu, type the maximum length of the playlist in minutes in the box. If you selected songs, enter the maximum number of songs that can be included in the playlist.

tip

If you want to remove a condition from a smart playlist, click the Remove button for the condition you want to remove.

note

If you include more than one condition based on the same attribute, you usually don't want to use the All option because the conditions will likely be mutually exclusive, and using the All option will result in no songs being included in the playlist because no song will be able to meet all the conditions at the same time.

14. Select how you want iTunes to choose the songs it includes based on the limit
    you selected by using the **selected by** menu. This menu has many options,
    including to choose songs randomly, based on your rating, how often the
    songs are played, and so on (see Figure 6.12).

15. If you want the playlist to include only songs whose check box in the
    Content pane is checked, check the **Match only checked songs** check box.
    If you leave this check box unchecked, iTunes will include all songs that
    meet the playlist's conditions, even if you have unchecked their check box in
    the Content pane.

16. If you want the playlist to be dynamic, meaning that iTunes will update its
    contents over time, check the **Live updating** check box. If you uncheck this
    check box, the playlist will include only those songs that meet the playlist's
    conditions when you create it.

17. Review the playlist to see whether it contains the conditions and settings you
    want (see Figure 6.13).

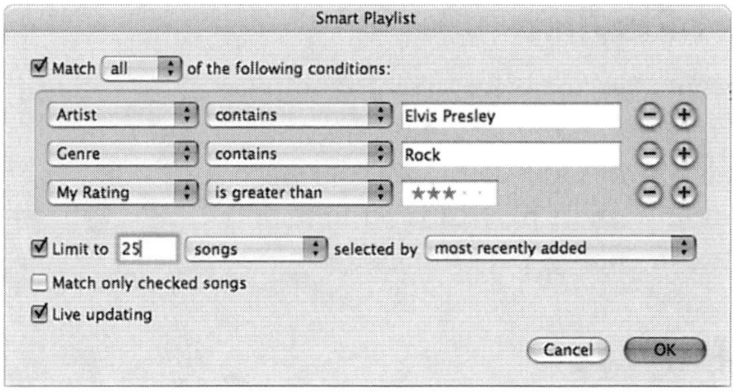

FIGURE 6.13

This playlist will include up to 25 songs of the best (rated at four stars or more) of my Elvis music from the Rock genre; as I add music to my Library, it will also be added to this playlist if it meets these conditions.

18. Click **OK** to create the playlist. You will move to the Source list, the smart playlist will be added and selected, and its name will be ready for you to edit. Also, the songs in your Library that match the criteria in the playlist will be added to it and the current contents of the playlist will be shown in the Content pane.

19. Type the playlist's name and press **Enter** (Windows) or **Return** (Mac). The smart playlist will be complete (see Figure 6.14).

FIGURE 6.14

If you compare the songs in this smart playlist to the criteria shown in the previous figure, you will see they match.

Listening to a Smart Playlist

Listening to a smart playlist is just like listening to other sources: You select it on the Source list and use the playback controls to listen to it. The one difference is that, if a smart playlist is set to be live, its contents can change over time.

Changing a Smart Playlist

To change the contents of a smart playlist, you change the smart playlist's criteria (remember that iTunes actually places songs in a smart playlist). Use the following steps to do this:

1. Select the smart playlist you want to change.

2. Select **File**, **Edit Smart Playlist**. The Smart Playlist dialog box will appear, and the playlist's current criteria will be shown.

3. Use the techniques you learned when you created a playlist to change its criteria (see Figure 6.15). For example, you can remove conditions by clicking their Remove buttons. You can also add more conditions or change the other settings for the playlist.

> **note**
>
> The smart playlist I built as an example in these steps can be interpreted as follows: Include songs by Elvis Presley in the Rock genre that I have rated at four or five stars. Limit the playlist to 25 songs, and if I have more songs that meet the conditions than this time limit allows, select the songs to include based on those I have most recently added to my Library. Finally, keep adding songs that meet these conditions as I add new Elvis music to my Library.

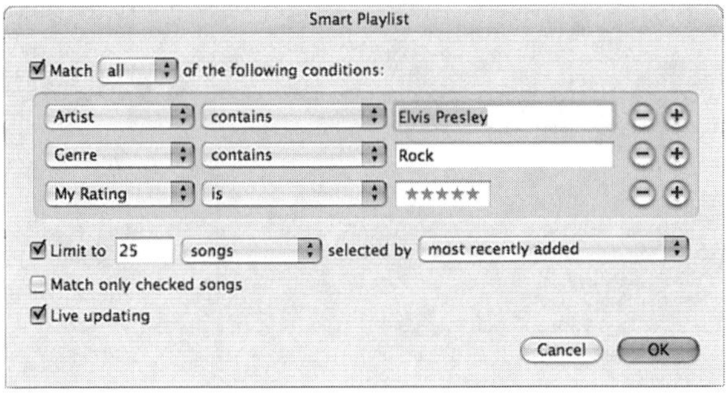

FIGURE 6.15

I changed the conditions on this smart playlist so that only five-star songs are included.

4. Click **OK**. Your changes will be saved and the contents of the playlist will be updated to match the current criteria.

You can also change a smart playlist using the same techniques you use on other sources, such as sorting it, selecting the columns you see when you view it, and so on.

Doing the Party Shuffle

iTunes includes some "built-in" playlists (such as Purchased Music) you might not even recognize as being playlists based on the chapter so far. But, these special playlists are playlists indeed.

One of the most useful of these is the Party Shuffle that you'll see near the top of the Content pane. This is actually a playlist that enables you to play a source you select in shuffle mode. If you like to keep things interesting, the Party Shuffle is a good way to do so because you can hear the songs in any source in a random order without having to change the source itself. After you try this special playlist, you'll probably use it as often as I do, which is to say, quite a lot. To do the party shuffle, follow these steps:

1. Select **Party Shuffle** on the Source pane. You'll see a dialog box explaining what the Party Shuffle is; read it, check the **Do not show this message again** check box, and click **OK**. You'll see songs fill the Content pane and some controls will appear at the bottom (see Figure 6.16).

2. Select the source of music you want to shuffle on the **Source** pop-up menu. You can choose your Library or any playlist (standard or smart).

3. If you want songs you have rated higher to be played more frequently, check the **Play higher rated songs more often**

note

Just like other sources, when you select a smart playlist, its information will be shown in the Source Information section at the bottom of the window. This can be useful if you want to create a CD or just to see how big the playlist is (by number of songs, time, or file size). Remember, though, that because a smart playlist's contents can change over time, its source information can also change over time. So, just because a smart playlist will fit on a CD today doesn't mean it still will tomorrow (or even later today).

tip

You can also edit a smart playlist by selecting it and opening the Info window (which also opens the Smart Playlist dialog box). Plus, you can open the playlist's contextual menu by right-clicking (Windows or Mac) or Ctrl-clicking it (Mac) and selecting Edit Smart Playlist.

check box. This causes iTunes to choose songs with higher star ratings more frequently than those with lower or no star ratings.

4. Use the two **Display** pop-up menus to choose how many songs are shown that have been played recently and that are upcoming. Your choices range from 0 to 100 on both menus. When you make a selection, the songs in the Content pane will reflect your choice.

tip

To delete a smart playlist, select it on the Source list and press **Delete**. Confirm the deletion at the prompt, and the playlist will be removed from the Source list.

FIGURE 6.16

The Party Shuffle source might seem odd to you at first, but once you get to know it, you'll love it.

The current song is always highlighted in the Content pane with a blue bar. Songs that have played are grayed out and are listed above the current song. Songs that will be played are in regular text and appear below the current song.

5. If you want to change the order in which upcoming songs will play, drag them up or down in the Content pane.

6. When you are ready to hear the tunes, use the same playback controls that you use with any other source.

The Party Shuffle source will play forever. After it plays a song, it moves one of the recently played songs off that list, moves the song it just played into the recently played section, highlights and plays the next song, and adds another one to the upcoming songs section. This process will continue until you stop the music.

As the Party Shuffle plays, you can keep moving upcoming songs around to change the order in which they will play. You can also press the right-arrow key to skip to the next song.

In addition, you can manually add songs to the Party Shuffle. View a source to find the song you want to add. Open the song's contextual menu by right-clicking it (see Figure 6.17). Select **Play Next in Party Shuffle** to have the song play next, or select **Add to Party Shuffle** to add the song to the end of the upcoming songs list.

note

The Party Shuffle is one item for which the Source Information data doesn't make a lot of sense. Because the list is always changing, the source information doesn't really mean a lot. It simply shows information based on the songs currently shown in the Content pane, which change after each song is played.

FIGURE 6.17

To add a song to the Party Shuffle, use one of the Party Shuffle commands on its contextual menu.

The Absolute Minimum

Playlists are a great way to customize the music in your Library for listening purposes, to create a CD, or to manage the music on an iPod. As you learned in this chapter, playlists include a specific collection of songs that you choose, whereas iTunes chooses the songs in a smart playlist based on the conditions you specify.

Playlists are a great way to select specific music to which you want to listen. You can make them as long or as short as you like, and you can mix and match songs to your heart's content.

Use the Party Shuffle playlist to spice up your music experience by keeping it fresh.

Smart playlists can really enhance your listening experience. Following are some ideas you might find interesting for your own smart playlists:

- Be diligent about rating your songs. Then create a smart playlist for one of your favorite genres that also includes a rating condition. Enable this playlist to be updated live. Such a playlist would always contain your favorites songs in this genre, even as you add more songs to your Library.

- Create a smart playlist based only on genre and allow it to be updated live. This playlist would make it easy to listen to that genre, and it would always contain all your music in that genre.

- Create a smart playlist that includes several of your favorite artists (remember to choose Any in the top menu) and limit the number of songs to 20 or so. Have iTunes select the songs in a random order. Playing this playlist might provide an interesting mix of music. If you include a My Rating condition, you can cause only your favorite music to be included in this group. Make a dynamic list, and it will change over time as you add music to your Library.

- Create a smart playlist for your favorite artists and allow them to be updated live. As you add music by the artists to your Library, just play the related playlist to hear all the music by that artist, including the new music you add.

- If you like to collect multiple versions of the same song, create a playlist based on song name. Allow it to be updated live, and this playlist will contain all the versions of this song you have in your Library.

In this chapter

- Get an overview of how to build your iTunes music Library.

- Determine how much iPod space you need and how much you have.

- Understand and configure your iPod update options.

- Update specific songs and playlists on your iPod automatically.

- Update your iPod's music manually.

- Manage the music on an iPod shuffle.

Building an iPod's Music Library

The first time you connected your iPod to your computer, all the music in your iTunes Library was transferred to your iPod automatically—that is, all the music that would *fit* within the iPod's disk or memory space limitations. If your iPod has enough storage space to hold all your iTunes music, then everything is just fine. However, as you build your iTunes Library, there may come a day when this isn't true anymore and you can't just let everything run on automatic to keep your iPod's music library current. That's where this chapter comes in. Here, you'll learn how to take control over the music stored on your iPod, especially if your iPod's storage space isn't large enough to hold all your iTunes music.

FOR IPOD SHUFFLE READERS

If you use an iPod shuffle, and only an iPod shuffle, most of this chapter doesn't apply to you. Like just about everything else you do with an iPod, you manage the music on a shuffle quite differently from how you manage music with the other iPod models. So, if you are an iPod shuffle-only user, you can skip to the section "Adding Music to an iPod shuffle" on page 134.

> **note**
>
> Throughout this chapter, I assume that you have a good working knowledge of iTunes. You need to at least read Chapter 3, "Touring iTunes," so you understand the basics of the application.

Creating an iTunes Music Library

As your learned in Chapter 2, "Getting Started with an iPod," and read in each of the subsequent chapters, you manage the music you store on your iPod within the iTunes application. The iTunes Library and the playlists you create within iTunes are the sources of music you listen to with an iPod. The two general steps to creating these music sources are building your iTunes Library and creating iTunes playlists.

Building an iTunes Music Library

You can get music for your iTunes Library from three main sources: audio CDs, the iTunes Music Store, and the Internet. Although the specific steps you use to add music from these various sources to your Library are a bit different, the end result is the same. Your iTunes Library will contain all the music in your collection.

I don't provide the details of building and managing an iTunes Library here because Part II is dedicated to iTunes and provides all the information you need to use this excellent application. The chapters that specifically focus on building your Library are Chapter 4, "Building, Browsing, Searching, and Playing Your iTunes Music Library," and Chapter 5, "Labeling, Categorizing, and Configuring Your Music."

Creating iTunes Playlists

From the earlier chapters in this part of the book, you learned that the playlists stored within iTunes are transferred to your iPod so you can listen to them. You create and manage these playlists within iTunes. Chapter 6, "Creating, Configuring, and Using Playlists," provides an in-depth look at playlists and gives you all the information you need to create and manage your playlists.

Assessing the Size of Your iTunes Library and How Much Disk Space Your iPod Has

To determine how you are going to have to manage the music on your iPod, you need to understand how large your music collection is and how much storage space is available on your iPod. This information will determine the way in which you build and maintain your iPod's music library.

Determining the Size of Your iTunes Library

You can determine how much storage space you need to move your entire music collection in just a few steps. Open iTunes. Select **Library** in the Source list. With the Browser open, select **All** in the Genre or Artist column. The iTunes window will show all the music you have placed in your Library. Look at the Source Information area at the bottom of the iTunes window (see Figure 7.1). Here, you will see the number of songs, the total playing time, and the disk space required to store all the music in your Library. The number you should be most interested in is the disk space required because that is what you use to determine whether all your music can fit onto your iPod's disk.

Determining How Much Storage Space You Have on an iPod

You have three ways to determine how large the storage space is on your iPod.

One is to refer to the documentation that came with your iPod, or perhaps you can simply remember the size of iPod you purchased. At press time, the possibilities were about 4GB or 6GB for an iPod mini, 20GB or 60GB for an iPod, or 512MB or 1GB for an iPod shuffle. This method is easy and provides a pretty good estimate of the storage capability of your iPod.

If you can't remember or want to determine the disk space on an iPod or iPod mini more accurately, you can get this information directly from the iPod itself. To do this, select **Main** menu, **Settings**, **About**. On the resulting About menu, you'll see the capacity of your iPod's disk (see Figure 7.2).

FIGURE 7.1

At this point in time, my Library required 12.78GB of disk space.

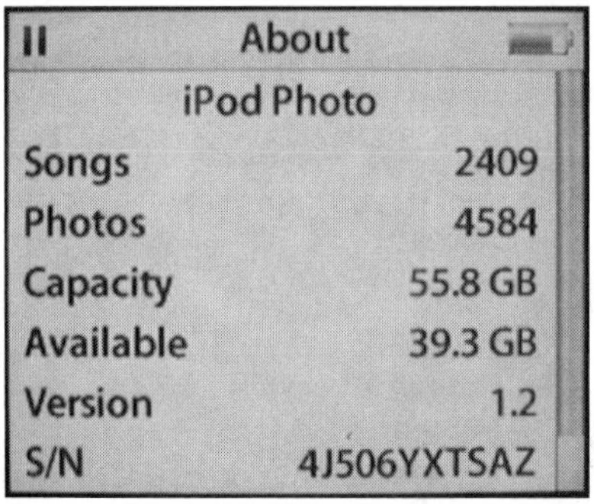

Source Information

FIGURE 7.2

This iPod has a disk capacity of 55.7GB.

The capacity shown on the About menu is the amount of storage space available for your music. Some space is required to store the files needed for the iPod to function; this is the reason the capacity you see will always be slightly less than the rated size of the iPod's disk.

You can also get information about the status of the iPod's disk by connecting it to your computer and selecting it on the Source list. Just above the Source Information area, you'll see information about the iPod's disk, including used space and free space (see Figure 7.3).

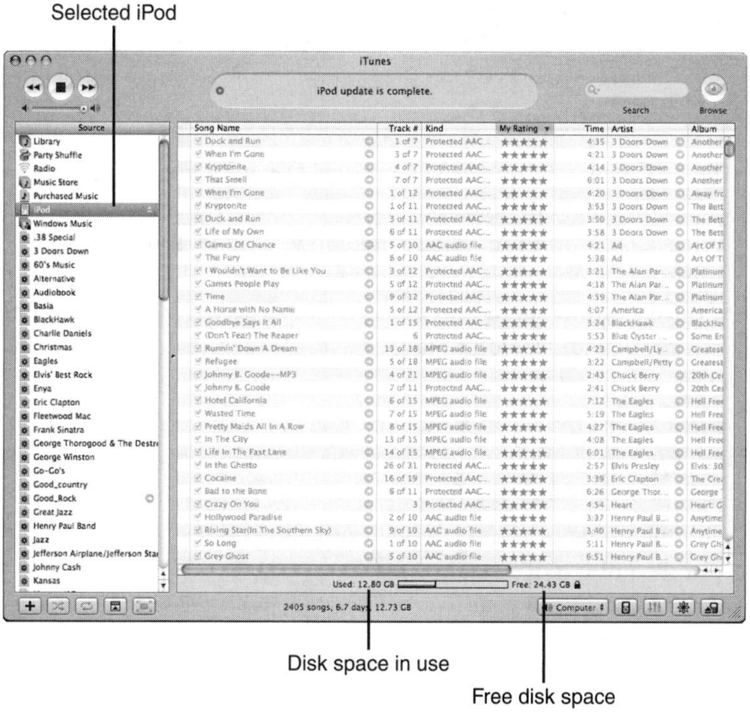

FIGURE 7.3

Here you can see
that this iPod
has stored my
entire Library
with lots of room
to spare.

Selected iPod

Disk space in use

Free disk space

Understanding and Configuring iPod Synchronization Options

After you know how much space you need to store all your music (the size of your
iTunes Library) and how much space is available on your iPod (its disk capacity),
you can choose how you want to build and manage your iPod's music library.

Understanding Your Synchronization Options

Three basic options are available for managing the library of music on your iPod:

- **Automatically update all songs and playlists**—When you use this
  method, the entire process is automatic; iTunes ensures your iPod's music
  library is an exact copy of your iTunes Library each time you connect your
  iPod to your computer. This is the ideal method because you don't have to do
  any additional work and you always have all your music on your iPod.

- **Automatically update selected playlists only**—When you use this
  method, iTunes still manages the update process for you, but it updates only
  the specific playlists you select. This option is useful when you have more
  music in your iTunes Library than will fit on your iPod and don't want to
  have to manually update your iPod's music.

■ **Manually manage songs and playlists**—When you use this method, you manually move songs and playlists onto your iPod. This option is mostly useful in special situations, such as when you want to use the same iPod with more than one computer.

The first time you connected your iPod to your computer, an automatic method was used to move songs onto your iPod. However, if there were more songs in your iTunes Library than could be stored on your iPod, some slight of hand was done by iTunes so you wouldn't have to get into the details of this process before listening to music on your iPod. In that case, iTunes created a playlist containing a selection of your music that would fit on your iPod and iTunes moved that music to your iPod so you could listen to it.

After the first time, you need to choose the synchronization method you want to use. Finding the right method for you is a matter of preference, but I can provide some general guidelines for you.

If all the music in your iTunes Library will fit onto your iPod (the space required for your iTunes Library is less than your iPod's disk capacity), I recommend you use the option Automatically update all songs and playlists. This option is the easiest because it requires literally no work on your part. Each time you connect your iPod to your computer, the update process is performed automatically and you will have your complete music collection available on your iPod. That's because with this option, your entire iTunes Library is moved to your iPod along with the playlists you have created. So, even if some music is not part of your playlists, it still gets moved onto the iPod.

note

Even if you have enough space on your iPod for all your iTunes music, you can still choose one of the other update options if it suits your preferences better.

If the size of your iTunes Library is larger than the disk capacity of your iPod, managing the music library on your iPod is slightly more difficult.

If your iPod isn't large enough to store your entire Library and you take full advantage of iTunes playlists to create collections of music to which you listen, using the option Automatically update selected playlists only is a good choice. After you choose the playlists you want to be updated, iTunes handles the process of keeping them up-to-date for you so you don't have to think about it each time you connect your iPod to your computer. Of course, you need to make sure you create and can select playlists that contain the music you want to be able to listen to on your iPod. This can require some effort, but because playlists are so useful, you will likely do that work anyway so you can listen to them on your computer. And, be aware that only music in the selected playlists is moved onto your iPod.

Finally, if you don't use a lot of playlists or you simply want to choose the specific music you want to place on your iPod, you can use the manual method to do so.

After you have determined how you want to manage your iPod's music library, you need to configure iTunes to implement your decision.

Understanding How iTunes Updates Playlists on the iPod

When iTunes updates a playlist on your iPod, it takes a "snapshot" of that playlist and places it on the iPod. If you change the playlist in some way, the next time you update your iPod, the previous "snapshot" is replaced by the new playlist.

For example, suppose you have a smart playlist that is dynamic and plays the 50 songs you have played most frequently. As you listen to songs in iTunes, the contents of that playlist change to reflect the songs you have listened to. When that playlist is moved to the iPod, it contains the songs as they were in the playlist when you performed the update. The playlist on the iPod will remain unchanged until you perform the next update. At that time, if the contents of the playlist have changed, the revised playlist will replace the one currently stored on the iPod.

caution

If you use the same iPod with more than one computer, you need to be careful before selecting one of the automatic methods. When you use an automatic method, iTunes will copy its Library onto the iPod. When it does this, it will also remove any songs on the iPod that aren't in its Library so the music on the iPod is an exact copy of the music in the iTunes Library. If you share the iPod on more than one computer, you should not use the Automatically update all songs and playlists method for both computers if you have different music in the iTunes Library on each computer. Fortunately, you can leave one computer set to automatic and the others set to manual.

The same principle applies when you make changes to a playlist manually. For example, if you sort a playlist to change the order in which songs play, that order will be reflected in the playlist when you update it onto your iPod. If you change the order of the songs in the playlist again in iTunes, the next time you update the iPod, the songs will play in the new order on the iPod.

Using the Automatically update selected playlists only option, when iTunes moves a playlist from its Library onto an iPod, it moves only the songs in that playlist onto the iPod. This can sometimes be confusing. For example, if you purchase an album by a specific artist and then include only some of the songs on that album in a playlist that gets moved to an iPod, only those songs by that artist in the playlist get moved onto the iPod. As an example, this can be confusing the first time you browse your iPod by artist and can't figure out why a song you know you have by that artist is not on your iPod.

Configuring iTunes to Automatically Update All Songs and Playlists

Choosing the "fully automatic" method is automatic in itself, in that this is the default option. However, should you ever need to choose this option, you can do so with the following steps:

1. Connect your iPod to your computer (remember Chapter 2!). iTunes will open automatically and the iPod will appear on the Source list.

2. Select the iPod on the **Source** list and click the **iPod Options** button (see Figure 7.4). You'll see the iPod pane of the iTunes Preferences dialog box. If you use a Mac, make sure the Music tab is highlighted.

tip

By default, when iTunes performs an update, it moves all the songs from each affected source onto the iPod. If you don't want specific songs to be moved onto an iPod, open the iPod Preferences dialog box and check the Only update checked songs check box. If a song's check box is not checked, it won't be included in the music moved onto the iPod during an update.

Selected iPod

FIGURE 7.4
To choose an update method, select the iPod and click the iPod Options button.

iPod Options

3. Click the **Automatically update all songs and playlists** radio button (see Figure 7.5). On a Windows computer, the **Music** tab must be selected to see this option.

4. Click **OK**. The dialog box will close, and the update will start. If your iPod can store all the music in your Library, the process will continue until the update is complete. The next time you connect your iPod to your computer or update the iPod with a command, iTunes will attempt to update its Library automatically. As long as there is enough space on your iPod, you won't need to do anything else.

tip

There are two other ways to open the iPod pane of the iTunes Preferences dialog box. One is to open the iPod's contextual menu and choose iPod Options. Another is to open the iTunes Preferences dialog box and click on the iPod pane.

FIGURE 7.5

The iPod Preferences dialog box enables you to configure the update process for your iPod.

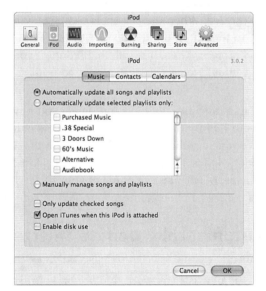

If your iPod doesn't have enough room to store all your music, you'll see a warning prompt telling you so. iTunes will offer to choose a selection of songs to put on the iPod.

If you click Yes in this dialog box, iTunes will create a special playlist called *nameofyouripod* Selection, where *nameofyouripod* is

note

If you use a Windows computer, you won't see the Contacts or Calendars tab shown in Figure 7.5. These options are available only on a Mac.

the name you gave your iPod when you configured it. This playlist contains a selection of music from your iTunes Library that will fit on your iPod. iTunes will move the music in this playlist onto the iPod to complete the update.

If you don't change the update option, iTunes will update this playlist (and only this playlist) each time you connect your iPod to your computer. (iTunes actually changes the update mode to Automatically update selected playlists only and chooses the *nameofyouripod* Selection playlist on the playlists list in the iPod Preferences pane.) You can use this playlist just like the others in your iTunes Source List, such as adding songs to it, removing songs from it, changing their order, and so on.

If you click No in the dialog box instead, the update will be aborted and you'll have to use one of the other update options.

Every time you connect your iPod to your computer, the update will be performed. You will see the update information in the Information area of the iTunes window, and the iPod icon will flash red. When the process is complete, you will see the iPod update is complete message in the Information area and the OK to disconnect message will be displayed on the iPod's screen. Then, it is safe to disconnect your iPod from your computer. Of course, you should leave the iPod connected until its battery is fully charged.

You can also activate the update manually, such as when you have added or changed the music in your Library (maybe you created a new playlist) after the automatic update was complete. You can do this by opening the iPod's contextual menu and selecting Update Songs. Or, you can select File, Update Songs on *nameofyouripod*, where *nameofyouripod* is the name of your iPod. This will perform the same update that is done when you connect your iPod to your computer.

Configuring iTunes to Automatically Update Selected Playlists

To have iTunes automatically update selected playlists only, use the following steps:

1. In iTunes, create the playlists you want to place on your iPod.

2. Connect your iPod to your computer. It will appear on the Source list, and an update determined by the current update option (such as fully automatic) will be performed.

3. Select the iPod for which you want to set an update option and click the **iPod Options** button. The iPod Preferences dialog box will appear.

4. Click the **Automatically update selected playlists only** radio button (see Figure 7.6). (If you use a Windows computer, the **Music** tab must be selected to see this option.) Just below this button you will see a list of all the

playlists configured in your iTunes Library. Next to each is a check box. If that box is checked, that playlist will be updated automatically; if that box is not checked, that playlist will be ignored.

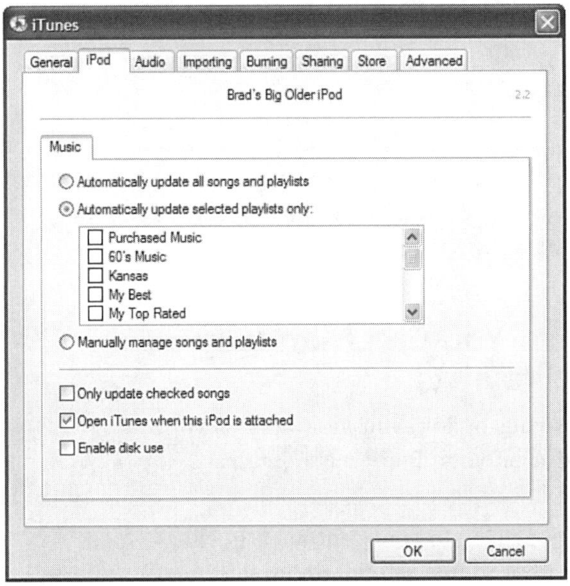

FIGURE 7.6

You can choose the playlists that are updated automatically by checking their check boxes.

6. Click **OK**.

If the playlists you selected will all fit on the iPod, the dialog box will close and the playlists you selected will be updated on your iPod. The next time you connect your iPod to your computer, the playlists you selected will be updated automatically and you can skip the rest of these steps.

If the playlists you selected are too large to fit on the iPod, the update will start but a warning dialog box will appear (see Figure 7.7). Click **OK** to stop the update; the update can't continue because iTunes doesn't know what music to move to the iPod.

note

When you change the update method, you will see a warning prompt telling you that the current music on the iPod will be replaced by the new update method. This should be what you expect, so just click OK to clear the prompt.

FIGURE 7.7

When you see this, the playlists you selected for automatic update won't fit on your iPod.

In this situation, you have two choices. You can deselect some of the playlists until the selected ones fit on your iPod, or you can remove songs from the selected playlists until they fit. (Remember that the only way to remove songs from smart playlists is to change their criteria.)

Configuring iTunes So You Can Manually Manage Songs and Playlists

When you choose this option, you manually place songs and playlists on your iPod. To choose this option, do the following steps:

1. Connect your iPod to your computer. It will appear on the Source list and an update determined by the current update option (such as fully automatic) will be performed.

2. Select the iPod for which you want to set an update option and click the **iPod Options** button. The iPod Preferences dialog box will appear.

3. Click the **Manually manage songs and playlists** radio button (on a Windows computer, this is located on the Music tab). You will see a prompt explaining that with this option, you must manually unmount the iPod before disconnecting it; read the information and click **OK** to close the prompt. (I'll explain what this means in a later section.)

4. Click **OK**. The dialog box will close and a brief update will be performed. An expansion triangle will appear next to the iPod on the Source list, and all the playlists stored on it will be shown under its icon. You can then manually add or remove songs or playlists (the steps to manually move music onto an iPod appear in a later section).

note

If you use the Automatically update selected playlists only option, smart playlists are even more useful because their content can be dynamic (see Chapter 6, "Creating, Configuring, and Using Playlists"). For example, you can create a playlist that automatically contains all the new music in your iTunes Library. If you choose to have this playlist updated automatically, each time you connect your iPod to your computer that playlist will be updated and so your newest music will always be placed on your iPod.

Updating Specific Songs and Playlists Automatically

If you chose the Automatically update selected playlists only option, the playlists you selected are updated on your iPod each time you connect it to your computer. To change the contents of your iPod's music library, change the contents of the playlists you have selected to update. When you connect the iPod to your computer, those playlists will be updated. For example, you can add songs to the selected playlists, remove songs from them, change a smart playlist's criteria, and so on. The next time you connect your iPod to your computer or activate the Update Songs command manually, the changes you made will be reflected on the iPod's version of those playlists.

note

Smart playlists can change over time automatically. These playlists will automatically change on your iPod each time you connect it to your computer. This is a great way to keep the music on your iPod fresh.

Every time you connect your iPod to your computer, the update will be performed. You will see the update information in the Information area of the iTunes window, and the iPod icon will flash red. When the process is complete, you will see the `iPod update is complete` message in the Information area, and the `OK to disconnect` message will be displayed on the iPod's screen. Then, it is safe to disconnect your iPod from your computer.

Manually Updating an iPod

If you choose the manual option, you must manually move songs and playlists onto the iPod. To do this, use the following steps:

1. Connect your iPod to your computer.

2. Select the iPod you want to update. If it isn't expanded already, click the expansion triangle next to the iPod on the **Source** list. In the iTunes Content pane, you will see all the songs in the iPod's music library. Under the iPod's icon on the Source list, you will see the playlists it contains (see Figure 7.8).

3. To add a playlist to the iPod, drag it onto the **Source** list and drop it on the iPod's icon (see Figure 7.9). When you are over the iPod, the plus sign will appear next to the pointer to show that you can release the mouse button. When you do so, the playlist and the songs it contains will be moved onto the iPod.

FIGURE 7.8

When you con-
figure an iPod
for manual
updating, you
can expand it on
the Source list to
see the playlists
it contains.

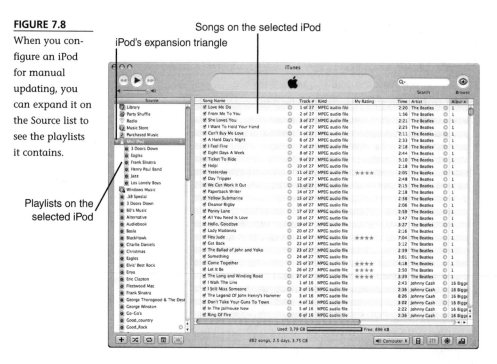

Songs on the selected iPod

iPod's expansion triangle

Playlists on the
selected iPod

FIGURE 7.9

When you drag
a playlist into an
iPod, it and the
songs it contains
will be moved
into the iPod's
library.

4. To remove a playlist from the iPod, select it by clicking it in the list of playlists
    under the iPod and pressing the **Delete** key. Unless you have disabled it, you
    will see a prompt asking you to confirm that you want to delete the playlist. If
    you have disabled the warning prompt, the playlist and its songs will be
    removed from the iPod and you can skip step 5.

5. Click **OK**. The playlist will be deleted from the iPod.

6. To add songs to the iPod, select the source containing those songs, such as the Library. The contents of that source will be shown in the Content pane. Drag the songs you want to add from the Content pane and drop them on the iPod's icon. The songs you selected will be copied into the iPod's music library.

7. To remove songs from the iPod, select the iPod, then select the songs you want to remove in the **Content** pane, and press the **Delete** key. These songs will be deleted from the iPod and will also be deleted from any playlists on the iPod containing them.

8. When you are done updating the iPod, unmount it by selecting its icon and clicking the **Eject** button that appears next to the iPod or in the lower-right corner of the iTunes window (see Figure 7.10). After the iPod has been successfully unmounted, it will disappear from the Source list and you will see the OK to disconnect message on its screen.

tip

If you don't want to be bothered by the confirmation prompts, check the **Do not ask me again** check box.

Eject button

FIGURE 7.10
Before you disconnect an iPod that you have manually updated, you must eject it.

9. Disconnect your iPod from your computer.

You must eject an iPod that you manually update before disconnecting it because iTunes doesn't know when it should shut down any processes it is using that are related to the iPod. Because it is, in effect, a hard disk, the iPod must not be in use when you disconnect it; otherwise, its data can be damaged. When you do the update manually, you need to tell iTunes that you are done (by "ejecting" the iPod) so that it can prepare the iPod to be disconnected safely.

> **note**
>
> To reiterate this slightly confusing behavior, when you delete a playlist from an iPod, only the playlist itself is removed—the songs it contains remain on the iPod. You have to select the songs and delete them to remove them from your iPod.

Adding Music to an iPod shuffle

Like in all other areas, managing the music on an iPod shuffle is different. There are different update options, and one of those is a special tool that is not available for other iPod models.

The reason for this is that, unless your music library is very small, it won't fit on a shuffle and likely not that much of it will fit because the largest memory in current shuffle models is 1GB. So, the shuffle does things a bit differently.

There are two ways to get music onto an iPod shuffle: You can use the Autofill tool to have iTunes move music onto the shuffle for you. Or, you can manually configure the songs the shuffle contains.

Prior to updating its music, configure your shuffle's preferences.

Configuring an iPod shuffle

The shuffle also has a different set of options you can configure using the following steps:

1. Plug your shuffle into an available USB 2 port on your computer. iTunes will open if it isn't already open, and the shuffle will appear on the Source list.

2. Click the **iPod Options** button, which has an iPod icon and is located to the immediate left of the Equalizer button in the lower-right corner of the iTunes window. The iPod pane of the iTunes Preferences dialog box will appear (see Figure 7.11).

> **caution**
>
> Don't disconnect your iPod from your computer unless the OK to disconnect message is displayed on its screen. If you do so, you can damage its data. It is also safe to disconnect your iPod when the large battery charging icon or battery charged icon appears on the iPod's screen.

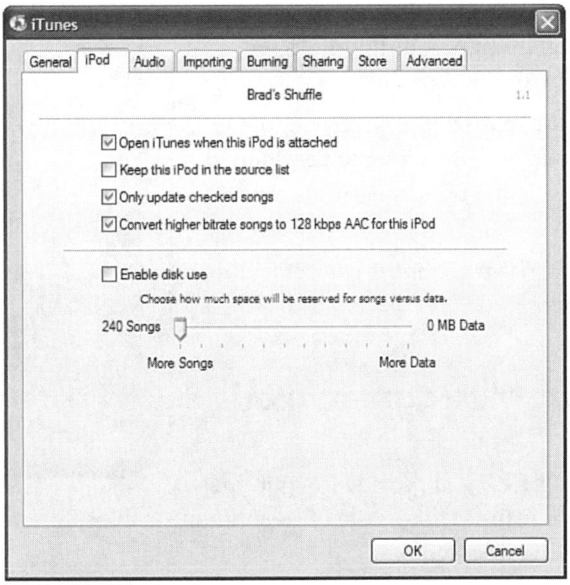

FIGURE 7.11

The iPod shuffle offers preferences that are much different from other iPod models.

3. Set the options for the shuffle. These options are explained in the following list:

- **Open iTunes when this iPod is attached**—When this is checked, which it is by default, iTunes will open whenever you plug your shuffle into your computer.

- **Keep this iPod in the source list**—If you check this, the iPod shuffle always appears in the Source list even if it isn't plugged into the computer. You can update it just like it was connected. The next time you plug your shuffle in, it will be updated with the current music configuration.

> **note**
>
> In most cases, you can update an iPod shuffle using an USB 1 port too. But, the process will be a lot slower and might not recharge your iPod. For these reasons, you should use a USB 2 port if your computer has one.

- **Only update checked songs**—If you check this, only songs with their Song check box checked will be moved onto the shuffle.

- **Convert higher bitrate songs to 128 kbps AAC for this iPod**—This option is useful if you have a lot of music that uses a higher-quality encoder, such as Apple Lossless. With this option checked, when you put music like this on the shuffle, it is converted into the 128Kbps AAC format so that it takes up less memory. You should leave this option checked so you can get the maximum amount of music on your shuffle.

■ **Enable disk use**—You use this check box and slider to configure a shuffle so you can use it as a flash drive.

4. Click **OK**. The preferences you set will take effect.

Using Autofill to Put Music on an iPod shuffle

tip

You also open the iPod pane by opening the shuffle's contextual menu and selecting iPod Options. Or, you can open the iTunes Preferences dialog box and click the iPod tab.

Using the Autofill tool, you provide the parameters for an update and iTunes takes care of moving music to or from the shuffle as needed based on your criteria.

To perform an Autofill update, do the following steps:

1. Plug your shuffle into an available USB port. iTunes will open (assuming you left this preference on).

2. Select the shuffle on the **Source** list. The Autofill tool will appear at the bottom of the Content pane (see Figure 7.12).

FIGURE 7.12

You can use the Autofill tool to place music onto an iPod shuffle.

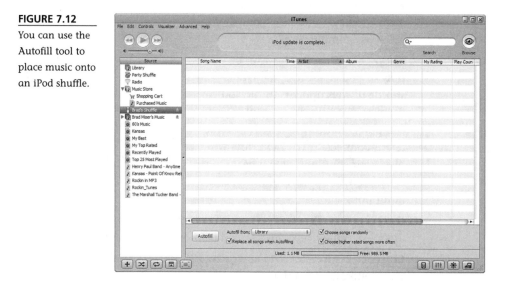

3. Choose the source of music you want to place on the shuffle on the **Autofill from** pop-up menu. You can choose your Library or any of your playlists. When it autofills your shuffle, iTunes will choose only music from the selected source.

4. If you don't want all the songs currently on the shuffle to be replaced by the Autofill, uncheck the **Replace all songs when Autofilling** check box. If this check box is checked, the entire contents of the shuffle are replaced. If it isn't checked, iTunes will try to add the Autofill songs until the shuffle's memory is full.

5. If you want to Autofill with songs selected at random from the source you selected in step 3, leave the **Choose songs randomly** check box selected. If you uncheck this check box, Autofill will select songs in the order in which they are listed in the source you selected in step 3 and add them to the shuffle until its memory is full.

6. If you rate songs and want Autofill to choose higher-rated songs more frequently, leave the **Choose higher rated songs more often** check box selected. This option is only available when you use the random option described in step 5. If you uncheck this box, Autofill will select songs truly at random and ignore your ratings.

7. Click **Autofill**. The Content pane will fill with the songs that Autofill has selected and the update process will start (see Figure 7.13). It will continue until the shuffle's memory is as full as it can get or until all the music you selected has been moved onto the shuffle, whichever comes first. The amount of your shuffle's memory that is being consumed will be shown on the bar just above the Source Information area at the bottom of the iTunes window.

8. When the update process is complete, click the **Eject** button next to the shuffle's icon on the Source list or the one located in the bottom-right corner of the iTunes window.

9. Unplug the shuffle from your computer and enjoy some tunes! (Of course, you should leave the shuffle plugged in to charge its battery.)

tip

If you have elected the random option, each time you click Autofill, a new set of songs will be placed on your shuffle.

caution

Don't unplug a shuffle if its orange status light is flashing. That means an update is in progress.

FIGURE 7.13

This shuffle is getting filled up with the good stuff.

If you checked the preference to keep your shuffle on the Source list, its icon will remain after you have unplugged it. The only way to tell this is that when the shuffle isn't plugged in, the Eject buttons don't appear (because there isn't anything to eject). You can still use the Autofill tool to manage your shuffle's music. When you plug it in the next time, that music will be moved onto your shuffle.

Manually Adding Songs to an iPod shuffle

You can also add songs to a shuffle manually by performing the following steps:

1. Plug your shuffle into an available USB port. iTunes will open (assuming you left this preference on), and the shuffle will appear on the Source list.

2. Select the source containing music that you want to place on the shuffle. You can move music from the Library or any playlist.

3. Drag the songs you want to place on the shuffle from the **Content** pane onto the shuffle's icon. When the pointer is over the shuffle, its icon will be highlighted. Release the mouse button and the songs will be copied onto the shuffle (see Figure 7.14).

tip

You can combine methods. For example, you can use Autofill and then manually add more songs. However, if you have the Replace all songs when Autofilling check box checked, each time you Autofill all the songs currently on the shuffle will be replaced.

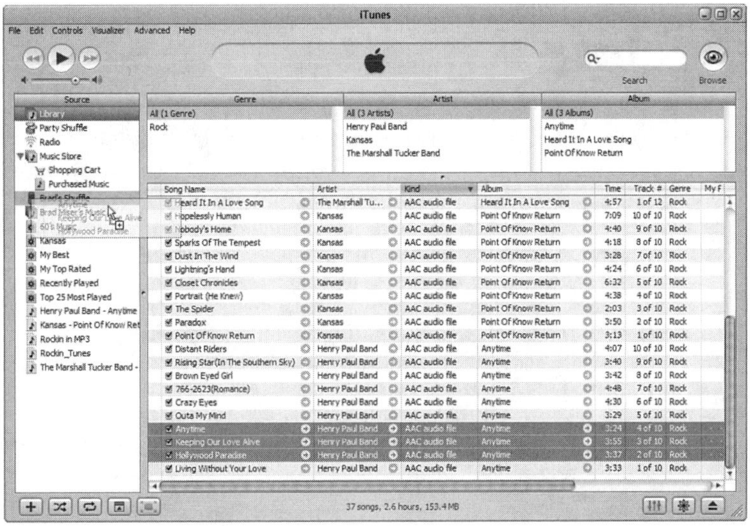

FIGURE 7.14

You can drag
songs from any
source onto the
shuffle's icon to
add those songs
to it.

4. Continue dragging songs from your sources until you have added all you
    want or until the shuffle's memory is full.

Removing Songs from an iPod shuffle

You can also manually remove songs from the shuffle whether you put them there
manually or they were added by Autofill. Select the shuffle on the **Source** list and
then select the songs you want to delete. Press the **Delete** key. If you are prompted,
click **Remove** and the songs will be removed from the shuffle. If you have previously checked the **Do not ask me again** check box, you won't see any prompt
that the songs will be immediately removed.

The Absolute Minimum

Managing the music on your iPod is essential if you are to be able to listen to the music you want to when the mood strikes you. Fortunately, maintaining your iPod's music library isn't all that hard. As you build and maintain your iPod's music library, keep the following points in mind:

- You use the iTunes application to create the music library on your iPod.

- You can determine the amount of used and free space on the iPod's hard disk in a number of ways, including by using the iPod's About command. This is important so you know whether you can fit all your music on your iPod.

- There are three ways to synchronize the music in your iTunes Library and on your iPod.

- When you use the "fully automatic" option, this is done for you automatically and your iPod will be updated with your current iTunes Library each time you connect the iPod to your computer.

- You can also choose to have only specific playlists updated automatically.

- You can manage the music on your iPod manually as well.

- If you have more than one iPod, such as an iPod and an iPod mini, you can choose different update options for each. For example, you might want to use the Automatically update selected playlists only option for the iPod mini and the fully automatic option for the iPod.

- Most of this list doesn't apply to the shuffle. You update its music using the Autofill tool or by manually configuring its music.

8

IN THIS CHAPTER

- Pick some music, any music.
- Control your music like a pro.
- Create and listen to an On-The-Go playlist.
- Check your battery.

Listening to Music on an iPod or iPod mini

In this chapter, you'll learn how to listen to and control your iPod tunes. Like any other device on which you listen to music, listening to music on an iPod is a two-step process. You first select the music you want to listen to. Then you play and control that music.

As you rock on, jazz up, classical out, and so on, you'll also find some other tasks useful, such as creating and using an On-The-Go playlist, rating your tunes, and monitoring your battery.

Selecting Music You Want to Listen To

The iPod is cool, but it isn't psychic. You need to tell it what music you want to listen to. There are two primary ways you do this: You can use playlists or you can browse the music stored on the iPod in various ways.

Selecting Music with Playlists

When you transfer music from your iTunes Library to an iPod, the playlists you have created and that are shown in the iTunes Source List come over too. You can select music to listen to by choosing a playlist using the following steps:

1. Select **Main** menu, **Music**, **Playlists**. You'll move to the Playlists menu (see Figure 8.1).

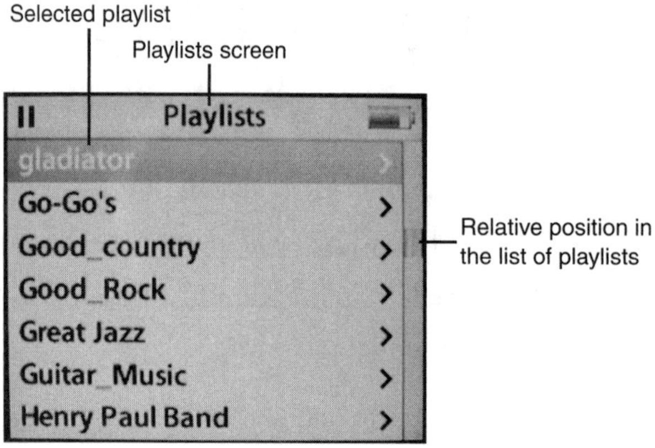

note

To play music on an iPod, you must have music stored on it. You do this by loading music into your iTunes Library and then transferring that music to the iPod.

Selected playlist

Playlists screen

FIGURE 8.1
Almost all the playlists you see on an iPod's Playlists menu should look familiar because they are the same playlists that appear in your iTunes Library.

Relative position in the list of playlists

2. Highlight the playlist you want to listen to and press the **Select** button. The songs in that playlist will be shown (see Figure 8.2).

3. If you want to play the entire playlist, press the **Play/Pause** button. If you want to start with a specific song, high-light it and press the **Select** button. The

tip

Remember that you can scroll up or down any menu, including the Playlists menu, by sliding one of your digits around the Click Wheel.

Now Playing screen will appear, and the first song in the playlist or the one you highlighted will begin playing (see Figure 8.3).

Playlist title

FIGURE 8.2

This playlist is called "gladiator" because it contains the *Gladiator* soundtrack. Here, you see the list of songs in the playlist.

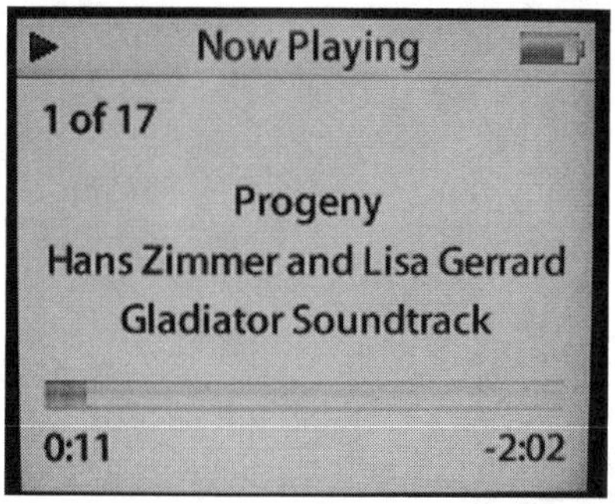

```
❚❚          gladiator          ▭
Progeny
The Wheat
The Battle
Earth
Sorrow
To Zucchabar
Patricide
```

FIGURE 8.3

One of the songs from the selected playlist is now playing.

```
▶          Now Playing          ▭
1 of 17

              Progeny
   Hans Zimmer and Lisa Gerrard
        Gladiator Soundtrack

▬▬▬▬▬▬▬▬▬▬▬▬▬▬▬▬▬▬▬▬▬▬▬▬
0:11                        -2:02
```

4. Use the techniques you'll learn throughout this chapter to control the tunes.

Browsing Your iPod's Music

Choosing music with playlists is great, and you might often find that method to be the one you end up using most because it gets you to specific music quickly. However, some music stored on your iPod might not be in a playlist, you might want to listen to all the music by a specific artist, and so on. In these cases, you can browse the music stored on your iPod to choose the music to which you want to listen. You can browse your music by the following categories:

■ Artists

tip

You can customize the iPod menu's to match your preferences. For example, if you listen to music mostly through playlists, you can move the Playlists command to the Main menu. You'll learn how in Chapter 10, "Configuring an iPod to Suit Your Preferences."

- Albums
- Songs
- Podcasts
- Genres
- Composers
- Audiobooks

To browse your iPod's music, do the following:

1. Select **Main** menu, **Music**. You'll see the Music menu, which contains the categories listed previously (see Figure 8.4).

2. Highlight the category by which you want to browse your music, such as Artists to browse by artist, and press the **Select** button. You will see the menu that shows you all the music that is associated with the category you selected in step 1. For example, if you select Artists, you will see all the artists whose music is stored on your iPod (see Figure 8.5).

> **note**
>
> If you are wondering how this information gets associated with your music, don't wonder any longer. It all comes from your iTunes Library. See Chapter 5, "Labeling, Categorizing, and Configuring Your Music," to learn how data is associated with your music.

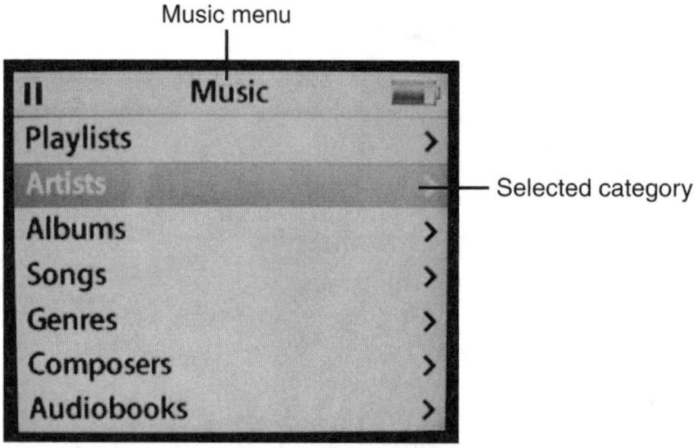

FIGURE 8.4
The Music menu enables you to browse your music by various categories.

Music menu

II	Music	🔋
Playlists		>
Artists		Selected category
Albums		>
Songs		>
Genres		>
Composers		>
Audiobooks		>

FIGURE 8.5
When you browse by a category, such as Artists, you will see all the music on your iPod organized by that category.

II	Artists	🔋
Amy Grand/Sandi Patti		>
Andy Williams		>
Antonio Vivaldi		>
Arthur Rubinstein & Greg...		>
Avril Lavigne		>
B.B. King		>
Bach		>

3. Browse the resulting list of music that appears until you find the specific category in which you are interested; then press the **Select** button. You will see the list of contents of the category you selected. For example, when I was browsing by artist and chose B.B. King, the list of my B.B. King music was displayed (see Figure 8.6).

tip

If you select the All option on any of the category screens, all your music for that category will be shown on the next screen.

FIGURE 8.6
This screen shows all the music on this iPod by B.B. King.

4. To move down to the next level of detail, select an item on the current list and click the **Select** button. The resulting screen will show you the contents of what you selected. For example, I selected the B.B. King album called *Spotlight on Lucille* and saw that album's contents (see Figure 8.7).

tip

You can start playing music at any time by making a selection and pressing the Play/Pause button. The entire contents of what you select will begin to play. For example, if you select the name of an artist on the Artists list, all the music by that artist will start playing, beginning with the first song on the first album. You don't have to drill down to lower levels of detail as these steps show.

FIGURE 8.7
Here, I am looking at the contents of a specific album by B.B. King.

5. To play everything shown on the screen, starting at the top, press the **Play/Pause** button. To start with a specific song, select it and press the

Play/Pause button. The Now Playing screen will appear, and the first song or the song you selected will start to play (see Figure 8.8).

FIGURE 8.8
I drilled down to
a specific album
and pressed the
Play/Pause but-
ton to hear it.

Although the previous steps used the Artists category as an example, you can browse and select music in any of the other categories in just the same way.

Controlling Your Music

Okay, so now you have selected music and started to play it. What's next? Learn to control it, of course.

Playing the Basic Way

Here are the basic controls you can use:

- **Play/Pause button**—When music is not playing or is paused, pressing this button will cause it to play again. When music is playing, pressing this button will cause the music to pause.

- **Previous/Rewind button**—If you press this button once quickly, you will jump back to the start of the song. If you press this button twice quickly, you will jump back to the start of the previous song. If you press and hold this button, the music will rewind; release the button when you get to the point at which you want it to start playing again.

- **Next/Fast-forward button**—Press this button once and you will jump to the start of the next song. Press this button and hold it, and you will fast-forward the song; release the button when you get to the point in the song where you want to be.

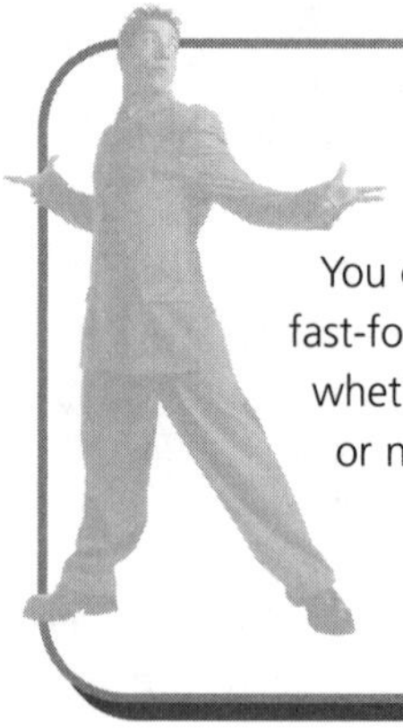

tip

You can rewind or fast-forward music whether it is playing or not.

■ **Click Wheel**—When the Now Playing screen is shown, drag a digit clockwise to increase the volume or counterclockwise to decrease the volume. When you touch the Click Wheel, the Volume bar will appear on the screen to visually indicate the current volume level; the shaded part of the bar represents the current volume level (see Figure 8.9). As you change the volume, the shaded area will expand or contract, depending on whether you increase or decrease the volume. When you release the Click Wheel, the Volume bar will disappear.

FIGURE 8.9

When you touch the Click Wheel, the Volume bar appears and you can drag on the Wheel to change the volume level.

Volume bar

Current volume level

You can only change the volume using the Click Wheel when the Now Playing screen is shown. That is why the Now Playing option is listed on the Main menu. You can quickly jump to this screen to change the volume when you need to.

Playing the iPod Way

The basics of listening to music are cool. Now let's take a look at some of the cool iPod playback features that aren't so obvious.

You can move around menus while music is playing just like you can when it isn't. As you choose other menus, the music will continue to play until you pause it or choose different music and play that instead.

If music is playing and you move away from the Now Playing screen, such as to change a setting on a menu, you'll automatically move back to the Now Playing screen a couple of seconds after you release the Click Wheel. So, as long as music is playing, you'll always wind up back at this screen.

tip

Remember that you move "up" the menu structure by pressing the Menu button.

The Now Playing screen provides lots of information about the music that is currently playing or paused (see Figure 8.10).

Number of song out of total selected

FIGURE 8.10
The Now
Playing screen is
packed with fea-
tures, some of
which might not
be obvious.

Album art (iPod photo only)

Song title

Artist

Album title

Played portion

Elapsed time   Timeline bar

Time remaining

At the top of the screen, you'll see the number of the current song out of the total you selected. For example, if you are playing the first song in a playlist containing 50 songs, this will be 1 of 50. This information helps you know where you are in the selected source.

In the center of the screen, you will see information about the song currently selected, including the song title, artist, and album. If any of this information is too long to be shown on one line, it will begin scrolling across the screen a second or two after a song starts playing. If you have artwork associated with music in iTunes and are using an iPod with a color screen, the album art will appear next to the song information.

At the bottom of the screen, you will see the Timeline bar. In the normal mode, this gives you a visual indication of the song's length and how much of the song you have played so far (represented by the shaded part of the bar). Under the left edge of the bar, you will see the amount of time the current song has been playing. Under the right end of the bar, you will see the time remaining to play (this is a negative number and counts up to zero as the song plays).

If you click the Select button one time, the Timeline bar changes to indicate that you can now rewind or fast-forward using the Click Wheel (see Figure 8.11).

note

Sometimes when song information is too long to fit onto one line, it's cut off and ellipses are used to indicate that there is more text. Frankly, I wasn't able to determine why some song information scrolls and some doesn't.

FIGURE 8.11
When the Timeline bar looks like this, you can rewind or fast-forward using the Click Wheel.

Current Location marker

When the Timeline bar is in this mode, you can drag the Click Wheel clockwise to fast-forward or counterclockwise to rewind the music. As you drag, the Current Location marker moves to its new location and the time information is updated. When you release the Click Wheel, the Timeline bar will return to its normal mode in a second or so.

If a song with artwork is playing on an iPod with a color screen and you click the Select button twice, the artwork will expand so it fills most of the screen. After a second or two, you'll return to the normal Now Playing screen.

If you click the Select button three times rapidly on an iPod with a color screen or twice on an iPod mini, the Timeline bar will be replaced by the Rating display. If the song currently playing has been rated, you will see the number of stars for that song (see Figure 8.12). If the song hasn't been rated, you see five dots instead (see Figure 8.13). You can rate the current song by dragging the Click Wheel clockwise to give the song more stars or counterclockwise to reduce the number of stars. A second or so after you stop touching the Click Wheel, the Timeline bar will return to its normal mode.

FIGURE 8.12
You can rate your music in iTunes and display the rating on your iPod.

FIGURE 8.13

You can rate your iPod music by choosing one of the dots shown here.

The neat thing about this is that the next time you connect your iPod to your computer, the rating information you set on the iPod is carried over to that music in your iTunes Library. So, you need to rate a song in only one place.

note

You can rate your music in iTunes. For more information on why and how you do this, see Chapter 5 for details.

Creating and Using an iPod On-The-Go Playlist

Working with playlists that you create in iTunes is useful, but you can also create a single playlist (called the On-The-Go playlist) on the iPod and listen to that playlist as much as you'd like. This enables you to create a playlist when you are away from your computer to listen to a specific collection of music.

To add a song to your On-The-Go playlist, view a list—such as the list of songs on an album—on which the song is listed. Highlight the song you want to add and hold down the **Select** button until the highlighting on the song flashes. Continue adding songs using the same process until you have added a group of songs to the playlist.

tip

When you are viewing a playlist—including the On-The-Go playlist—that contains the song that is currently playing, it is marked with a speaker icon.

To see the contents of your On-The-Go playlist, select **Main** menu, **Music**, **Playlists**, **On-The-Go**; the current On-The-Go playlist will always be at the bottom of the Playlists menu. You will see the contents of the On-The-Go playlist you have created. You can play this playlist just like any other playlist on your iPod.

When you connect your iPod to your computer, the On-The-Go playlist will be transferred into iTunes and will be available on the iTunes Source List.

If you want to clear the On-The-Go playlist, select **Main** menu, **Music**, **Playlists**, **On-The-Go**, **Clear Playlist**, **Clear Playlist** (no, that isn't a mistake, you select this command twice, but each is on a different screen). All the songs that were in the playlist will be removed, and it will become empty again. (The songs that were in that playlist are not removed from your iPod; the playlist is just cleared of those songs.)

After you have transferred the On-The-Go playlist to your iTunes Library, you can create a new On-The-Go playlist on your iPod by using the steps you learned in this section. When you connect your iPod to your computer again, this version of the playlist will also be added to your iTunes Source List, but a sequential number will be added to its name to keep the versions straight (as in On-The-Go 14).

note

As far as I know, you can't remove just a single song from the On-The-Go playlist; you have to remove all of them or none of them. Also, you can't use the same techniques to add songs to or remove playlists you created in iTunes. This works only for the On-The-Go playlist.

Each time you synch your iPod with your iTunes Library and these playlists are part of the synch options, each On-The-Go playlist will be added to your iPod. You can listen to them just like other playlists.

No matter how many of these playlists you accumulate, the current On-The-Go playlist will always be the last entry on the Playlists menu.

Monitoring an iPod's Battery

Even though the iPod's battery lasts a long time, it will eventually run out of juice and your music will come to a crashing halt. To prevent this, keep an eye on your iPod's Battery icon (see Figure 8.14). As your battery drains, the shaded part of the battery will decrease to indicate how much power you have left. When 1/4 or less is shaded, you should think about recharging your iPod. (For more information about the iPod's battery, see Chapter 13, "Maintaining an iPod and Solving Problems.")

FIGURE 8.14

This iPod mini's battery still has plenty of juice.

Now Playing — Battery icon

8 of 43

When I'm Gone

3 Doors Down

2:00   -2:20

The Absolute Minimum

Now you know just about everything you need to listen to music on your iPod. It isn't that difficult because the iPod's controls are well designed. Not to get controlling on you, but here are few more control points for your consideration:

- The first step in listening to music is to choose the music you want to listen to. You do this by choosing playlists or browsing your iPod's music.

- After you've selected music, you can use the pretty-obvious playback controls to control it. You also learned some useful but not so obvious ways to control it.

- After you have used it for a bit, you'll find that you can easily control an iPod with a single thumb. Often, the best way to hold an iPod is to set it in your palm and use your thumb to control it. It doesn't take long until you can navigate like a pro.

- When you use the Click Wheel to move around the iPod's screens or to control music, don't think you have to drag on it slowly or in small increments. You can move quite rapidly by dragging your finger or thumb quickly. The faster you move your finger, the faster things will happen on your iPod. You can move even faster by moving your digit in complete circles.

- You can use the On-The-Go playlist to create a playlist on the iPod.

- As you play your music, keep an eye on your iPod's battery so you don't run out of power.

9

In This Chapter

- Get your shuffle ready to groove.
- Turn on your shuffle, control it, and then turn it off.
- Sometimes, you need to put your shuffle on Hold.
- Keep an eye on your battery status so your shuffle doesn't run out of gas...whoops, I mean, electricity.

Listening to Music on an iPod shuffle

The iPod shuffle is the newest and most different member of the iPod family. While sometimes having someone so different in a human family can be not such a good thing (you know, like that Uncle Fred no one ever talks about), the shuffle is very different in a good way. One of the "good" things about the shuffle is that it is simple to use. The previous two chapters were required to go into all the details of playing music on the other iPods, but this short chapter will tell you all you need to know about playing music on a shuffle.

Getting Ready to Play

To hear the music stored on your iPod shuffle, you must attach a sound output device to it. The most common one you might think of is the earbud headphones that were included in the package.

To use these, you connect the mini-jack on the earbud cable to the Headphone jack located on the top of the iPod shuffle (see Figure 9.1). When you do so, you'll hear any sound coming from the iPod through the earbuds.

Although you are likely to use earbuds or other headphones with an iPod shuffle, those are certainly not the only audio output devices through which you can play a shuffle's music. For example, you can also connect this jack to powered speakers to play its music on those speakers. Using an adapter, you can also connect the shuffle to a home stereo receiver, as you will learn in Chapter 8, "Using an iPod with a Home Stereo or Car Stereo."

note

Before you can play music on a shuffle, you have to put some music on the shuffle. To do that, you first need to install its software; see Chapter 2, "Getting Started with an iPod," for help with that. You also need to load music onto the shuffle, which you probably did as part of configuring it. You can also use a special iTunes tool to fill your shuffle with great tunes (see "Adding Music to an iPod shuffle" on page **134**).

FIGURE 9.1

It's easy to figure out where to plug headphones into a shuffle because there is only one option.

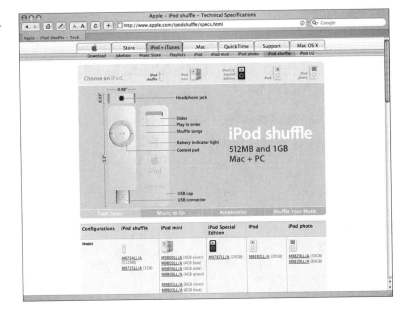

Turning On, Controlling, and Turning Off an iPod shuffle

Playing music on a shuffle couldn't be much easier. First, you choose how you want the music to play. Then, you use the shuffle's simple controls to control that music. When you are done, you turn off the shuffle.

Turning On a shuffle and Choosing How Music Will Play

One limitation of a shuffle is that you can't select the music that plays on it. You can, however, choose whether the music plays in the order you loaded it from the first song to the last or choose to have the music play at random with the iPod shuffle choosing the order in which it plays the music it contains.

Conveniently enough, when you let the shuffle know how you want the music to play back, you turn it on at the same time.

To get the shuffle going, use the slider on the back side of the shuffle's case (refer to Figure 9.1). Slide the slider one notch down to have music play straight through in the order it was loaded onto the shuffle. Slide the slider all the way down to have the shuffle, well, shuffle its music.

Notice that when you slide the slider to one of the "on" positions, a green area under the switch is exposed. This helps you know that the shuffle is turned on.

If you look at the front side of the shuffle (the side with the Control pad) while you turn it on, you'll notice that the status light (located above the Control pad) blinks green for a moment to let you know it is ready to play.

Using the iPod shuffle's Playback Controls

After the shuffle is powered up and ready to go, controlling it is a snap. You use the controls on the Control pad to play, pause, change the volume, and so on (see Figure 9.2).

The following controls are available on the Control pad:

- **Play/Pause**—When the music is stopped, pressing this makes it play. When it is playing, pressing this pauses the music.
- **Increase Volume**—Press and hold this one to increase the volume.
- **Next/Fast-Forward**—Press this once to move to the next song. Press it and hold it down to fast-forward in a song.

note

Using the Next or Previous button is affected by whether you have the shuffle set to shuffle. For example, if you have the shuffle shuffling and press the Next button, you'll move to the next song at random, not in the order in which they are loaded onto the shuffle.

■ **Decrease Volume**—Press and hold this one down to decrease the volume.

■ **Previous/Rewind**—Press this once to move to the previous song. Press it and hold it down to rewind a song.

FIGURE 9.2

Everything you need to control your music is on the shuffle's Control pad.

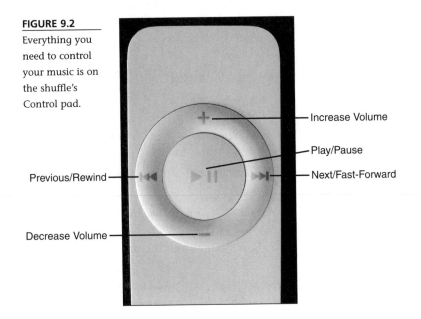

Increase Volume

Play/Pause

Previous/Rewind

Next/Fast-Forward

Decrease Volume

Each time you press a button, the green status light on the front of the shuffle will light up to indicate that your input was received. It will go out as soon as you stop using the control.

Turning Off an iPod shuffle

When you are done playing music, you should turn off the shuffle to conserve battery power. To do so, slide the slider on the back all the way to the off position; if you don't see any green in the slider, you know the shuffle is powered down.

tip

To move to the beginning of the music on the shuffle, press the **Play/Pause** button quickly three times. That will move to the beginning of the shuffle's playlist. If you press Play/Pause again, the music will start playing from there.

Putting an iPod shuffle on Hold

Because the shuffle is so small and light, you are likely to stuff it in a pocket or other place where it might get jostled. If it gets jostled in just the right place, one of the buttons might get pushed accidentally and disrupt your musical experience. And we can't have that!

To inactivate the buttons on the shuffle, press the **Play/Pause** button and hold it for about 3 seconds. The green status light will go out and the orange one will come on. When this happens, the shuffle is in Hold mode and its controls will have no effect. If you press a button, the orange status light will light up so you know the shuffle is still in Hold mode, but the control itself will have no effect.

> ## caution
>
> Because the shuffle doesn't have a screen, nor does a status light remain lit while the shuffle is on, it is easy to leave it playing when you don't mean to. Remember that if you see green in the slider on the shuffle's back, it is turned on.

To make the controls active again, press and hold the **Play/Pause** button for about 3 seconds. When the green status light appears, release the button. The shuffle's controls will become active again.

Monitoring an iPod shuffle's Battery

Just like all iPods, the shuffle has an internal battery. You should monitor its charge level occasionally so you don't run out of music.

To check the shuffle's battery level, press the **Battery** button on the shuffle's backside (see Figure 9.3). The status light will illuminate. If it is green, your shuffle has plenty of charge; if it is yellow, you should think about recharging your shuffle soon. If it is red, your world is about to become a lot quieter so get thee to a USB port immediately.

Remember that every time you plug your shuffle into a computer, its battery will be charged. And, as you'll learn in Chapter 13, "Maintaining an iPod and Solving Problems," it is actually good for an iPod's battery to be charged frequently. So, it's a good idea to plug your shuffle into your computer regularly, whether you have been listening to it a lot or not.

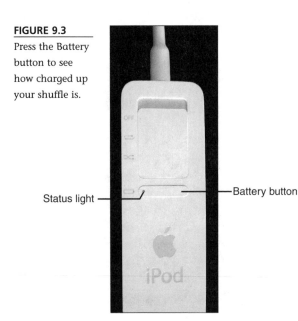

FIGURE 9.3
Press the Battery button to see how charged up your shuffle is.

Status light —

— Battery button

The Absolute Minimum

This is a short chapter because there just isn't that much to controlling a shuffle. But, in case your mind wandered, here are the highlights:

■ You can listen to a shuffle's music with the included earbuds, but you can also connect it to a set of powered speakers.

■ Turn on a shuffle and choose how its music will play (straight through or shuffling) with the slider on the back of its case.

■ Use the Control pad to control music playback and volume.

■ Use the slider to turn off the shuffle when you are done with it.

■ Use the Hold mode to prevent unintentional control presses.

■ Check on the shuffle's battery every so often by pressing the Battery button on the back and looking at the status light.

■ If you've read this chapter and don't have a shuffle yet, what are you waiting for? shuffles make great companions to your other iPods (don't worry, they won't get jealous).

10

IN THIS CHAPTER

- Use some cool music playback options, such as Shuffle and Repeat.

- Customize the Main menu.

- Set the contrast of your iPod's screen.

- Set the Sleep Timer.

- Get rid of the clicker—or not.

- Change the iPod's language.

- Restore all your settings to their default states.

Configuring an iPod to Suit Your Preferences

iPods are personal devices; because they are, you can customize them to work the way you want them to. You can control many aspects of how your iPod works by using the Settings menu. In this chapter, you'll learn about many of these settings that you can use to customize an iPod to suit your personal preferences.

Configuring Music Playback

Several of the iPod's settings relate to the way in which music plays. These include Shuffle, Repeat, Sound Check, and the Equalizer. If you only use an iPod shuffle, you can skip this chapter because none of its information is applicable to the shuffle.

Shuffling Music

There are two ways to shuffle music on your iPod. You can configure music to shuffle using the Shuffle settings. You can also use the Shuffle Songs command that is on the Main menu by default.

Shuffling Music with Shuffle Settings

You can use the iPod's Shuffle feature to have songs play in a random order. To shuffle music, use the following steps:

1. Select **Main** menu, **Settings**. You'll see the Settings menu.

2. Highlight the **Shuffle** command (see Figure 10.1).

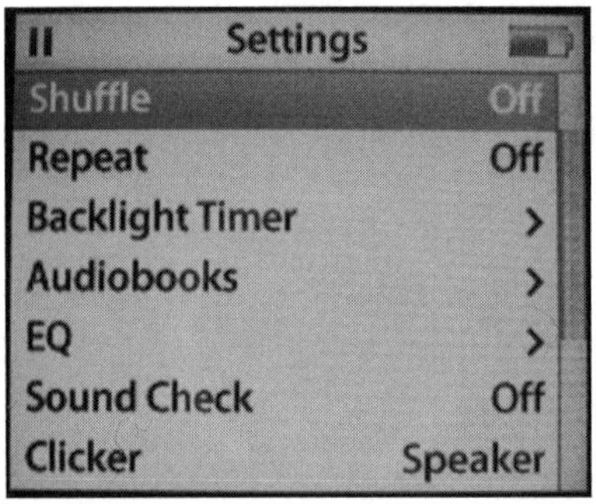

note

In the opening paragraph, I included the word *many* because you won't learn about all the available settings in this chapter. Some are covered in the chapters related to the features controlled on the Settings menu, such as the Contacts setting.

FIGURE 10.1

You can use the Shuffle setting to have an iPod play your music in a random order.

II	Settings	▬▭
Shuffle		Off
Repeat		Off
Backlight Timer		>
Audiobooks		>
EQ		>
Sound Check		Off
Clicker		Speaker

3. If you want the songs within a selected Browse category or playlist to play in a random order, press the **Select** button once. The Shuffle setting will become Songs. This causes the iPod to shuffle the songs within a music source when you play it.

4. If you want the iPod to select random albums when you select a Browse category or playlist, press the **Select** button twice. The Shuffle setting will become Albums. This causes the iPod to select an album randomly, play all

the songs on the album that are stored on the iPod, select another album randomly, and repeat this pattern until you turn off Shuffle again.

5. Select the music you want to play in a randomized fashion and play it. On the Now Playing screen, you'll see the Shuffle indicator to remind you that you are in Shuffle mode (see Figure 10.2).

6. To disable the Shuffle feature, move back to the Settings menu and press the **Select** button until you see Off next to the Shuffle setting. Your music will again play in a linear fashion.

> **note**
>
> The options you see on the Settings menu will vary among iPod models so don't be concerned if you don't see the exact same list of options on your iPod that you see in this chapter's figures.

Shuffling Music with Shuffle Settings

By default, the Shuffle Songs command appears on the Main menu. The command shuffles all the music on your iPod. This is different from the Shuffle setting you learned about in the previous section because you can select a specific source with that option. With the Shuffle Songs command, you can only shuffle through all your iPod's music. To shuffle this way, select **Main** menu, **Shuffle Songs**. When you play your iPod's music, you'll see the Shuffle indicator on the Now Playing screen. Music will move from one song to the next at random.

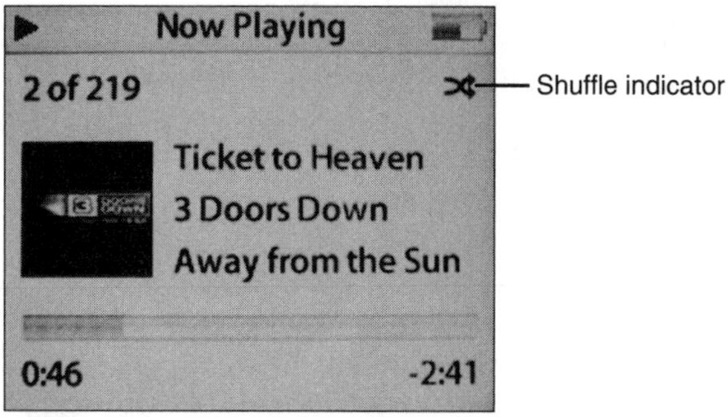

FIGURE 10.2
The Shuffle indicator reminds you that you are playing in the Shuffle mode.

Shuffle indicator

Now Playing
2 of 219
Ticket to Heaven
3 Doors Down
Away from the Sun
0:46   -2:41

There is some interaction between this command and the Shuffle setting. If you have Off as the Shuffle setting, this command does what I described in the previous two paragraphs. If the Shuffle setting is Songs, both are doing the same thing and work as expected. If the Shuffle setting is Albums, using the Shuffle Songs command randomly selects an album, plays all the songs on that album, chooses another album, plays all its songs, and so on.

When you want to stop shuffling music after you have selected the Shuffle Songs command, you have to select and play a music source, such as a playlist, an artist's music, and so on.

Repeating Music

The Repeat feature enables you to repeat an individual song as many times as you'd like or to repeat all the songs in a selected music source as many times as you can stand.

To repeat the same song ad infinitum, select **Main** menu, **Settings**. Highlight **Repeat** and press the **Select** button once so that One is displayed next to the Repeat setting. Select the song you want to hear and play it. It will play and then play again until you pause the iPod or choose a different song. While the song plays, the Repeat One indicator will appear on the Now Playing screen (see Figure 10.3).

note

The Shuffle feature works on any source of music you select, including playlists or any of the Browse categories, such as Artists, Albums, Genre, and so on. When you use the Songs mode, all the songs will be selected and play in a random fashion.

Repeat One indicator

FIGURE 10.3
You can make the same song play over and over until you just can't take it anymore.

To repeat all the songs within a selected music source, select **Main** menu, **Settings**. Highlight **Repeat** and press the **Select** button twice so that All is displayed next to the Repeat setting. Select the music source (such as a playlist) you want to hear and play it. It will play and then repeat until you pause the iPod or select a different music source. While the music source plays, the Repeat All indicator will appear on the Now Playing screen (see Figure 10.4).

note

Like the Shuffle feature, the Repeat feature works with any music source you select, including playlists or any of the Browse categories.

Repeat All indicator

FIGURE 10.4

You can use the
Repeat All mode
to repeat all the
songs in a
selected music
source, such as a
playlist.

> ▶ Now Playing ▬
>
> **2 of 29** ↻
>
> **Hollywood Paradise**
> **Henry Paul Band**
> **Anytime**
>
> 0:56 -2:41

To turn off Repeat, select **Main** menu, **Settings**.
Highlight **Repeat** and press the **Select** button until
Off is displayed next to the Repeat setting. Music
will again play one time through and then stop.

The Repeat feature also interacts with the Shuffle
Songs command. If Repeat is Off, Shuffle Songs
plays all the songs on your iPod once (randomly of
course). If Repeat is set to One and you use the
Shuffle Songs command, one song will be selected
and played until you stop it or the iPod runs out of
battery. If Repeat is set to All and you select
Shuffle Songs, all the songs are played at random
and then start over again and play in the same
order until you stop playing or the iPod runs out
of power.

note

When you have
Repeat set to One,
don't be fooled by
the 1 of X indicator on
the Now Playing screen. "X" will
continue to be the number of
songs in the selected source, but
the number of the current song
(such as 1 of) won't change
because that song gets repeated.

Using Sound Check

iTunes' Sound Check feature causes songs to play back at the same relative volume
level—if you have ever been jolted out of your chair because of one song's volume
level being much higher than the next one, you know why this is a good thing.
Using the iPod's Sound Check setting, you can cause the iPod to use the volume levels set by iTunes when Sound Check is on.

To use Sound Check, make sure it is active on the Audio pane of the iTunes
Preferences dialog box. Then, connect your iPod to your computer so the iPod's
music will be updated, or you can perform a manual update if that is how you
have configured iTunes for your iPod. After the update is complete, on the iPod
select **Main** menu, **Settings**. On the Settings menu, highlight **Sound Check** and
press the **Select** button. The Sound Check setting will become On to show you that

it is in use. When you play music back, it will play at the same relative volume level.

To return the volume level to the "normal" state, select **Main** menu, **Settings**. Highlight **Sound Check** and press the **Select** button so that Off appears as the Sound Check setting.

Using the iPod's Equalizer

The iPod also has a built-in Equalizer you can use to improve (*improve* being a relative term, of course) the music to which you listen. The iPod includes of number of presets designed to enhance specific kinds of music and other audio sources. To use the iPod Equalizer, do the following steps:

1. Select **Main** menu, **Settings**.

2. Highlight the **EQ** setting and press the **Select** button. You'll see the EQ menu (see Figure 10.5). On this menu, you will see all the available presets. The list is pretty long, so you will need to scroll down to see all your options. The presets include those designed for specific styles of music, such as Acoustic, Classical, Jazz, and so on, as well as for situations in which you might be using your iPod to play music, such as Small Speakers.

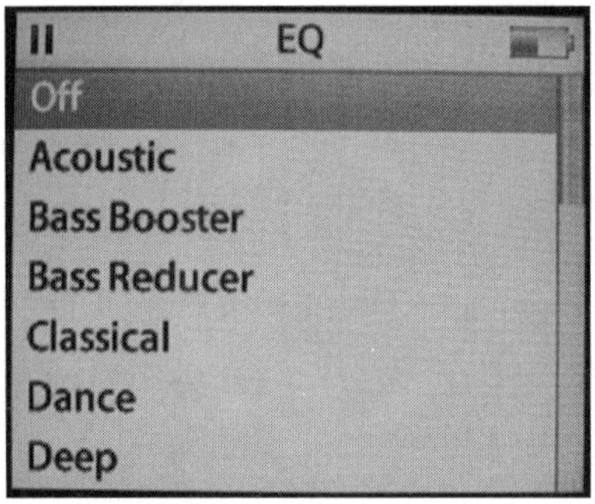

FIGURE 10.5
Choose an Equalizer preset on the EQ menu to activate it.

3. Highlight the preset you want to use and press the **Select** button. You'll return to the Settings menu. When you play music, the Equalizer will adjust the volume levels of various frequencies to enhance certain frequencies and to reduce the levels of others.

note

If you have created your own presets on the iTunes Equalizer, they won't be available on your iPod. The iPod includes a set of presets, and those are all you can use. Fortunately, the list of presets is quite large, so this isn't much of a limitation.

Setting Up Your Main Menu Preferences

You can configure the commands on the iPod's Main menu to customize it to suit your preferences. For example, suppose you frequently browse your music by artist. You can add the Artists command to the Main menu so you don't have to drill down through the Music menu to get to this category you use frequently. To configure your Main menu, do the following steps:

1. Select **Main** menu, **Settings**. The Settings menu will appear.

2. Highlight **Main Menu** and press the **Select** button. You'll see the Main menu (see Figure 10.6). On this menu, each command is listed along with its current Main menu state. If On is listed next to a command, it appears on the Main menu. If Off is listed next to a command, it doesn't appear on the Main menu. The commands are grouped into categories, including Music, Extras, and so on.

FIGURE 10.6
You can add items to the Main menu by turning them on or remove them by turning them off.

3. To add a command to the Main menu, highlight it and press the **Select** button so that On is listed next to that command (see Figure 10.7). That command will then appear on the Main menu.

FIGURE 10.7
When On appears next to a command, such as the Artists command, it will be on the Main menu.

4. To remove a command from the Main menu, highlight it and press the **Select** button so that Off is listed next to that command. That command will not appear on the Main menu.

5. Repeats step 3 or 4 for each command until you have set all the commands you want on the Main menu to On and all those you don't want to appear on the Main menu to Off. When you view the Main menu, your command preferences will be in effect (see Figure 10.8).

tip

To return the Main menu to its default commands, select **Main** menu, **Settings**, **Main Menu**, **Reset Main Menu**. Select **Reset** again to confirm the command. The iPod's Main menu will be just like it was when you first powered it up.

FIGURE 10.8
Using the Main menu settings, I customized the Main menu on this iPod (notice that I can use the Artists command on the Main menu to more quickly browse this iPod's music by artist).

Setting the Screen's Contrast

On an iPod mini, you can adjust the contrast of the iPod's screen so it's easier to read. To do this, select **Main** menu, **Settings**, **Contrast**. You'll see the Contrast menu, which consists of the Contrast slider (see Figure 10.9). Drag the **Click Wheel** clockwise to increase the contrast (which makes the text and background darker) or counterclockwise to decrease the contrast (which makes the text lighter). As you drag, the shaded part of the Contrast bar indicates the current relative contrast level. When you think you have a setting that suits you, move to other menus to see whether the setting is correct for your eyes and viewing conditions. Otherwise, continue to adjust it until it is correct.

FIGURE 10.9
Increasing the
contrast of the
iPod's screen can
make it easier to
read.

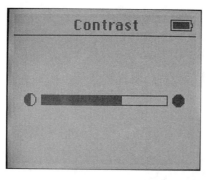

Setting the Sleep Timer

You can configure your iPod to turn itself off
automatically after a specific period of time
passes. To do this, use the following steps:

1. Select **Main** menu, **Extras**, **Clock**,
   Sleep Timer. You'll see the Sleep menu,
   which consists of a list of sleep time periods, from Off (meaning that the Sleep
   Timer is turned off) to 120 Minutes
   (meaning that the iPod will shut off in 2
   hours).

2. Select the **Sleep Timer** setting you want by highlighting it and pressing the
   Select button.

tip

You can reset an
iPod's contrast to the
default setting by
pressing and holding
the **Menu** button
for about 4 sec-
onds.

When you have the Sleep Timer on and view the Now Playing screen, the current
amount of time until the iPod sleeps is shown at the top of the screen (see Figure
10.10). When the counter reaches zero, the iPod will turn itself off. This happens
regardless of whether you happen to be listening to music at the time. So, if your
iPod suddenly shuts off and you don't first see a battery low warning, this is likely
the reason.

Time remaining until the iPod sleeps

FIGURE 10.10
This iPod will
turn itself off in
29 minutes.

▶ Now Playing ▬

1 of 17   ⊙29

Clear Horizon
Basia
The Best Of Basia

0:41   -3:34

Configuring the Clicker

As you select various menu options, your iPod "clicks" to give you audible feedback. There are two ways the clicker can sound: through the iPod's internal speaker or through the Headphones jack. You can also turn off the Clicker or have it play in both ways at the same time. To configure the Clicker, select **Main** menu, **Settings**. Then highlight the **Clicker** option and press the **Select** button until the setting you want is selected. You have the following options:

■ **Off**—The Clicker is silent.

■ **Speaker**—The Clicker plays through the iPod's speaker only.

■ **Headphones**—The Clicker plays through the Headphones jack only.

■ **Both**—The Clicker plays through the iPod's speaker and the Headphones jack.

Working with the iPod's Language

When you first turned on your iPod, you selected the language in which you wanted it to communicate with you. In most cases, you will never need to change that initial setting. However, you can if you do need to for some reason.

To choose a different language, select **Main** menu, **Settings**, **Language**. You'll see the Language menu (see Figure 10.11). Highlight the language you want your iPod to use and press the **Select** button. The menus will change and use the language you selected.

FIGURE 10.11

If I were multi-lingual, more of these settings might be useful, but because I am language limited, only one is applicable.

Returning an iPod to That Factory-Fresh Feeling

On occasion, all your work configuring your iPod might not be what you intended. Fortunately, you can return the iPod settings to their default values with a single menu command.

To do this, select **Main** menu, **Settings**, **Reset All Settings**. You'll see the Reset All menu. Highlight **Reset** and press the **Select** button. Your iPod's menus and all other settings will be returned to their default condition. You'll see the Language menu you use to select the language you want your iPod to use. Do so and you'll move to the Main menu.

> **tip**
>
> If you accidentally select a language you can't read, you can use the information in the next section to reset the language even if you can't read the iPod's menus.

If you have set your iPod to use a language you can't read, you can reset it by selecting the Settings command, which is the fourth command on the Main menu (by default) and then selecting the last command on the Settings menu (which is the Reset All Settings command). On the resulting menu, choose the second command and press the **Select** button to reset the iPod. Of course, if you have customized the Main menu, the Settings command might or might not be the fourth one down. When you customize the Main menu, it is a good idea to remember where that command is, just in case.

The Absolute Minimum

In this chapter, you've explored many of the options on the Settings menu and learned a number of ways to make your iPod suit your personal preferences. Check out the following list to review what you have learned and to pick up a few more pointers:

- Use the Shuffle, Repeat, Sound Check, and Equalizer to configure how music plays on your iPod.

- You can determine which commands appear on the Main menu by using the Main menu settings.

- Use the Contrast setting to set the contrast of the iPod's screen for an iPod mini.

- Use the Sleep Timer to have your iPod go to sleep automatically.

- If you don't like the clicking sound the iPod makes when you press a button, you can turn it off.

- Your iPod is multilingual; use the Language settings to determine which language your iPod uses.

- You can restore your iPod to its factory settings with the Reset All Settings command.

- The About command on the Settings menu provides important information about your iPod, including its name, its disk capacity, its available space, the software version installed on it, its model, and its serial number.

- The Date & Time settings enable you to configure and work with your iPod's clock.

- You use the Contacts setting to choose how contacts on your iPod are displayed.

- The Legal setting takes you to the oh-so-useful Legal screen, which contains lots of legalese you can read should you have absolutely nothing else to do.

11

IN THIS CHAPTER

- Listen to your iPod with a home stereo.
- Use your iPod as a home stereo.
- Listen to your iPod with a car stereo.

Using an iPod with a Home Stereo or Car Stereo

One of the cool things about an iPod is how versatile it is. You can use one to play music just about anywhere and in about any situation. In fact, the iPod can be the one constant in your musical universe. Wherever you go, you can take your trusty iPod along to provide the soundtrack for your life. That's because you can interface an iPod with other devices to play your iPod's music through those devices. In this chapter, we'll look at two of the most common music components with which you might want to listen to your iPod's music: your home sound system and your car stereo. You'll also see how the iPod can easily be transformed into a home stereo or boombox.

Using an iPod with a Home Stereo

You can connect your iPod to your home stereo and then listen to your iPod's music over that stereo. There are two fundamental ways you can do this: using wires or by using an FM transmitter.

Hard-Wiring an iPod to a Home Stereo

You can connect your iPod to your stereo system using cables similar to those you use to connect other audio components, such as a lowly CD changer. After you have connected the iPod to your amplifier/receiver, you can listen to it just like that lowly CD changer or DVD player.

The only challenge to this is choosing and connecting the proper cables to get the output of your iPod connected to the input of your receiver. Fortunately, this isn't all that challenging. You just need a cable that connects the Headphones jack on your iPod to an audio input port on your home stereo receiver. In most cases, you need a cable that has a stereo mini-jack on one end and two RCA connectors on the other end. The mini-jack connector goes into the Headphones jack on your iPod, while the RCA connectors go into the audio input ports on your home stereo's amplifier/receiver.

note

Although this section is focused on connecting an iPod to a home stereo receiver, the same techniques enable you to connect an iPod to many other audio devices, such as boomboxes.

The cable you need is available in just about any store that carries home electronics. Or, you can buy a kit that includes all the cables you need to connect your iPod to other devices, such as the Apple iPod Stereo Connection Kit with Monster Cable (available at the Apple online store).

There are two basic ways to connect an iPod to a home stereo using a cable: You can connect the iPod directly to the cables or you can use a Dock. Each method has its pros and cons.

Connecting an iPod Directly to a Home Stereo

To connect an iPod to a stereo receiver, simply plug the mini-jack end of a Mini-jack to RCA cable into the iPod's Headphones port. Then connect the RCA connectors to the audio input ports on the receiver. Figure 11.1 shows a diagram of a typical connection scheme.

FIGURE 11.1
Connecting an
iPod to a home
stereo isn't hard.

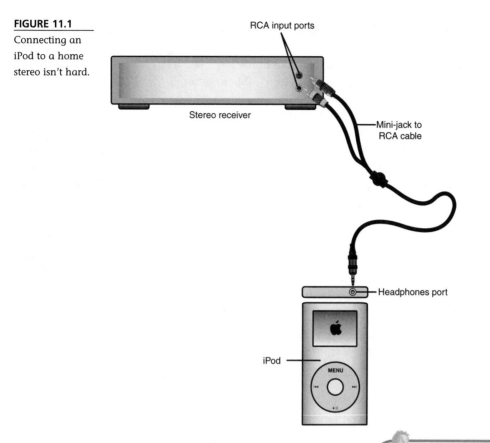

If you also want to power the iPod while it is connected to the receiver, connect the Dock connector port to the Dock connector end of a USB or FireWire cable. Then connect the USB or FireWire end of that cable to an AC adapter and plug the adapter into a wall outlet.

Pros: Easy setup; inexpensive.

Cons: Somewhat messy because you need to have a cable connected to the receiver, whose input ports typically aren't accessible, so you leave the cable connected and "loose"; you need a separate power adapter and cable to charge the iPod while using it with the stereo.

tip

If you want to use a shuffle to play music on a stereo system, you can plug an AC adapter into a wall socket and then plug the shuffle into the USB port on the adapter. This will charge the shuffle while you play its music.

Using a Dock to Connect an iPod to a Home Stereo

The best way to connect an iPod to a home stereo is to first use a Mini-jack to RCA cable to connect a Dock to the stereo and then use the USB 2 or FireWire cable to connect the Dock to an AC adapter (see Figure 11.2). Then, you can connect the iPod to the stereo by simply placing it in the Dock. When connected, your iPod also charges, so you don't have to worry about running out of battery power.

tip

You can use any input port on a receiver to accept an iPod's input. For example, you can connect the cable to the CD ports, Aux input ports, and so on. Any ports that include a left and right channel will work.

FIGURE 11.2

Using a Dock to connect an iPod to a home stereo enables you to connect the iPod to a stereo by simply placing the iPod into the Dock.

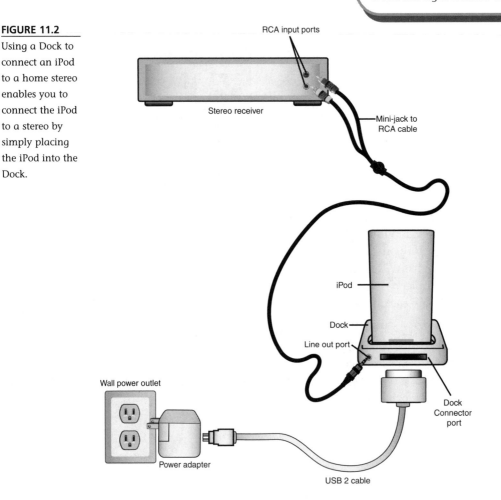

RCA input ports

Stereo receiver

Mini-jack to RCA cable

iPod

Dock

Line out port

Dock Connector port

Wall power outlet

Power adapter

USB 2 cable

Pros: Easy setup; clean installation because you don't have loose wires—after it's set up, you only need to have the Dock exposed; it's easiest to use because you connect the iPod to the stereo by placing it in the Dock.

Cons: Relatively expensive because, to be practical, you need to have a Dock and an AC adapter dedicated to this purpose, which means buying at least one Dock and AC adapter or purchasing an Apple iPod Stereo Connection Kit with Monster Cable.

Broadcasting iPod Music over FM

You can use an FM transmitter to broadcast your iPod's music on standard FM radio frequencies. Then, you can tune in the frequency on which you are broadcasting on any receiver, such as the tuner in your stereo system's receiver, to listen to your music.

Obtaining an FM Transmitter

To broadcast your iPod's music over FM, you need a transmitter that connects to your iPod and then sends its output over the airwaves. Because you are more likely to use one of these devices in your car, they are covered later in this chapter.

Broadcasting iPod Music to a Home Stereo

Depending on the type of FM transmitter you use, setting up an iPod and FM transmitter so you can tune in your iPod's music requires from little to no work. You simply plug the transmitter into your iPod's Headphones or Dock Connector port and play your iPod. Then, you set the tuner you are going to use to listen to the same frequency over which you are broadcasting your iPod's output.

Pros: Using an iPod with any audio device that can receive FM is easy; simple setup and use; no messy wires.

Cons: Subject to interference; it can be difficult to find an unused FM station in a metropolitan area.

Playing an iPod over a Home Stereo System

After you have installed or connected the components necessary to send your iPod's output to a home receiver, listening to your iPod's music is as simple as simple gets (however simple that is). On the receiver, select the iPod source, such as an Aux input or the FM tuner tuned to the frequency on which you are broadcasting your iPod's output. Then use the iPod controls to play the music and use the receiver's controls to set the volume level.

Typically, if you connect the iPod through its Headphones jack, you should leave the iPod's volume set at a mid-range point when using it with a home receiver. That prevents any distortion that might occur when the iPod is using its maximum output level. If you connect it via the Dock Connector port, the volume level on the iPod doesn't matter.

Using an iPod in this way is no different from other sources, such as a standard CD player.

Using an iPod As a Portable Home Stereo or Boombox

If you want to be able to listen to your iPod without headphones, use it as a home stereo, or use it as a portable boombox, you can obtain a set of iPod speakers. Typically, the iPod drops into a Dock-like port on the speakers. When powered via an AC adapter, the iPod also charges while you are using it. Some speakers can be battery powered too, so you can use the iPod boombox anywhere.

Many iPod speakers are available, and most offer similar features. My favorite is the Altec Lansing IM3c (see Figure 11.3). These speakers are about the size of a small hardcover book and fold flat for easy storage. They can be run on the included AC adapter or on batteries. The unit also includes a remote control so you can control the iPod music from a distance. But the best part about these amazing speakers is how good they sound; you won't be sacrificing anything for the unit's small size. I take my set with me whenever I travel so I can have my own stereo system in hotel rooms or wherever I happen to be.

FIGURE 11.3

Altec Lansing IM3c speakers are small and compact, but the sound they produce is anything but small.

If the cost of a set of speakers like this is prohibitive for you, you can purchase an inexpensive set of computer speakers and plug them into the Headphones jack on the iPod. You'll need to make sure you get a powered set of speakers because the iPod won't be able to provide enough volume to unpowered speakers.

Using an iPod with a Car Stereo

Being able to take all your music with you on an iPod is cool everywhere, but no place more so than in your car. Forget trying to carry CDs with you (if you are like me, you never have the one you really want to listen to anyway). Just grab your iPod and you are ready for the open road.

note

One of the features I like best about the IM3c speakers is that they also include a Line In port to which you can connect other devices. For example, when watching DVDs on my laptop computer, I connect its audio output to the IM3c speakers. This provides much better sound quality than the tinny speakers on most laptops.

Getting Sound from an iPod to a Car Stereo

There are two basic ways to get the output from your iPod to your car stereo: use a cassette adapter or use an FM transmitter.

Connecting an iPod to Your Car Stereo with a Cassette Adapter

A cassette adapter looks like a standard cassette, but it also has a wire coming from it that ends in a mini-jack. You connect this plug into the iPod's Headphones port. There are many brands and types of cassette adapters, and you can obtain one through most electronics retailers.

You then insert the cassette into a standard cassette player that is installed in many cars and use the car stereo's controls to play it.

When that is done, you can control the music from the iPod, just as if you were listening to it with headphones.

Cassette adapters are convenient, but don't be surprised if the sound quality doesn't seem as good as you get when you listen to a CD or an FM radio station. These adapters often cause music to sound a bit muted. If this bothers you, try an FM transmitter instead.

The other issue is that cassette players are going the way of 8-tracks and other obsolete devices. Once common, cassette players are seldom installed in new vehicles because CDs are better on all counts.

Connecting an iPod to Your Car Stereo via FM

You can also use an FM transmitter to broadcast your iPod's output. Then, you use your car's tuner to tune into the frequency you are broadcasting on. At that point, you can play your iPod and listen to its output over your car radio.

Many types of FM transmitters are available. The best units provide the ability to transmit over all available FM frequencies, power the iPod while it is broadcasting, and hold the iPod securely. My current favorite is the Digital Lifestyle Outfitters TransPod FM All-In-One Car Solution (see Figure 11.4). This unit includes a variety of attachment devices, including a solid boom that plugs directly into your car's power outlet (in the old days, this used to be where the cigarette lighter was installed). The unit holds your iPod securely and recharges it whenever you drop it into the TransPod's iPod bay. It has a digital tuner so selecting any FM frequency is a snap (it also enables you to memorize your favorite broadcast channels). When you use the boom to connect the unit to power, you don't have any wires to mess around with. Just drop the iPod into the unit and you're ready to play.

> **tip**
>
> Combined with a good frequency, broadcasting your iPod's music over FM results in the best sound quality. In fact, it might be so good that it will sound much better than it does when you use headphones.

FIGURE 11.4

The DLO TransPod enables you to listen to your iPod in the car while powering it and holding it securely.

Powering and Charging an iPod While You Are on the Road

You can power and charge your iPod while you are on the road by obtaining and using an auto power adapter. These devices plug into the 12-volt power outlet that is available in all cars and connect to the Dock port on your iPod to power it. Many of these devices are available, too.

If you use FM to broadcast your iPod's music, try to get a unit that also powers your iPod. Otherwise, you'll need a separate power adapter. If you use a cassette adapter, you'll likely also want a separate power adapter to keep your iPod charged when you use it in the car.

Mounting an iPod in Your Car

Finding a good spot to place your iPod in your car is probably the most difficult part of using an iPod in a car. You need the iPod within arm's reach, but you don't want it sliding around or falling off the dash. So, you want it close to you but want it held firmly, too. Let's see, what is designed to keep something in place but needs to be close enough to reach? Yep, you got it. A cup holder. It is likely that you have one or more of these near your radio and within arm's reach. The odds are that one of these is a good place to keep your iPod while you are driving.

You can just drop the iPod in a cup holder. Depending on the size and configuration of the cup holder and the size of your iPod, this might work just fine. However, in most cases, you should put your iPod in a holder or case before doing this to protect it from scratches and to keep it from bouncing around. Several devices are designed to hold your iPod in a cup holder securely, such as the Belkin TuneDok Car Holder for iPod.

In what is probably a familiar song by now, if you use an FM transmitter, get one that also holds the iPod securely. The TransPod does this and so does the Griffin Technology RoadTrip.

caution

If you use wires, such as a power and cassette adapter, be sure you route them such that they don't interfere with any of your car's controls. It is easy to get them wrapped around something without knowing it until you are in a bad spot.

caution

If the cup holder you use is in plain sight from outside the car, make sure you remove your iPod and put it out of sight before you leave your vehicle. An iPod in plain sight will tempt any thief who happens by your car.

Controlling an iPod While You Are on the Road

If there is one dangerous topic in this book, this is it. Playing around with an iPod while you are driving is not a good idea. It is very easy to get focused on the iPod instead of where you are going, and your day can suddenly be ruined. To practice safe iPodding while you are on the road, consider the following tips:

> **caution**
>
> Take the information in this section seriously. Listening to music is not worth risking your life or property, not to mention the others who share the road with you (myself included!).

- **Choose the music to which you are going to listen while you are stopped**—The iPod's screen is just not large enough to be able to see it clearly and look around you at the same time. Choosing music is at least a one-hand and two-eye operation. That doesn't leave much left for driving. So fire up your iPod, connect it to the radio with a cassette adapter or configure the FM transmitter, choose your music source and play it, place your iPod in its holder, and then drive.

- **Consider creating playlists for driving**—You can make these long enough so you never have to change the music that is playing while you drive.

- **If you must fiddle with your music while you drive, at least use a remote control**—You can't change the music source with these devices, but you can change the volume, skip to the next song, and so on.

- **Remember that you don't need to change the volume on the iPod itself**—Set it at mid-level and leave it alone. Use your car radio's controls instead. (If you use an FM transmitter that connects to the iPod's Dock Connector port, you don't need to bother with the iPod's volume control at all.)

- **Keep your iPod secure, as explained in the previous section**—Nothing is more distracting than the thought of your precious iPod flying around the car as you drive. If that does happen, remember that fixing you and your car (plus other people) will cost a lot more than a new iPod!

- **Remember the road rule of the day: Road first, music last.**

The Absolute Minimum

Using an iPod with a home or car stereo is easy to do and lets you listen to your iPod's music in many situations. Perhaps the best way to do this is to use an FM transmitter so you can tune in your iPod's music on your car radio or receiver's tuner. If you do this, check out the following pointers:

- Don't worry about other people being able to listen to your music when you use an FM transmitter. These devices have very limited range. If you are in a vehicle, someone might be able to pick up your iPod station if his vehicle is right next to yours; however, as soon as you separate even a few feet, he will lose the signal.

- Because you move around a lot when you drive, finding a good (meaning never used) FM frequency to use while you are on the road can be a challenge, especially if you are in a large metropolitan area. If a frequency isn't being used directly, it still might suffer bleed-over from stations on other frequencies. If you choose a frequency that is being used or has bleed-over, your iPod's music might be interrupted occasionally. For best results, select a station you think is unused and listen to it for a while as you drive around. (Yes, you will feel kind of silly listening to static, but hey, it will help in the long run.)

- When you find a good candidate for an unused frequency, set one of your radio's buttons to that frequency so you can easily return to it. If you use an FM transmitter in more than one car, you might want to set it on the radio in each one.

- Don't be surprised if you still have occasional static while using FM, even if you find a good unused station. Hopefully, you will be able to find a station with which this is a rare occurrence, but it is likely to happen once in a while. If you can't find a frequency/transmitter combination that works satisfactorily, try using wires or the cassette adapter method instead.

- Remember that, as you move among different areas, there are different radio frequencies being used. You might have to use different frequencies in the different areas in which you drive.

IN THIS CHAPTER

- Understand that iPods aren't just for music any more.

- Move photos onto an iPod.

- View pictures on an iPod.

- Add some flair by viewing your pictures in slideshows.

- Connect your iPod to a TV to show your slideshows on a bigger screen.

- Turn things around and move photos from the iPod to your computer.

Using the iPod for Images

The current pinnacle of the iPod line is the iPod itself. There are a number of reasons for this, including the color screen, bigger hard drives, and so on. One of the coolest things about an iPod is that it can work with photos as well as it does music.

iPods and Photos

What does *work with* photos mean? That means you can

- Use iTunes to move photos from a computer onto an iPod.
- View photos on the iPod individually or in slideshows.
- Use an iPod to display photos and slideshows on a TV.
- Connect a digital camera to an iPod and move photos from the camera to the iPod, where you can view them (with an optional iPod Camera Connector).
- Move photos from the iPod onto a computer.

> ## note
>
> This chapter really only applies to the iPod and the variant that once existed called the iPod photo (which became the iPod). If you have an iPod with a monochrome screen (such as in iPod mini), you can store photo files on it just like any other computer files, but you can't view or work with them without moving them onto a computer. And since it doesn't have a screen at all, none of the information in this chapter applies to the iPod shuffle.

Moving Pictures onto an iPod

To view photos on an iPod, you have to move them onto the iPod. There are three ways to do this:

- Use a supported application to move images onto an iPod via iTunes.
- Manually move photo files from a computer onto an iPod.
- Transfer photos from a digital camera onto an iPod.

Card readers for iPods enable you to transfer photos from the memory cards in digital cameras onto your iPod. You can use these devices with any iPod (except the shuffle) to store photo files on the iPod. However, you can't view photos on the iPod with this method. You can only use the iPod to transport those files, in which case, this is like using the iPod as a disk with any other kind of computer file. While this is useful in some cases, this isn't covered in this chapter. The focus here is on using the iPod to view photos along with transporting them.

Using an Application to Move Pictures from a Computer onto an iPod

With a supported application, you can transfer photos from your photo albums onto an iPod. To use this technique, you must store your photos in one of the following applications:

- Adobe Photoshop Album, version 1.0 or later (Windows)

- Adobe Photoshop Elements, version 3.0 or later (Windows)

- iPhoto, version 4.0.3 or later (Macintosh)

If you use an application other than one of these to manage your photos, you can still move those photos onto an iPod; you just have to manage them outside the application itself, which you'll learn how to do in the next section.

If you do have one of these applications, use the following steps to move images from the application onto an iPod:

note

These steps use iPhoto on a Mac as an example. Using Photoshop Album or Elements on a Windows PC works similarly.

1. Connect the iPod to your computer.

2. Select the iPod on the **Source** list and click the **iPod Options** button.

3. Click the **Photos** tab. You'll see the Photos synchronization tools (see Figure 12.1).

FIGURE 12.1

Use the Photos tab of the iPod Options dialog box to move photos from a supported application onto an iPod.

> iPod
>
> General iPod Audio Importing Burning Sharing Store Advanced
>
> iPod Photo   1.1
>
> Music **Photos** Contacts Calendars
>
> ☑ Synchronize photos from: 🖼 iPhoto   ⬍
>   ⦿ Copy all photos and albums
>   ○ Copy selected albums only
>
> | Last Roll (10) | iTunes will first copy all of your music onto your iPod. |
> | Last 12 Months (1377) | iTunes will then copy your photos onto your iPod in the |
> | CA_NV Vacation 2004 (570) | order shown in the list until the iPod is full. You can drag |
> | House_remodel_2004 (156) | the albums in the list to |
> | Photobooks (112) | change their order. |
>
> ☐ Include full-resolution photos
> Copy full-resolution versions of your photos into the Photos folder on your iPod, which you can access after enabling disk use in the Music tab.
>
> 4293 photos
>
> Cancel   OK

4. Check the **Synchronize photos from** check box.

5. On the pop-up menu, choose the application you want to use. If you use a Mac, select **iPhoto**. If you use a Windows PC, select either **Photoshop Album** or **Photoshop Elements**.

6. If you want to move all the photos and photo albums stored in the selected application onto your computer, click the **Copy all photos and albums** radio button and skip the next step.

7. If you want to move only selected photo albums onto the iPod, click **Copy selected albums only** and then click the check box next to each album you want to import.

8. If you also want to move full-resolution photo files onto the iPod, check **Include full-resolution photos**. When viewing photos on an iPod, it uses an optimized version of the photo to display on the screen. If you want to use the iPod to move full-resolution files, say from one computer to another, this option will copy those files onto the Photos folder on the iPod. You can then use the iPod as a disk to move the files from that folder onto a different computer.

9. Click **OK**. The dialog box will close and the photos you selected will be moved onto the iPod, ready for you to view.

tip

If you look closely at Figure 12.1, you'll notice that the iPod menu appears at the top of the pane. That's because I had two iPods connected to the computer at the same time. You can use this menu to choose the iPod you want to configure. In this example, I have the iPod called iPod Photo selected.

Moving Image Files from a Computer onto an iPod

If you don't use a supported photo application, you can still transfer images onto an iPod for viewing. This requires slightly different steps, as you will see here:

1. Prepare the photos you want to move onto the iPod using the application you use to transfer photos from a digital camera.

2. Create a folder on your computer.

3. Copy or move the photo files into the folder you created in the previous step.

4. Connect the iPod to your computer.

5. Select the iPod on the **Source** list and click the **iPod Options** button.

tip

You can use an iPod to back up your photo files by checking **Include full-resolution photos**. Each time you synch your iPod, copies of your photo files will be placed on your iPod. If you ever need to recover them on your computer, you can use the iPod as a disk to do so.

6. Click the **Photos** tab. You'll see the Photos synchronization tools.

7. Check the **Synchronize photos from** check box.

8. On the pop-up menu, select the folder in which you placed the photos you want to move onto the iPod. The menu will show the folder you selected (see Figure 12.2).

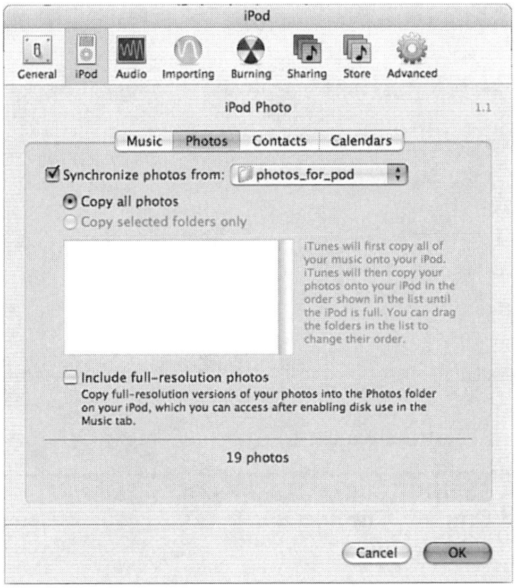

FIGURE 12.2

The menu next to the Synchronize check box shows the name of the folder containing images I want to move onto an iPod.

9. If you also want to move full-resolution photo files onto the iPod, check **Include full-resolution photos**. When viewing photos on an iPod, it uses an optimized version of the photo to display on the screen. If you want to use the iPod to move full-resolution files, say from one computer to another, this option will copy those files onto the Photos folder on the iPod. You can then use the iPod as a disk to move the files from that folder onto a different computer.

10. Click **OK**. The dialog box will close and the photos you selected will be moved onto the iPod, ready for you to view.

Moving Photos from a Digital Camera onto an iPod

Using the iPod Camera Connector accessory (available at the online Apple Store), you can connect the USB cable you use to transfer images from your digital camera to your computer to also transfer them onto an iPod (see Figure 12.3). In addition to being able to view those images on the iPod, you can also transfer them from the iPod to your computer.

FIGURE 12.3

Using the iPod Camera Connector, you can transfer images directly from a digital camera onto an iPod.

To transfer photos from a digital camera to an iPod, use the following steps:

1. Connect the iPod Camera Connector to the Dock port on the iPod.

2. Connect the USB cable for your camera to the camera and to the iPod Camera Connector, and put your camera in transfer mode. On the iPod, you'll see the Import screen. On this screen, you'll see the number of photos that are ready to transfer and how much disk space they will consume.

3. Highlight the **Import** command and press the **Select** button. The photos will be imported onto the iPod. On the Photo Import screen, you'll see a thumbnail of each image as it is moved from the camera onto the iPod.

When the process is complete, you'll see the Import Done screen.

4. To exit the Import mode, select **Done**. You'll move to the Photo Import screen that shows each import session identified by Roll (see Figure 12.4). For each roll, you'll see the number of photos imported.

> # tip
>
> This is a great way to expand the number of images you can capture without a computer. If you fill up your camera's memory card, you can move the images on that card to the iPod, erase the card, and then shoot more photos.

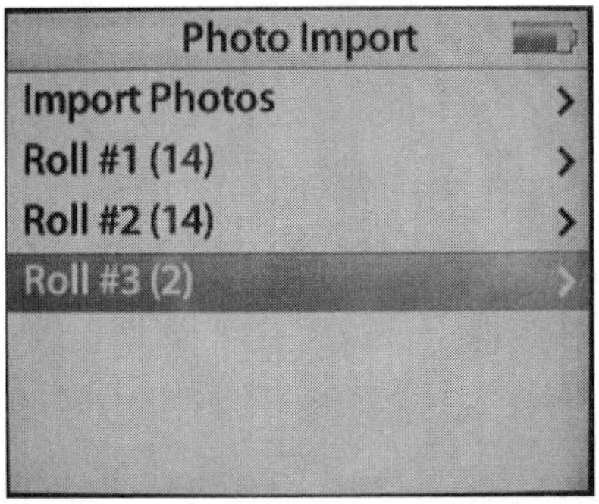

FIGURE 12.4

So far, I've used the iPod Camera Connector to import three "rolls" of photos from my camera onto this iPod.

Photo Import	
Import Photos	>
Roll #1 (14)	>
Roll #2 (14)	>
Roll #3 (2)	>

tip

If you want to stop the process before it is complete and save the images you have imported so far, select **Stop** and **Save**. If you don't want to save any of the images, select **Cancel**.

After you have imported images from a camera onto the iPod, you can work with them on the iPod (to view them or move them to a computer), just like photos you move onto the iPod with one of the other methods, which brings us to the next section.

To erase the camera's memory card, select **Erase Card**. Then select **Erase Card** again on the Erase Card screen.

Viewing Photos on an iPod

After you have stored photos on an iPod, using any of the methods you learned earlier in this chapter, you can view them using the following steps:

1. Select **Main** menu, **Photos**. You'll see the Photos menu (see Figure 12.5). On this menu, you'll see the photos you have imported to the iPod organized in photo albums if you used a compatible application to import them. If you've imported photos using an iPod Camera Connector, you'll also see the Photo Import option, which leads you to images you have imported from a camera.

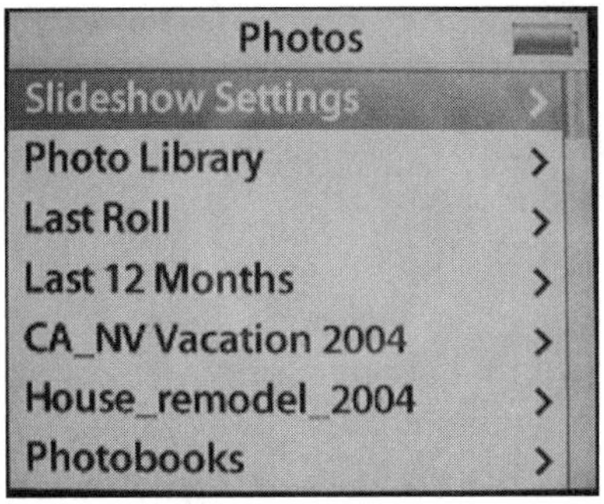

FIGURE 12.5

When I imported photos onto this iPod, I used the iPhoto application, so I see my photo albums on the iPod.

Photos	
Slideshow Settings	>
Photo Library	>
Last Roll	>
Last 12 Months	>
CA_NV Vacation 2004	>
House_remodel_2004	>
Photobooks	>

2. Select the source of the photos you want to view. For example, to view the images in a photo album, select it on the menu. To see all the images on the iPod, select **Photo Library**. To see images you have imported from a camera, select **Photo Import** and then select the roll you want to view.

3. Press the **Select** button. You'll see thumbnails of all the images in the selected source (see Figure 12.6). The current image will be indicated by a yellow box.

FIGURE 12.6
Here, I've selected a photo album and can see thumbnails of the images it contains.

4. Use the **Click Wheel** to move to the image you want to view.

5. Press the **Select** button. The image you selected will fill the iPod's screen (see Figure 12.7).

FIGURE 12.7
This image is filling the iPod's screen.

6. Press the **Fast Forward** button to view the next image in the source or the **Rewind** button to view the previous image.

7. When you are done viewing images in the selected source, press the **Menu** button to move back to the source's menu and then press **Menu** again to move back to the Photos menu.

note

When you get to the last photo in the source, pressing the Fast Forward button won't do anything. That's how you know you have seen all the images in the source.

Viewing Slideshows on an iPod

tip

If you press the Play or Select button when you are viewing an image, you'll jump to the Slideshows menu.

You can view the images on your iPod in a slideshow. There are two general steps to do this. First, configure the slideshow options. Then, watch the show.

Setting Up an iPod Slideshow

To configure a slideshow, perform the following steps:

1. Select **Main** menu, **Photos**, **Slideshow Settings**. You'll see the Slideshow Settings menu (see Figure 12.8).

FIGURE 12.8

Your iPod offers a number of options for its slideshows that you can configure on the Slideshow Settings menu.

Slideshow Settings	
Time Per Slide	>
Music	>
Repeat	Off
Shuffle Photos	Off
Transitions	>
TV Out	Ask
TV Signal	NTSC

2. Select the option you want to configure and press the **Select** button.

3. Use the resulting menu to choose the specific options you want to configure. See Table 12.1 for a description of the available settings.

Table 12.1   Slideshow Settings Options

Setting	What It Does	Options
Time Per Slide	Controls the amount of time each image is displayed	Manual; means you must press the Fast Forward button to advance the slideshow
		2, 3, 5, 10, or 20 seconds; plays the image for the selected amount of time

Table 12.1 (continued)

Setting	What It Does	Options
Music	Chooses the music that should be played when the slideshow is playing	From iPhoto (Mac only); plays the music associated with the source in iPhoto
		Now Playing; uses the music currently playing
		Off; no music
		Playlist name; plays the selected playlist
Repeat	Repeats the slideshow	Off; don't repeat the slideshow
		On; repeats the slideshow
Shuffle Photos	Displays photos at random	Off; plays the photos in order
		On; displays the images randomly
Transitions	Chooses the transition used between photos	Off; no transition is used
		Random; uses a random transition between each image
		Transition name; uses the selected transition between all images
TV Out	Sets the iPod to play to a TV	Ask; displays a prompt for you to select to play to a TV each time you play a slideshow
		On; always sets to display on a TV
		Off; always sets to play on the iPod only
TV Signal	Chooses a format for the signal sent to a TV	NTSC; uses the NTSC format (standard for the United States)
		PAL; uses the PAL format (standard for Europe)

4. Press the **Menu** button to move back to the Photos menu.

Playing an iPod Slideshow

To view a slideshow, perform the following steps:

1. Select **Main** menu, **Photos**. You'll see the Photos menu.

2. Highlight the source of the images you want to view in a slideshow. The options are the same as when you are viewing images individually.

3. Press the **Play** button. The slideshow will play using the current slideshow settings (see Figure 12.9). Sit back and enjoy the show!

FIGURE 12.9
Although you can't tell it from the figure, this slideshow includes a nice soundtrack and transition effects.

4. When the last image in the slideshow appears, press the **Menu** button to return to the slideshow.

Using an iPod to Display Slideshows on a TV

Using the optional iPod AV Cable, you can connect your iPod to a TV and display slideshows on the TV (see Figure 12.10). Connect the cable to your iPod and to the RCA input jacks on your television. Then, play a slideshow using the TV Out option set to Yes, or select the Ask option and then select the TV On option. The slideshow will be played on the TV.

note

If you configure slideshows with the Manual setting, you'll need to press the Fast Forward button to advance the images in the show.

FIGURE 12.10

Using this cable, you can display images and slideshows on a TV.

You can use the iPod Dock for this as well. The benefit of this is that you can use an S-video cable to connect the Dock to your television, which will improve the quality of the images on the TV. Then, you connect the Audio out port on the Dock to the Audio In ports on the TV. Drop your iPod in the Dock and play a slideshow.

While a slideshow plays, you'll see full-screen images on the TV. On the iPod, you'll see thumbnails of the previous, current, and next images. You'll also see how many images are in the slideshow and the amount of time remaining for each image being displayed (see Figure 12.11).

FIGURE 12.11

While you're watching a slideshow on a TV, you'll see the Slideshow screen on the iPod.

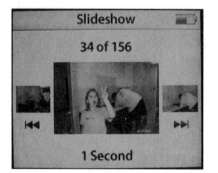

Moving Photos from an iPod onto a Computer

You can move photos from an iPod to a computer. For example, you might want to move images you have moved from a camera onto the iPod to your photo collection on your computer or move images from one computer to another.

tip

You can stop the slideshow by pressing the Menu button.

Using an Application to Move Photos from an iPod onto a Computer

You can transfer photos from the iPod to a computer just like you do from a digital camera. The steps to do this are as follows:

1. Connect the iPod to your computer, just as you do when you want to update it.

2. Open the application you use to import images from your digital camera.

3. Import the images from the iPod (see Figure 12.12).

FIGURE 12.12

Here I am importing images from an iPod into my iPhoto Library.

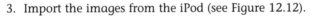

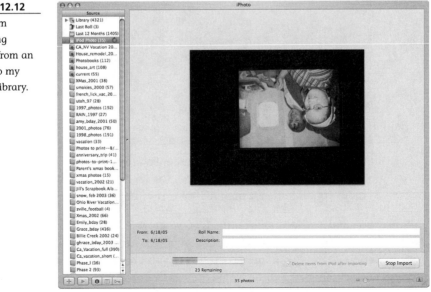

Manually Moving Files from an iPod to a Computer

You can store images on an iPod and move those to a computer similar to how you store and move any other files. To do so, perform the following steps:

1. Enable your iPod for disk use.

2. Connect your iPod to your computer.

3. Open a window on the desktop that shows the contents of your iPod (see Figure 12.13).

4. Drag the image files from the iPod to a location on your computer to copy them there.

note

If your iPod is not recognized by the application, you'll have to use the method described in the next section to move images from the iPod to your computer.

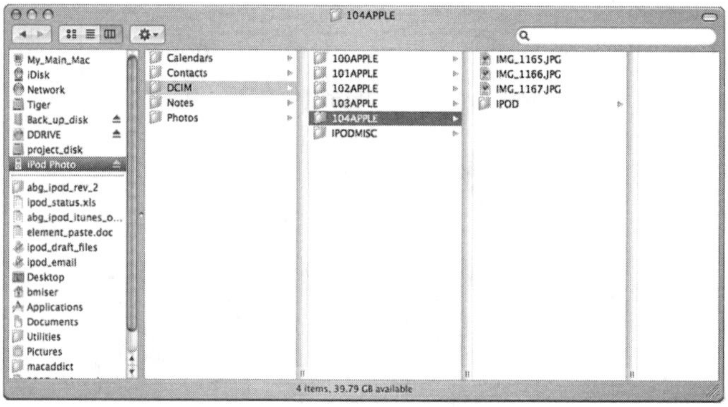

FIGURE 12.13
On this Mac, I've selected the iPod and can see the folders and files it contains.

5. Open the application you use to manage your images.

6. Import the images you copied from the iPod into that application. From this point on, the images you moved from the iPod can be used in the same way as those you imported from a digital camera.

There are a couple of locations on the iPod where your photos might be stored. If you manually moved photos from your computer onto the iPod, look in the folder you placed them in. (You might do this when you are moving image files from one computer to another.) If you imported images from a digital camera onto the iPod, the photos will be stored in the folder called DCIM (which stands for Digital Camera Images). Open this folder and you will see a folder for each import. Open a folder to access the files it contains, such as to import them into your photo application.

The Absolute Minimum

The iPod is the king of the iPod family for several reasons, the foremost of which is its capability to handle photos along with music. If you are fortunate enough to have one of these amazing devices, keep the following points in mind:

- The iPod enables you to store images and view those images individually or in slideshows.

- There are three ways to move images onto an iPod so you can view them. You can use iTunes to synchronize your photos stored in a supported photo application (Photoshop Elements, Photoshop Album, or iPhoto) on your iPod. You can also use iTunes to move photos stored in a folder on your computer onto your iPod. With an iPod Camera Connector, you can download images directly from a digital camera onto an iPod.

- You can select and view images on your iPod individually.

- You can also view photos on an iPod in slideshows that can have music and transition effects.

- With the optional cable or Dock, you can connect an iPod to a TV and show your slideshows on the TV.

- You can also move photos from an iPod onto your computer. You can do this by importing its images into your photo application or from your computer's desktop.

- If you don't have a color iPod yet, what are you waiting for?

IN THIS CHAPTER

- Maximize your iPod's battery life and durability.
- Update or restore your iPod's software.
- Identify and solve iPod problems.

Maintaining an iPod and Solving Problems

The iPod is a well-designed device, and it is more likely than not that you won't ever have any trouble with it, especially if you practice good battery management and keep its software up-to-date. In this chapter, you'll learn how to do those two tasks, plus you'll also learn how to handle any problems in the unlikely event they do occur.

Maintaining Your iPod's Power

Like any other portable electronic device, your iPod literally lives or dies by its battery. When not connected to a power source, your iPod's battery is the only thing standing between you and a musicless life. Fortunately, working with your iPod's battery isn't very difficult, but it is something you need to keep in mind.

Monitoring and Maximizing Battery Life

The Battery icon in the upper-right corner of the screen always tells you what your battery's status is at any point in time for all iPods except the shuffle.

When your iPod is running on battery power, the amount of shading within the icon provides a relative—and I do mean *relative*—indication of your battery's current state (see Figure 13.1). As you use battery power, the shaded part of the battery will decrease until your iPod runs out of gas. When it does, you'll see an icon of a battery with an exclamation point that indicates your iPod is out of power and that the battery will have to be charged before you can use the iPod again.

note

There has been a lot of controversy regarding the iPod's battery, including several lawsuits and some awards from those lawsuits. Getting into the details of the iPod battery's legal and other history isn't the point of this section. Unless you have an older iPod, you'll probably not encounter any battery problems anyway.

Battery icon

FIGURE 13.1

Keep an eye on the battery icon to make sure you don't run out of juice while you're on the move.

Determining the state of the iPod shuffle's battery is much harder (not really). On the back of the shuffle, press the Battery Status button. The small light next to the button will illuminate. If it is green, you are good to go. If it's orange (Apple calls this *amber*), you are running somewhat low and should recharge when you can. If it is red, you are close to being empty and need to recharge ASAP. If the light doesn't appear at all, your shuffle is out of power and you are out of luck if you want to listen to music.

To maximize your iPod's playing time per battery charge, you can do the following:

- Keep the iPod's software up-to-date (you'll learn how later in this chapter).

- Use the Hold feature (the Hold switch on the iPod and iPod mini or press and hold the Play button for 3 seconds on the shuffle) to prevent your iPod's controls from being unintentionally activated when you carry it around. You'd be amazed how easy it is for the iPod to be turned on and start playing without you knowing it, especially if you carry it in your pocket, backpack, or computer bag. (It's no fun trying to listen to tunes only to find out your iPod's battery has been accidentally drained—not that this has ever happened to me, of course.)

- When you aren't listening, don't keep your iPod playing; press the Pause button to stop the music. Playing music uses power at a greater rate than not playing music.

- Put your iPod to sleep by turning it off when you aren't using it. The Sleep, or Off, mode uses the least amount of power. (You can press and hold the Play/Pause button to turn off the iPod. You can also add the Sleep command to the Main menu if you prefer to use that instead. You can turn a shuffle off by using the slider on its back.)

- Keep backlighting at a minimum level. Backlighting is very helpful to be able to see the iPod's screen, especially in low-light conditions. However, it does use additional power, so you should use it only as necessary to maximize battery life. When you don't need it, such as in daylight conditions, turn it off. When you do need it, set it such that it remains on only a few seconds when you press a control.

- Minimize track changes. Each time you change tracks, the iPod uses more power than it would just playing tracks straight through. Likewise, using the Shuffle mode consumes power at a faster rate because the iPod's disk has to be accessed more frequently.

> **note**
>
> The batteries on different iPod models and different generations of the same models are rated for different amounts of playing time. At press time, the iPod's battery is rated for up to 15 hours (music only, 5 hours for slideshows with music), the iPod mini's for up to 18 hours, and the shuffle's for 12 hours. Of course, these ratings are based on ideal conditions, which means the iPod plays straight through for these periods with no controls being used, no backlighting, and so on. Should you expect to get that much time under actual conditions? Probably not. Later in this section, you'll learn how to test your iPod's battery to ensure it is in good condition.

- Turn off the Equalizer. The Equalizer uses more power than playing music without it.
- Every 30 recharges or so, fully drain and recharge the battery.
- Keep the iPod at a comfortable temperature. Using the iPod in very cold or very hot conditions lowers its battery life.

Charging an iPod's Battery

Fortunately, there are a number of ways to charge your iPod's battery, including the following:

- If your iPod includes an AC adapter, use it to charge the iPod's battery.
- Connect the iPod to a high-power USB 2 or a FireWire port either directly with a cable or via a Dock. This has the benefit of updating your iPod at the same time you charge its battery.
- Plug the shuffle into a high-power USB 2 port on a computer's case.
- Use a power adapter designed for 12-volt sources, such as the power outlets in your vehicle, along with the iPod's AC adapter to charge the iPod on the move.

The iPod lets you know it is charging in two different ways.

When your iPod's battery is charging via a connection to a computer, the Battery icon will include a lightning bolt symbol and display a filling motion from the left to the right of the icon (see Figure 13.2). When the battery is fully charged, the icon will be completely filled and the motion will stop.

tip

When an iPod is turned off, it still uses some power. For example, its internal clock keeps ticking. And, it takes some power to maintain the iPod's memory. If you don't use your iPod for 14 days or more, you should charge its battery to keep it ready to play.

Battery being charged
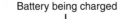

FIGURE 13.2
This iPod is getting its battery charged via a FireWire cable.

Do not disconnect.

When you charge your iPod's battery through a separate power adapter only, the battery icon fills the iPod's screen and flashes (see Figure 13.3). When the process is complete, the battery icon remains steady and the fully charged message appears.

FIGURE 13.3
This iPod is
being charged
with the power
adapter.

When you are charging a shuffle, its status light will be orange while the battery is charging. When it's fully charged, the light will be green.

According to Apple, it takes only 2 hours (iPod shuffle, iPod mini) or 3 hours (iPod) to charge a drained battery to 80% of its capacity. It can take up to 4 hours (iPod shuffle) or 5 hours (iPod) to fully charge a drained battery.

Getting More Life Out of an iPod's Battery

The iPod uses a lithium-ion batter. Any battery, including the iPod's, will eventually wear out and no longer provide the power it once did. In my research, most lithium-ion batteries are rated for 300–500 charges. In this context, a charge can't be precisely defined, but it does include a full discharge and then a full recharge. A partial charge doesn't "count" as much, but the precise relationship between the amount of charge and how much that charge "counts" can't be specified.

Batteries like that in the iPod actually last longer if you don't let them fully discharge before you recharge them. Frequent "topping off" will not reduce the battery's life and in fact is better for your battery than letting it run very low on power before you recharge it.

Every 30 recharges or so, do run your iPod until it is completely out of power and then perform a full recharge. This will reset the battery's power gauge, which tends to become more inaccurate if the battery is never fully discharged.

note

Unlike some other rechargeable batteries, lithium-ion batteries don't have a memory, which means their performance is not degraded by not being fully discharged and then recharged each time.

note

The fact that the iPod's battery will eventually wear out is nothing unique to the iPod. All batteries die eventually and must be replaced. However, some early iPods (the Original iPod for one) did have major battery problems that have left the iPod with a now-underserved reputation for having defective batteries.

It doesn't hurt the battery to do frequent and short recharges, such as by placing the iPod in a Dock every day after you are done using it.

However, you should be sure to run the iPod on battery power for significant periods of time. If you constantly run the iPod from the power adapter or while it is in the Dock connected to a power source, the iPod's battery's performance will degrade.

Solving Battery Problems

Frankly, your iPod's battery will eventually wear out. You'll know this by the time it can play on battery power becoming shorter and shorter. And, the battery is the most likely problem you might experience.

Testing Your iPod's Battery

If your iPod doesn't seem to play for a reasonable amount of time, you should test it to get an idea of what its current battery life is. Test your iPod by performing the following steps:

1. Fully charge your iPod.

2. Remove the iPod from the charger so it is running on battery power.

3. Make a note of the current time.

4. Use the Settings commands to turn off the Equalizer, Shuffle, and Backlight.

5. Set **Repeat** to **One**; on the shuffle, use the slider to have music playback straight through.

6. Select an album or a playlist and play it.

7. Let the iPod play until it runs out of power. While the iPod is playing, don't use any of its controls. Anytime you cause the iPod to perform an action, you cause it to use additional power. In this test, you are attempting to determine what its maximum life is so you can compare it to the rated life.

8. When the iPod stops playing and the low power icon appears in the display, make a note of the time.

9. Calculate the battery life by figuring out how much time passed since you started the iPod playing (compare the time you noted in step 8 with what you noted in step 3).

The rated life of iPod batteries changes regularly, but when I wrote this, the following ratings applied:

tip

If you are testing an iPod, use the slideshow with music mode because the test will be done much more quickly.

■ **iPod shuffle**—Rated for up to 12 hours of playing time. If yours lasts more than

8–10 hours, your battery is in good shape. If it won't last more than 6 hours, you likely have a battery problem.

- **iPod mini**—Rated for up to 18 hours of playing time. If yours lasts more than 14–16 hours, your battery is in good shape. If it won't last more than 8, you likely have a battery problem.

- **iPod**—Rated for up to 15 hours of music playing time or 5 hours of slideshows with music. If yours lasts more than 8–12 hours of music or 2–3 hours of slideshows, your battery is in good shape. If it won't last more than these general guidelines, you likely have a battery problem.

Getting Help from Apple for iPod Battery Problems

If your iPod doesn't play for the expected time, the battery probably needs to be replaced. If the iPod is still under warranty (1 year without the AppleCare Protection Plan or 2 years with it), Apple will replace the battery for free. If the iPod is not under warranty, Apple will replace the battery for you (currently this costs $99 plus $6.95 shipping). To get more information and start this process, go to www.apple.com/support/ipod/power/ and click the **iPod battery service request form** link.

> **note**
>
> Batteries are manufactured items, which means they aren't always made just right. You should test your new iPod's battery life to ensure yours is performing up to snuff prior to the warranty expiring.

Updating or Restoring an iPod's Software

Apple is continually improving the iPod's software to add features, make it even more stable, and so on. You should periodically check for new iPod software and, when you find it, install it on your iPod—this is called *updating* the iPod's software.

When you are having major problems with your iPod or just want to completely reformat it, you can also *restore* its software to return it to factory settings.

You do both of these tasks in the same way, as the following steps show:

1. Open a Web browser and move to www.apple.com/ipod/download/. You'll see the iPod Updater page (see Figure 13.4). Along the right side of the screen you'll see a table listing each model of iPod and the current software version. If your iPod is already using the most current version, you don't need to download or install the iPod Updater application because it is already installed on your computer and so you can skip to step 6.

FIGURE 13.4

Apple's iPod
Updater page
provides access
to the latest iPod
software.

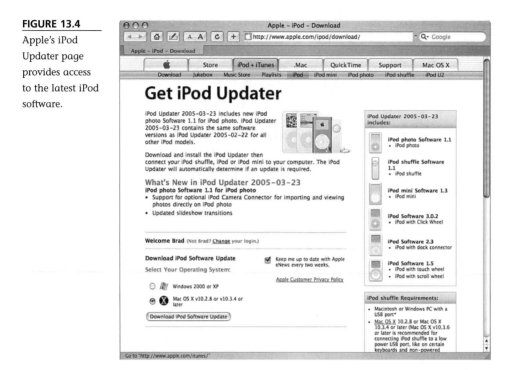

2. Click the radio button for either **Windows 2000 or XP** or
   Mac OS X and then click **Download iPod Software
   Update**. The download process will start
   automatically; if not, click the link to
   manually start it.

3. Notice the name of the application you
   downloaded and where you stored it on
   your computer.

4. Launch the iPod Updater installer application you downloaded—in some cases, it
   will run automatically after you download it.

5. Follow the onscreen instructions to install
   the iPod Updater application on your
   computer.

caution

According to
Apple, your iPod
will be replaced
with an equivalent
model rather than just
the battery being replaced. Make
sure you have all the data you need
from your iPod before you send it in
for service.

6. Connect the iPod you want to update or restore to your computer.

7. Launch the iPod Updater application. To do this on a Windows computer,
   select **Start** menu, **All Programs**, **iPod**, **iPod Updater** (with the most
   recent date), **iPod Updater**. On a Mac, open the **Applications**, **Utilities**,

and **iPod Software Updater** folders. Then open the iPod Updater application with the most recent date.

When the iPod Updater launches, it will locate the iPod connected to your computer and display information for it, such as its name, serial number, software version, and capacity (see Figure 13.5).

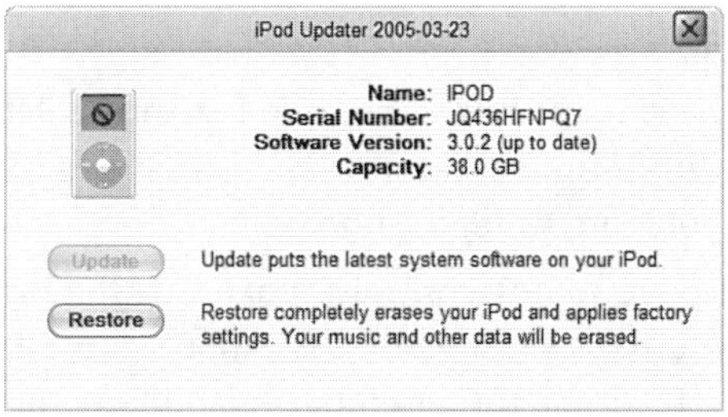

FIGURE 13.5
You use the iPod Updater application to update your iPod's software or to restore it to original condition.

iPod Updater 2005-03-23

Name: IPOD
Serial Number: JQ436HFNPQ7
Software Version: 3.0.2 (up to date)
Capacity: 38.0 GB

Update — Update puts the latest system software on your iPod.

Restore — Restore completely erases your iPod and applies factory settings. Your music and other data will be erased.

8. If you want to install the latest version of the iPod software on your iPod, click the **Update** button. If the most current version is already installed, the Update button will be inactive and you'll see (up to date) in the software version information section. If you want to restore your iPod, click **Restore** instead.

9. Follow the onscreen instructions to complete the update or restore process.

After you have updated your iPod, you can continue using it as you did before the update.

If you restored your iPod, you will have to perform an update from iTunes to load your music back onto it. You'll also have to replace any calendar or contact information you want to store on it.

Identifying and Solving iPod Problems

Okay, I admit it. The iPod isn't perfect. Once in a while, it might not act the way you expect it to. Hey, no one or no technology is perfect, after all.

caution

When you restore an iPod, all of its data is erased, including its music, calendar data, contacts, and so on. If you have stored files on the iPod that aren't stored elsewhere too, make sure you copy the files you want to save from the iPod to another location before you restore it.

In this section, you'll read some information that will help you in the event you do experience problems.

Solving iPod Problems

Troubleshooting iPod problems isn't all that different from troubleshooting other kinds of problems. First, observe exactly what is happening. Determine what you are doing and how the iPod is responding or not responding, as the case may be. Then, use the information in the following sections to see whether you can solve the problem yourself.

Checking the Basics

We all do things that can be classified as something less than intelligent once in a while. And using the iPod can result in a few of these events, so use the following list to ensure you haven't done anything to shoot yourself in the foot:

- If the iPod won't respond to any controls, make sure the Hold feature isn't active. The Hold feature does just what it is supposed to—it prevents everything from working. It can be rather embarrassing to panic that your precious iPod has suffered a major failure only to realize that the Hold switch is on. (Of course, you understand that this has never happened to me personally.) If you use a shuffle, press a control; if the status light flashes orange, hold is on. Also on a shuffle, make sure the slider isn't in the Off position.

- If the iPod won't turn on, connect it to an AC power adapter or to a high-powered USB 2 or FireWire port on a computer. It might simply be that the battery is out of power. Remember that the iPod uses some battery power when you aren't using it, and after 14 days or so, it might not have enough battery power to wake up. Sometimes the empty battery icon will appear when you try to turn on a fully discharged iPod—and sometimes it won't. Use the Battery Status light on a shuffle to check its charge; if the light doesn't illuminate, the shuffle must be recharged before you can use it.

- If the Hold feature isn't on but the iPod won't respond to commands, try connecting the iPod to a computer. If it mounts, you probably just need to do a minor reset to get it to work again.

Resetting an iPod

If you can't get an iPod to do anything (and you've checked the Hold feature) or if it is behaving badly or locks up, try resetting it. When you reset an iPod, its temporary memory is cleared but your data (music) isn't affected.

How you reset an iPod depends on the specific model you are using. Fortunately, resetting the current models is relatively easy; you have to jump through some hoops for older models. You should check the documentation that came with your iPod to see how to reset it.

To reset current iPods, press and hold both the **Menu** and **Select** buttons for about 6–10 seconds until you see the Apple logo on the iPod's screen. This indicates that the reset process was effective.

To reset a shuffle, turn it off, wait 5 seconds, and then turn it on again using the slider on its back.

If you are using an older model and don't have its documentation, visit www.apple.com and click the **Support** tab. Then, search for "reset iPod." Open one of the documents that contains information about resetting an iPod. This will either provide you with the steps you need or lead you to documentation that does.

After your iPod is reset, it should work normally. If not, you should try restoring it.

caution

Restoring an iPod also deletes any data you have stored in its memory (hard drive or flash memory), so be sure you have any data that is unique to the iPod backed up before you restore it. As long as all of the music on the iPod is in your iTunes music library, you don't have to worry about its music because that will be replaced the next time you connect it to your computer to perform an update from iTunes.

Restoring an iPod

As you read earlier, you can also use the iPod Updater application to restore an iPod. When you restore an iPod, its memory is erased and a clean version of its software is installed. The purpose is to configure the iPod with factory settings that will likely solve many problems you are having.

For the steps to perform a restore, refer to "Updating or Restoring an iPod's Software" on page **205**.

Solving the Folder/Exclamation Point Icon Problem

In some situations, your iPod will display a folder and exclamation point icon on its screen. When it does so, this indicates there is a problem and you won't be able to use the iPod until you solve it. Unfortunately, this icon doesn't relate to one specific problem but can result from an incorrect software version being installed, which is easily remedied via a restore using the iPod Updater application. It can also be due to something being wrong with the iPod's disk, which will require a repair.

tip

Resetting or restoring an iPod is the solution to almost all the problems you will be able to solve yourself. Whenever you have a problem, always try to reset the iPod first. If that doesn't work, try to restore it. In the vast majority of situations, one of these will solve the problem.

Fortunately, while the cause of the problem won't be clear to you, the solutions available should be. First, try to reset the iPod. If that doesn't work, try to restore it. In most cases, one of these two actions will solve the problem. If not, your iPod probably needs to be repaired or replaced. See the section "Getting Help with iPod Problems" to see what to do next.

Solving the "I Can't See My iPod in iTunes" Problem

If you connect your iPod to your computer but it doesn't appear in the Source list, this means iTunes can't find your iPod. This can happen for a number of reasons. Use the following steps to troubleshoot this problem:

1. With your iPod connected to your computer, restart the computer and then open **iTunes**. This will sometimes get the devices communicating again. If you see your iPod on the Source list, you are good to go. If not, continue with the next step.

2. With your iPod connected to your computer, open the **iPod Updater** application. If it recognizes your iPod, this means your computer and iPod can communicate, which is a good thing. If the Update button is active, update your iPod's software. If not, restore its software instead. Then, repeat step 1. If iTunes still doesn't show the iPod, download and reinstall iTunes.

3. If the iPod Updater doesn't recognize your iPod and instead displays the message Connect an iPod to your computer to update it, there is a communication problem between your computer and the iPod. Try plugging the iPod into a different USB 2 or FireWire port. If the two devices still can't communicate, there is a problem either with the iPod or with your computer. You'll probably need some help to solve either of these issues.

Getting Help with iPod Problems

Although I probably could have added a few more pages to this book with specific problems you might encounter and potential solutions to those problems, that would have been wasteful for two main reasons. First, it is likely you won't ever experience the problems I would include. Second, Apple maintains an extensive iPod website from which you get detailed information about iPod problems. You can use this information to solve specific problems you encounter (that aren't solved with the information in the previous sections, such as a reset).

To access this help, use a web browser to move to www.apple.com/support/ipod. On this page, you can search for help, read FAQs, and get other information that will help you solve iPod problems (see Figure 13.6).

FIGURE 13.6

Need iPod help? You got it.

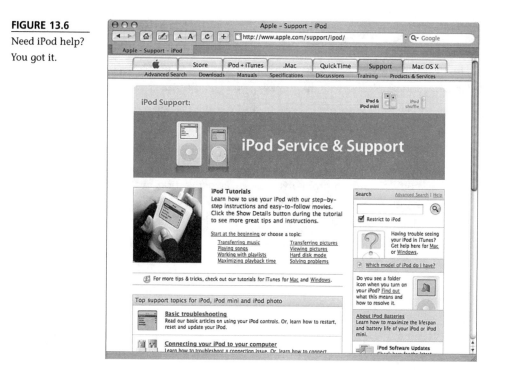

A number other websites might be helpful to you as well. These include www.ipodlounge.com and www.ipodhacks.com. You can also use www.google.com to search for iPod problems; you'll find no shortage of web pages on which those problems are discussed. It is highly likely that someone else has faced and solved the same problem you are having.

tip

Feel free to write to me with questions about your iPod or to ask for help with problems you are having with your iPod. You can reach me at bradmacosx@mac.com.

The Absolute Minimum

The iPod is what we hope most technology will be—it just works and works well. Here are some pointers to help you keep your iPod in tune:

- Understand your iPod's battery and use the practices described in this chapter to keep it maintained properly.

- Keep your iPod's software current by using the update software Apple releases periodically.

- If you do run into problems, check the last section in this chapter for help in solving them. Fortunately, many problems are easy to solve with a reset or restore. If those don't work, lots of help is available to you.

IN THIS CHAPTER

- Take care of iTunes, and it will take care of you.
- Be safe, not sorry, by backing up your music.
- Get help with those very rare, but possibly annoying, iTunes problems.

Maintaining iTunes and Solving Problems

As an application, iTunes is so well designed that you aren't likely to have many problems with it. And that is a good thing because who wants problems? However, you can minimize iTunes problems by keeping the application updated to the current release. You should also keep your music collection backed up just in case something bad happens to your computer.

In the rare event that you do have troubles, you can usually solve them without too much effort.

Keeping iTunes Up-to-date

iTunes is one of Apple's flagship applications, especially because it is the only current Apple application that runs on both Macintosh and Windows computers. Because of this, Apple is continuously refining the application to both make it even more trouble free and to enhance its features. You should keep your copy of iTunes current; fortunately, you can set up iTunes so it maintains itself.

Keeping iTunes Up-to-date on Any Computer Automatically

Setting up iTunes so that it keeps itself current automatically is simple. Open the **General** pane of the iTunes Preferences dialog box. Then check the **Check for iTunes updates automatically** check box (see Figure 14.1). Click **OK**.

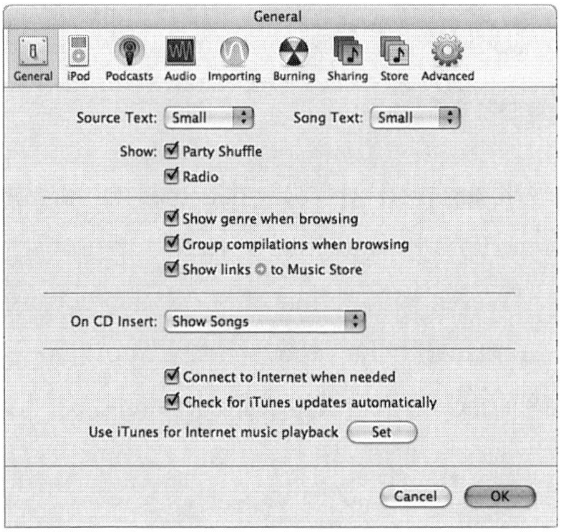

> **note**
>
> For automatic updates to work, you need to allow iTunes to connect to the Internet when it needs to. Check the **Connect to Internet when needed** check box on the General tab of the iTunes Preferences dialog box to grant iTunes permission to do this.

FIGURE 14.1

Using the General pane of the iTunes Preferences dialog box, you can have iTunes keep itself current.

Once per week, iTunes will connect to Apple's servers and check for updates. When it finds an update, you will be prompted to download and install it on your computer.

The benefit of this is that you don't have to remember to check for updates yourself. There isn't really a downside because you have the

> **caution**
>
> For iTunes to perform this check, it must be stopped and started once during the week. In other words, if you never quit iTunes, it won't ever perform this check.

opportunity to decline to install the update if you don't want it installed for some reason.

Keeping iTunes Up-to-date on a Windows PC Manually

You can check for an iTunes update manually any time you think one might be available or if you prefer to do manual updates for some reason. You can check for iTunes updates manually on a Windows computer by selecting **Help**, **Check For iTunes Updates**. iTunes will connect to the Internet and check for a newer version of the application. If a new version is available, you will be prompted to download and install it. If a newer version is not available, you will see a dialog box telling you that you are using the current version.

Keeping iTunes Up-to-date on a Macintosh

Because both Mac OS X and iTunes are Apple products, iTunes is one of the applications tracked by Mac OS X's Software Update feature.

If you have set Software Update to check for updates automatically, it will check for iTunes updates according to the schedule you set. When it finds an update, you will be prompted to download and install it.

To manually check for updates, select **Apple**, **Software Update** (see Figure 14.2). If an iTunes update is available, you will see it in the Software Update window. You can then select it and download it to your Mac. iTunes will then be updated to the latest and greatest version.

FIGURE 14.2

On a Mac, you can use Software Update to keep your version of iTunes current.

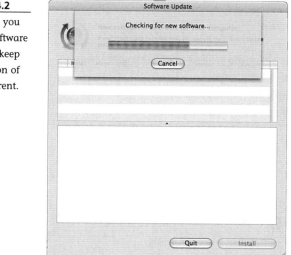

Backing Up Your iTunes Music Library

Hopefully, you have and use a good backup system to protect all your files, including your iTunes Library. If so, you get extra points from me and can skip the rest of this section.

If you don't use a backup system to protect yourself, shame on you. However, you can earn some points back by at least backing up your music collection to CD or DVD. You can do this by creating a playlist containing the music you want to back up. Then, you burn that playlist to a CD or DVD. That will place a copy of your music on disc so you can recover it should you ever need to. For detailed steps to burn discs, refer to Chapter 20, "Burning Your Own CDs or DVDs."

caution

Backing up is especially critical for music you purchase from the iTunes Music Store. If something happens to this music, you can't download it again without paying for it. If you lose music files you have purchased and don't have a backup, they are gone forever.

If the playlist you select contains more songs than will fit on a single CD or DVD, you will be prompted to see whether you want iTunes to place the playlist on multiple discs. If you allow this, iTunes will keep burning discs until all the songs in the playlist have been placed on a disc.

Solving iTunes Problems

iTunes is about as trouble-free as any application gets; this is especially amazing because iTunes offers so many great features. However, even the best application is bound to run into a few hiccups.

Because the odds of me including in this book the specific problem you might experience are small, it is more profitable for you to learn where you can access help with problems you might experience. So, I've included the solution to one problem you are likely to encounter here. Then, you'll learn how to get help for other problems should you experience them.

tip

When you back up your music, make sure you use the data format option, not the Audio CD or MP3 format. If you choose Audio CD format, you won't be able to fit many songs on a single disc. If you choose the MP3 options, music you purchased from the iTunes Music Store won't be able to be burned onto a disc.

Solving the Missing Song File Problem

One problem you might encounter occasionally has nothing to do with iTunes not working properly. This problem occurs when something happens to the file for a song in your Library. When this happens, iTunes doesn't know what to do because it can't find the song's file. To show its confusion, iTunes displays an exclamation point next to any songs whose files it can't find when you try to play them, or do anything else with them for that matter (see Figure 14.3).

Missing file icon

FIGURE 14.3

The missing file icon means iTunes can't find the file for a song.

To fix this problem, you have to reconnect iTunes to the missing file. Here are the steps to follow:

1. Double-click a song next to which the exclamation point icon is shown. You will see a prompt telling you that the original file can't be found and asking whether you would like to locate it (see Figure 14.4).

FIGURE 14.4

When you see this dialog box, iTunes can't find a song's file.

The song "Dry Your Tears, Afrika *" could not be used because the original file could not be found. Would you like to locate it?

Cancel   Yes

caution

iTunes depends on QuickTime to work. If you remove QuickTime from your system, iTunes will stop working. You'll have to reinstall QuickTime or run the iTunes Installer to get it working again.

2. Click **Yes**. You will see the Open dialog box.

3. Move to the song's file, select it, and click **Open**. You'll return to the iTunes window, and the song will begin to play. This will also restore the link from the iTunes Library to the song's file, and you will be able to play it again like before it was lost.

If the problem was that the file had been moved, you might want to cause iTunes to place it back within the iTunes Music folder to keep your music files nicely organized. To do this, select **Advanced**, **Consolidate Library**. In the resulting prompt, click **Consolidate**. iTunes will place a copy of any missing songs you have reconnected manually back into the proper location (within your iTunes Music folder).

Getting Help with iTunes Problems

When you run into a problem you can't solve yourself, the first place to go for help is Apple's Support website.

If you use iTunes on a Windows computer, go to http://www.apple.com/support/itunes/windows/. This page provides solutions to common problems, and you can search for specific problems you might experience (see Figure 14.5).

FIGURE 14.5

If you use iTunes on a Windows computer, check this website when you have problems.

Mac users are certainly not immune to problems either. For help with those, check out http://www.apple.com/support/itunes/ (see Figure 14.6).

FIGURE 14.6

Mac users can
get help here.

You can also access Apple's general support resources
at http://www.apple.com/support.

Many other websites contain useful iTunes
troubleshooting help. To find them, go to
www.google.com and search for the specific problem you are having. This will often lead you to a
forum or other place in which you can find information, including a solution, for many problems.

note

You can also write
to me with iTunes
questions. My email
address is bradmacosx@
mac.com.

The Absolute Minimum

Heck, who wants to spend time solving problems with a music application when the whole point is to spend time listening to and working with music? Not me, that's for sure. Fortunately, iTunes is designed and implemented so well that you aren't likely to experience any problems. If you do, help is available to you on the Web and from other sources.

- Of course, you can lower the chances that you will ever have problems with iTunes by keeping the application up-to-date. Fortunately, you can set iTunes to do this automatically.

- Just in case the worst happens, keep your music safe by keeping it backed up separately from your computer, such as on CD or DVD.

- You aren't likely to need to solve many problems. You might occasionally run into the "missing song file" problem. Fortunately, you learned how to solve that one.

- If you experience problems with iTunes, you can access the application's help system. You can also get help from the Apple Support web page or by writing to me.

Toys for Your iPod

Owning an iPod or iPod shuffle is only the start of a love affair with your music. Although the iPod alone is a great product, there is a plethora of Apple and third-party accessories that take your iPod to the next level.

Over the following pages, we take a look at the most popular add-ons for your iPod, including headphones, carrying cases, batteries, adapters, media readers, and much more. If you thought you were done spending money once you got the iPod, you were happily wrong!

Headphones

The first thing you will notice as a new iPod owner is that the white headphones that Apple Computer ships with your iPod leave a lot to be desired. Upgrading your headphones is the single most popular upgrade iPod owners make. All the following headphones work with all iPod, iPod mini, and iPod shuffle units.

Apple Headphones

Besides the headphones Apple bundles with the iPod, they also sell an in-ear headphone. These headphones fit completely in your ear (hence the name) and offer a noticeable improvement in sound quality over the stock iPod headphones.

They come with three sized caps, to ensure a fit with all the ear sizes out there.

There are much better sounding in-ear headphones out there, but none come close to the price range of these.

Price: $39.00

www.apple.com/ipod/accessories.html

Shure—www.shure.com

Shure makes a number of headphones that you can enjoy with your iPod. They range in price and performance, and are all in-ear. The models include the following.

E2 Sound Isolating Earphones

These are similar to the Apple In-Ear headphones. They perform well, and have a richer overall sound than stock Apple headphones.

Price: $99.00

E3 Sound Isolating Earphones with Extended Frequency Response

The only real difference between the E2 and E3 is better sound quality and price.

Price: $179.00

tip

Not all headphones sound the same to everyone. Your best bet is to actually try the headphones before you buy them.

tip

Even headphones that look alike don't feel alike. Comfort is very important in your choice of headphones. Try them on before you buy them! Remember, they will be sitting on your head or in your ear for long periods of time, so you want something that fits and feels well.

E5 Sound Isolating Earphones

The granddaddy of the Shure line of headphones, the E5 sports dual micro speakers per headphone. They sound terrific, look great, and cost as much as your iPod!

Price: $499.00

Learn more about the Shure line of headphones at www.shure.com.

Bose—www.bose.com

Known for years as one of the premium home speaker makers in the world, Bose is also known for their superior headphone audio quality. As an iPod owner, you obviously love music, and want to have it reproduced in the best sounding headphones you can afford. Bose has two headphones that you might be interested in, depending on your budget.

QuietComfort 2 Noise Cancellation Headphones

One of the problems you will encounter when trying to listen to your headphones is background noise. For those who try to enjoy your portable music on an airline or in a noisy room, you will appreciate the Noise Cancellation technology Bose has built in to the QuietComfort 2s.

In essence, these headphones cancel out any external background noise, such as an airliner's engines, loud air conditioning, and any other general "white noise" sound that can interfere with your listening enjoyment.

Combine the ability to cancel out the background noise with the superior sound quality of the QuietComfort 2 headphones, and you are in for a music lover's treat! These headphones are not earbuds or inner ear, but are more conventional looking, over-the-ear headphones. And for most people, they are much more comfortable to wear for extended periods than the inner ear or earbud variety (although obviously not a wise choice for joggers).

Price: $299.00

TriPort Headphones

Not as expensive as the previous QuietComfort 2s, and with no noise reduction technology, you will still be pleased at the tonal quality of the TriPort headphones. They, too, are over-the-ear headphones, so they are not ideal for joggers or more active iPod users. However, if you do not listen to your iPod while on the move or in an excessively loud environment, you will enjoy these headphones.

Price: $149.00

tip

Just because you don't recognize a name brand does not mean it is not as good, if not better, than the more advertised brand.

Sennheiser—www.sennheiserusa.com

Most of you reading this have probably never heard of the Sennheiser brand, but they are quickly making a big name for themselves in the world of audio. Not only are they making headphones for your iPod and computer, as well as for your home entertainment system, they are also making cutting-edge amplifiers for your iPod. But more on that later.

PXC250

I personally reviewed these headphones back in September of 2003, and they became the headphones I use more than any other. With noise reduction technology, similar to the above-mentioned Bose, the PCX250 does an admiral job of both quieting loud background sounds and reproducing music much better than the standard Apple earbud headphones. These are over-the-ear headphones, rather than the inner or earbud types. They are very comfortable, but you need two AA batteries for the noise reduction to work.

Price: $199.99

Sony—www.sony.com

Known for their top-quality products and brand recognition, Sony headphones will probably be the easiest to find in stores in your area. They make a wide range of headphones that will work great with your iPod. Here are some good choices if you are looking at Sony headphones.

MDR-EX71SL

These earbud type headphones are very similar to the earbuds that ship with the iPod, with two advantages. First, they sound much better, which is the reason you want to upgrade. Second, these earbuds are much more comfortable than the Apple earbuds.

Price: $49.99

MDR-V300

These over-the-ear headphones sound wonderful, and are very comfortable as well. Surprisingly, these are also very lightweight for their size, and perform well in office settings. They are not easy to transport, however, but more than make up for it with their folding design. These are nice headphones—you would not be disappointed.

Price: $49.99

MDR-G72LP

Although these are over-the-ear, they actually wrap around the back of your head, rather than the top. The MDR-G72LP sport a nonslip design, so that they do not fall off as easily as other behind-the-head designed headphones. The biggest drawback with these, however, is their not-so-superior sound quality. Only slightly better, if at all, than the iPod stock headphones.

Price: $39.99

Koss—www.koss.com

It is impossible to think about headphones without thinking about Koss. They have been making headphones since the 1950s. Koss has been at the forefront of headphone design and innovation for years, and continue to lead the industry in sales, service, and quality products.

UR29

These over-the-ear headphones are both comfortable and affordable, and more importantly, are very decent sounding. You can get much better headphones for twice the money, but they do sound better than the stock Apple earbuds.

Price: $25.99

tip

Another reason you might want to buy a third-party pair of headphones is for a safety reasons. The *New York Times* has reported that there have been muggings of iPod users when criminals spot the telltale white iPod earbud headphones lodged in people's ears. While this is not a widespread problem by any means, it has happened. Look at non-white headphones to confuse the bad guys!

SportaPro Traditional Collapsible Headphones

An earbud headphone is of a different flavor, in that they fit in your ear differently than most others. Don't let the differences sway you away from taking a closer look at the SportaPros, though, as they sound very good. They also have a volume control switch on the cord, though some people have reported problems with some iPod models. This is a nice headphone buy.

Price: $29.99

QZ-2000 Technology Noise Reduction

Another in the popular noise reduction category, the QZ-2000 sound fantastic, which, for the price, you would expect. These over-the-ear headphones are a bit bulky, and the twisted bulky cord is more "1970s" than any other headphone listed here. For the price, these are very nice headphones.

Price: $199.99

Ultimate Ears—www.ultimateears.com

UE-10 Pro

Ever wonder what the rock stars use? Look no further than the UE-10 Pro in-ear headphones. With a $900 price tag, these are not headphones just anyone can afford. But if money is no object, you can buy these custom-fit headphones that feature a 20Hz to 16k frequency response.

These are about the best headphones you can buy, and with a price tag that costs more than two iPods, it is probably only for the most diehard of audiophiles.

Price: $900

Nike Phillips—www.nike-philips.com

Nike Flight Lightweight Sport Headphones

Apple designed the iPod shuffle to be the perfect companion for those who like to exercise. Small and lightweight, the iPod shuffle is great for running or working out at the gym. Why not a pair of headphones that match?

Who knows more about working out than Nike? Teaming up with Phillips, these lightweight sports headphones are a behind-the-head, sweat-resistant unit that stays out of the way while you do your work. The 15mm Neodymium drivers in each headphone sound good, and the almost 4' cord assures easy reach to your iPod.

Price: $19.95

Bang & Olufsen—www.bang-olufsen.com

A8 Headphones

World renowned for high-quality audio gear, Bang & Olufsen has released the A8 headphones that sound as good as you would expect from the high-fidelity company.

The A8s are an earbud headphone that sports an ear-wrap fit so the listener's ears actually hold them in place. This is much more comfortable than earbud headphones in which the dangling cord actually pulls the headphones out of your ear.

Comfort and high-quality sound are what the A8s are known for. If you want your music quality to match your comfort, these are the headphones for you.

Price: $159.00

XtremeMac Audio Splitter for iPod shuffle

These are not headphones, but if you own an iPod shuffle, you can use this audio splitter to connect two headphones. You can then share your music with a friend!

Price: $12.95

www.xtrememac.com

Wireless Headphones

One of the biggest drags is, of course, that pesky cord that runs from your headphones to your iPod. It always seems to get in the way of whatever you're doing. But a few options exist for you to consider in a wireless headphone. Thanks to Bluetooth wireless networking, headphone wires might soon be a thing of the past.

The popularity of Bluetooth is growing by leaps and bounds. A few mobile devices such as cell phones and PDAs, as well as many Apple products, are all shipping with Bluetooth either built-in or as an optional add-on. Expect the availability of newer Bluetooth iPod accessories, and not just headphones, coming in the next few years.

BlueTake i-Phono BT420—www.bluetake.com

These Bluetooth wireless headphones sport a behind-the-head headphone and a small dongle that you plug into your iPod's headphone jack. The dongle then transmits the sound to your headphone wirelessly.

The dongle and headphones contain a rechargeable Li-Polymer battery, so there is no need to buy and maintain fresh batteries. You can also use this set with a mobile phone, as it has a retractable microphone as well. You can also change the color of the headphones with the included color plates: white, red, orange, blue, or green. (Only the white really match the iPod.)

Price: $229.00

Macally Bluewave Headphone—www.macally.com

Designed with the iPod in mind, Macally's wireless Bluetooth Bluewave headphones require a third generation or later iPod, including the iPod mini and iPod Photo.

The Bluetooth dongle is plugged into the top of your iPod and wirelessly transmits the sound to the headphones. The headphones themselves are large headphones, an over-the-ear type that is both comfortable and produces good audio quality.

The dongle does not draw any power from the iPod itself, but rather uses two AAA batteries for power. The headphones also require two AAA batteries for operation. Both have an on/off switch so you conserve power when not in use.

Price: $169.95

iPod Speakers

Because the iPod, iPod mini, and iPod shuffle use an industry-standard headphone jack, you are not limited to only using headphones to listen to your music. The iPod can act as a portable music player, as well. Although the iPod is great for personal use, sharing your music with family and friends or co-workers, can be even more enjoyable.

Because the iPod does not generate enough power through the headphone jacks, you need a powered speaker system or amplifier to get the most sound out of your iPod.

The term *portable speakers* really does not mean you can carry the iPod and these speakers around with you like a boombox. Rather, many of these speakers are designed to sit on a table or the like with your iPod plugged in. Some of these speakers can in fact turn your iPod into a boombox, allowing you to take your music on the go.

tip

Remember that price does not always equal quality! If you prefer one set of speakers over another, don't let the cheaper price deter you.

tip

If you plan to play your speakers outdoors, be certain to buy speakers that won't get ruined if it rains! Many speakers are waterproof, so do your homework before deciding which speakers fit your needs the best.

inMotion Portable iPod Speakers

There are now five InMotion Series of speakers, and prices vary depending on your wants and needs. Originally, the InMotion speakers came with a charging dock for third and forth generation iPods only, but Altec Lansing recently released a model that plugs into your iPod via the headphone jack. This opens up the InMotion Speakers to be used with any iPod, from the original to the shuffle.

Some of the InMotion speakers come with a remote control that can be used to control dock-mounted iPods. This is handy if you want to change volume or tracks from a distance.

All the InMotion speakers are portable and light, and draw power from either four AA batteries or the included AC Power adapter. Being a small

speaker system, the InMotions do not blast the sound for miles around, but they do turn your iPod into a boombox-like music player.

Price: $99.00–$179.99

www.alteclansing.com

Ezison Personal Speakers for iPod

These are small, battery-powered speakers similar to the inMotion speakers, but these work with any full-size iPod. Simply set the iPod in the cradle, plug them in via the headphone jack, and enjoy.

Price: $199.99

www.welovemacs.com

Sony SRS-T55 Folding Travel Speaker

These folding speakers work perfectly with any generation iPod, as they draw their sound from the headphone jack. They weigh about one pound, produce 2 watts of power, and fold up into a purse or bag.

Price: $49.99

www.sony.com

iPod Groove Bag Triplet and Tote

Think of this as a purse, but with built-in speakers and a slot for your iPod. This is an amazingly clever Gucci-like handbag, with nice-sounding speakers. Although obviously not for the male iPod owner, this speaker bag has been featured on TechTV (G4TV), Fox News, Style.com, and even Wired. 0.5 watts produces little in the way of real power, but this speaker bag is more about style than practicality—a neat item.

Price: $139.00

www.drbott.com

iPal Portable Speaker with Tuner

The iPal supports all iPods, as it uses the headphone jack to get the music from the iPod to its speakers. Unlike the previous speakers, the iPal is also an AM/FM radio using Automatic Frequency Control (AFC), which is one of the best ways to keep a radio station in tune. Because it is also a radio, the iPal has a telescoping antenna. Even better, the iPal has a rechargeable NiMH battery, which recharges in as little as three hours, and lasts longer than the charge in your iPod!

The iPal is an attractive, great-sounding external speaker for your iPod.

Price: $129.99

www.tivoliaudio.com

Cube Travel Speakers

Pacific Rim Technologies has created a truly portable system for the iPod with its Cube Travel Speakers. Inexpensive and easy to tote with you, the Cube Travel Speakers can be used with any iPod, as it plugs into the iPods headphone jack. The included iPod stand holds most iPods, although the mini and the shuffle are not very secure.

The Cube runs on four AAA batteries, which should last upwards of 16 hours, depending on the quality of batteries you use. You can also purchase, for an extra $5.00, an AC Power adapter.

The Cube Travel Speakers takes its name from the fact that it actually folds up into a 2.4"×2.4"×4" package. This is about the same size as a regular iPod.

The Cube is a two-speaker system, although you do not have to open the Cube all the way to listen to music. In a tight spot, for instance, you can pop only one of the speakers open. Sound quality is decent to good, considering the size of the speakers.

Price: $34.99

www.pacrimtechnologies.com

Bose SoundDock

Many feel that the Bose SoundDock is the very best-sounding iPod speakers you can buy. The price reflects the high quality and the high sound quality. With Bose, would you expect any less?

The SoundDock is not as portable as most other speakers for two reasons: weight and power. The SoundDock weighs in at a heavy five pounds, which might not

sound like much, but is a pain to move around often. The SoundDock is really designed to be put in one place and left there. Also a negative in portability is that it does not run on battery power, but rather on electricity from your wall. It does charge the iPod while in the dock, however.

The SoundDock only works with a third generation or later iPod with a dock connector.

Price: $299

www.bose.com

JBL On Stage

This is one of the most original speaker systems for the iPod. First, it only works with dock connector iPods, so if you have a first or second-generation unit, you are out of luck. Second, like the SoundDock, the JBL has to be plugged in, so it is not a portable speaker system.

Four speakers are mounted in the round base of the On Stage. They have a rich, full sound, considering the size of the unit. There are also touch-sensitive buttons that control the volume.

You can use the On Stage to not only power and charge your iPod, but there is even a port on the back of the unit to connect your iPod to your computer. Think of this as a multipurpose dock.

Great sound, midrange price, and neat features make the JBL On Stage a very nice unit.

Price: $199.95

www.jbl.com

JBL On Tour Portable Speakers

The On Tour speakers from JBL work with any iPod model, as it takes sound not from a Dock connection, but from the headphone jack. This provides older iPod owners with a really great sounding portable speaker system.

Because there is no way to dock an iPod to the On Tour, your iPod is basically connected to the speakers via the mini-jack wire connector. Be aware, then, that while the On Tour speakers are portable and able to run off both battery and while plugged in, there is no way for the On Tour to hold your iPod in place.

This speaker solution is small in size. You won't be carrying this around in a pocket, but it takes little space on a table or desktop. The great quality sound makes the On Tour a good choice, and the price makes it a winner.

Price: $99

www.jbl.com

Monster iSpeaker Portable

Remember back in the day, just a few years ago, when you had to carry your CD's along with you if you wanted to listen to music? Do you remember the two-disc CD cases, the ones that opened front and back? Keep that in mind, size-wise, when looking at the Monster iSpeaker Portable system.

Monster has been known for years as the high-quality cable maker, both in the home and car audio. In 2004, Monster jumped in the iPod arena and started making portable products that allow you to listen to your iPod on the go.

The Monster iSpeaker is a portable double CD jewel case–sized speaker system. It sports two smallish speakers on each foldout side of the unit, running off four AA batteries.

Sound quality is marginal; the draw here is size and portability. Still, for the price and the distinctive look and sound, Monster's iSpeakers are a neat solution to share your music with other people.

Price: $59.95

www.monstercable.com

Macally IceTune Speakers

Style plays an important role in purchasing equipment for iPod users. Most speaker systems with the iPod in mind have fairly conventional styling, but the unconventional styling is where the IceTune speaker system from Macally really shines.

The two speakers are round canister-like enclosures that can stack atop one another, spaced far apart, or close together, allowing the included iPod dock to sit atop them.

The IceTune iPod dock has a power button and a volume control knob, and emits a futuristic blue glow from underneath the dock, giving it a unique look. If speakers can be a conversation piece, the IceTunes would be the center of attention.

The IceTune works with all dock-connected iPods. (Sorry, first and second generation iPod and iPod shuffle owners, but your iPods are not compatible.) It uses AC power only, no batteries for portability, but it does charge your iPod while in operation. It also ships with different plates for each of the iPod dock connnector sizes, so your iPod mini will fit as sung as your full-size iPod Photo. The small size of the speakers and dock make it an ideal desktop or tabletop system.

Stylish, good audio quality, and like nothing else on the market today.

Price: $69.99

www.macally.com

Macally PodWave

If it is truly portable iPod speakers you are looking for, the PodWave from Macally is your cup of tea!

This small speaker system sits atop your iPod, plugging into the headphone jack. It is slightly larger in width than the full-size iPod, and has a speaker on either side of the unit. While the sound quality is decent, this system is really made for one-person enjoyment.

Keep in mind that while it would technically work fine with an iPod shuffle, the PodWave is really made for the full-size iPods or iPod minis. When using it with a iPod mini, be aware that it will hang over the right side further than on a regular iPod, due to the placement of the iPod mini's speaker jack.

Running on one AA battery, the PodWave is an ultra-portable and a fun addition to any iPod.

Price: $39

www.macally.com

DLO iBoom Speakers

Ah, the good old 1980s. For me, it meant hauling around a heavy boombox that sported a dual-cassette deck and radio. I usually carried it in my left hand, causing my left forearm to grow to Popeye proportions from all the heavy lifting. Thankfully, you are an iPod listener, so you enjoy much better music clarity than us poor souls who had to make do with cheap mix tapes from yesteryear. However, if you get nostalgic for that authentic boombox-like portable stereo system, the iBoom Speaker system from DLO is for you!

The iBoom is compatible with third and forth generation iPods and the iPod minis with a dock connector. (Note that it is not designed for the iPod Photo, which does not fit within the build-in iPod cradle.)

You fit your iPod in the front of the iBoom, where you would normally see a cassette deck on those older boomboxes. It also has a built-in FM tuner, so you can listen to your favorite radio station if you get bored with the music or PodCasts on your iPod. The front controls include a volume knob, a power button, FM on switch, FM tune controls, and two FM station preset memory buttons.

The iBoom runs on either the power cord or size D cell batteries for portability. Keep in mind that if your iBoom is plugged in, it charges your iPod. If you are using batteries, the batteries only power the iBoom itself, not your iPod.

There is a built-in handle to carry the iBoom, but it is not well designed and awkward to hold.

A neatly designed system with decent (if not inspired) sound quality, the iBoom brings the best of the boombox era to the iPod.

Price: $149.99

www.everythingipod.com

PocketParty shuffle

Not to be left out of the boombox market segment, the iPod shuffle also has the ability to become a tiny little boombox (boxette?) with the PocketParty shuffle from the company PodGear.

This tiny portable speaker system can run for up to 10 hours with one AA battery. The PocketParty shuffle sports two tiny speakers, each about the same size as the round iPod shuffle control button layout.

The iPod shuffle docks with the PocketParty via the USB port, and then the party can begin! The PocketParty delivers 1 watt of power, and is so light that it can be worn around your neck with a lanyard, just like your shuffle!

Price: $24.99

www.podgear.net

iPod in Your Car

Unless you own a 2002 or later BMW, and purchase the BMW iPod adapter for your car, you need to take a look at a few ways and products to get your iPod to play in your car. Sure, you can always listen to headphones while driving, but safety issues aside, how much fun is that? You want to listen to your music over all those speakers in your car, and here are the different ways to do it!

> **tip**
>
> Don't keep your iPod in your car in plain sight unattended. iPods are very popular, and one car window is a small price to pay for a determined thief who wants your iPod!

Sony CPA-9C Car Cassette Adapter

If you have a cassette player in your car, one of the easiest ways to get your iPod music to play over your automobile speakers is a handy cassette adapter. These have been around since the portable CD player was big. From the headphone jack of your iPod (or CD player), you plug in the cable, which connects at the other end to a cassette tape. It is not, actually, a cassette tape, but it acts as a go-between for your iPod and the tape player head in your cassette deck. The Sony CPA-9C is a very nice model. You can find cheaper models from other com-

panies, but I have found the Sony model to be a little superior in reliability.

Price: $19.99

www.sony.com

The Belkin TuneCast II Mobile FM Transmitter

The name is a dead giveaway for what this does. It broadcasts your music via FM radio wave, which you then dial in on your radio. This works in a car, home stereo, or even portable radio. The sound quality varies, depending on your stereo, antenna type, and distance from the antenna. I have found that antennas on the rear of a car have a harder time picking up the signal than do antennas in the front.

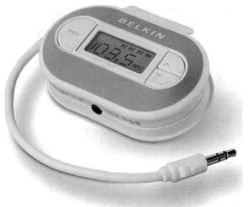

The Belkin TuneCast II Mobile FM transmitter broadcasts on any FM frequency, can memorize up to four channels, and runs for up to four hours on two AAA batteries. The unit plugs into your headphone jack on your iPod, rather than a dock. One drawback is that the Belkin unit does not directly attach to your iPod. It works with any iPod model.

Price: $39.95

www.belkin.com

Griffin iTrip

The Griffin iTrip and iTrip mini for the new iPod and iPod mini plugs into the top of your iPod directly, sitting atop the unit while broadcasting the signal on any FM radio frequency, just like the Belkin unit. The latest iTrip for iPod works with the third generation iPod only, and plugs not only into your headphone jack, but the FireWire port as well. In this way, the iTrip does not use batteries, it uses the iPod itself as a power source. What's more, it autopowers off after 60 seconds of silence, just as your iPod does.

The Griffin iTrip for third generation iPods is very stylish, blending in very well with the iPod design and aesthetics. Griffin also makes an iTrip for the iPod mini, as well as the first two generation of iPods.

Price: $35.00

www.griffintechnology.com

tip

Rechargeable batteries with a car adapter are a good way to keep your FM transmitter ready to go when you want it. Nothing is as sad as looking forward to listening to your iPod in your car and having dead batteries.

Monster iCarPlay Wireless

Another FM transmitter, the Monster iCarPlay Wireless plugs into your iPod headphone jack, but pulls its power from your automobile's cigarette lighter. Even better, the Monster iCarPlay Wireless also charges your iPod as it goes, filling up the iPod rapidly then turning into a trickle charge as to optimize performance.

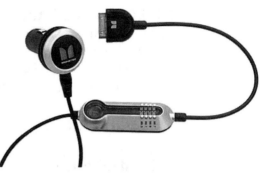

The Monster iCarPlay Wireless only works with dock connector iPods (meaning the third generation iPod and the iPod mini). Like other FM transmitters, you simply select which frequency you want to broadcast your iPod on, tune in your radio, and your iPod is playing over your car stereo.

Price: $69.95

www.monstercable.com

AirPlay for iPod shuffle

If you are the owner of an iPod shuffle, a great solution to play your music over your car audio system is the AirPlay FM Transmitter from XtremeMac. Not only does the AirPlay broadcast your music over a frequency between 88.1 and 107.9, but it also charges your shuffle as it does so.

This handy transmitter plugs into the USB port on your shuffle, and has an LCD display and changer controls to set the FM station frequency. This is handy, as you might have a powerful radio station on a channel to which a fixed FM frequency transmitter wants to broadcast.

The AirPlay plugs into your cigarette lighter in your car.

Price: $49.95

www.xtrememac.com

Auto Chargers

Although it is easy to play your iPod through your car audio system, you might simply want a way to charge your iPod in your car. Here are three products that do just that.

XtremeMac Car Charger for New iPods and FireWire Car Charger for Original iPods

They might look different, and plug into each of their respected iPods differently, but the XtremeMac car chargers do the same thing, charge your iPod from your cigarette lighter plug. The all-white design matches your iPod well, unless you have a colorful iPod mini.

Price: $19.95

www.xtrememac.com

Griffin PowerPod Auto Charger

Similar to the XtremeMac model, the PowerPod comes with a four-foot extension, so you can pretty much charge your iPod anywhere in the front of the vehicle. It works with all iPod models, and recharges your battery even when it is in use.

Price: $24.99

www.griffintechnology.com

Belkin iPod Auto Kit

The Belkin unit only works with newer, dock connector iPods (and iPod mini) but gives the added feature of also being able to power the Belkin TuneCast II FM transmitter. It also features an illumi-

nated indicator so you can tell at a glance if it is connected properly to your cigarette lighter.

Price: $49.99

www.belkin.com

iPod Automobile Mounting Kits

Although you can easily set your iPod in your lap while driving, it really is not a good idea. Nor is it a good idea to set your iPod on your dashboard; one sharp turn and your iPod might crash to the floor, or even fly out the window if you have a window down, which was the fate of my first portable CD player over a decade ago. Ouch!

The best solution is to securely mount your iPod in your car, and the following sections list a number of units that allow you to do that.

tip

Be certain you do not mount your iPod in a spot that will be in direct sunlight for extended periods of time. Prolonged exposure to sunlight is not good for your iPod.

Belkin TuneDok Car Holder

If you have a cup holder in your car, truck, or minivan, this is an inexpensive solution for holding your iPod securely. The TuneDok simply fits into your cup holder, and the iPod attaches to the Air Grip mount. It sports a ratcheting neck so that you can position your iPod to fit your reach more easily. There are two models—one for the regular iPod and one for the iPod mini.

Price: $29.99

www.belkin.com

DLO TransPod FM (New iPods and iPod mini Only)

This is an all-in-one type of unit. Not only does the DLO TransPod act as a mounting system and battery charger, it is also an FM transmitter. The unit allows for easy mounting of your third generation iPod, or the iPod mini, in your car, while transmitting the music to your car stereo system. It also sports a very nice LCD display so that you can easily view which FM station the iPod is playing on. This is a nice unit, well worth a look.

Price: $99.99

www.everythingipod.com

Voice Recorders

Do you regularly attend meetings, conduct interviews, or simply have a need to record conversations? If so, you could go out and buy a cheap mini cassette deck or a digital voice recorder. But if you already have an iPod, why bother? All you need is one of these three voice recorders.

The big benefit to using your iPod as a voice recorder is the massive amount of storage space. The ability to store said recordings on your computer, even using iTunes to catalog and sort them, is another huge benefit. Smaller digital voice recorders usually support less than 100MB, have poor audio quality, and can be quite expensive. Traditional cassette tapes are hard to manage and catalog; you cannot store the recordings on your computer, and must use cheap and easily damaged tapes. The iPod is the perfect voice recorder, and you already have one. (Note: The iPod mini does not support any voice recordings, only the third generation or later iPod with dock connector does.)

Belkin Voice Recorder for iPod

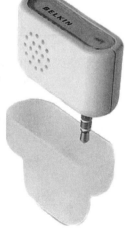

With the Belkin Voice Recorder, you simply attach the unit to the top of your iPod, and you are all set to record (after the Belkin software has been installed on your iPod, of course). You can then use it to record and play back your voice recording via the built-in speakers of your iPod's headphones. What's more, the Belkin Voice Recorder can also double as an alarm clock!

Price: $59.99

www.belkin.com

Griffin Technology iTalk

The iTalk, like the Belkin unit, plugs into the top of your iPod, and can be used to record sounds directly to your iPod. The iTalk records up to 100 feet away, and even supports the use of external microphones. It also has a 2-watt speaker built in, so that you can listen to your recordings without the need of a headphone.

Price: $39.99

www.griffintechnology.com

Belkin Universal Microphone Adapter

Perhaps you already own a monoaudio microphone and don't need all the features of the previous units. In that case, all you really need to get sound into your iPod is a Microphone Adapter, and Belkin iPod Microphone Adapter fits the bill. It allows a mono audio microphone with a 3.5mm plug to work with all iPods that have a dock connector (third generation iPods).

Price: $39.99

www.belkin.com

DLO VoiceNote Voice Recorder

The DLO is the latest addition for solutions to turn your iPod into a voice recorder. The VoiceNote plugs into the top of any third generation iPod or later via the microphone jack, and all recording is done via the iPods internal software. So there is no extra software you need to install on your iPod.

The VoiceNote is small and has a small speaker built-in. (A handy feature, as the VoiceNote takes the headphone jack as a plug so you cannot connect your headphones while using it) At the top of the unit is a microphone jack, which is used with the included lapel microphone. The microphone itself comes with a clip. The VoiceNote does not have to use the lapel microphone, however, as it is itself a microphone. Set it on a table and start talking; it picks up a surprisingly good amount of sound!

Price: $39.99

www.dlo.com

Digital Camera Adapters

As great as digital cameras are, they have one big problem: After the media card is full, you cannot take any more pictures until you empty the card again. If you are carrying your iPod anyway, with its huge amount of storage capacity, why not turn your iPod into a portable hard drive for your digital photos?

Belkin iPod Media Reader

This is a great unit, which acts as a digital media reader for most flavors of digital camera media cards. The iPod Media Reader allows you to take the media card out of your camera and transfer those files directly to your iPod. No more taking your expensive laptop out with you to hold your photos. Nor do you need to buy more than one digital media card for your camera.

Supported digital media card formats include CompactFlash (Type 1 and 2), SmartMedia, Secure Digital (SD), Memory Stick, or MultiMediaCard (MMC).

Price: $109.00

www.belkin.com

Belkin Digital Camera Link

Unlike the previous Belkin product that allowed you to plug your digital camera's media card into the media reader connected to your iPod, the Digital Camera Link actually connects your digital camera to your iPod. No more removing your camera's media card!

> **tip**
>
> Photo files take much more room on your iPod's hard drive than sound files do if you are using a high megapixel camera. If you plan to use your iPod to store photos, be certain to delete them from your iPod after you transfer them to your computer.

> **tip**
>
> As with all electronic gear, you would be well advised to check that these products work with your digital camera. Not all digital cameras are supported with these products. Buyers beware!

Operation is simple: Connect the included USB cable from your digital camera and the iPod dock connector to your iPod. One button push later, and all your digital photographs flow into your iPod.

The Digital Camera Link takes two AA batteries, so if you plan on taking this unit with you to the next photo shoot, be sure to replace them with a fresh pair. About the size of an iPod, this is a great addition for anyone who takes a lot of photos and fills up his digital camera's media card quickly.

Price: $79.99

www.belkin.com

Apple iPod Camera Connector

Made by the mother ship herself, the iPod Camera Connector is Apple's solution to transferring pictures from your digital camera to your iPod. Be aware, however, that this only works with the iPod Photo, not with any other iPod. If you don't have an iPod Photo, you can skip this section.

The Apple iPod Camera Connector is a small device that connects to the bottom of your iPod Photo via the dock connector. On the other side of the unit is a USB port, so you can connect the cable that came with your camera to it, and back to the camera's USB port.

Transfer speeds are good, faster in fact than the two Belkin devices listed previously. The Apple iPod Camera Connector also does not take batteries, so there is even less expense using it.

Price: $29

www.apple.com

Apple World Travel Adapter Kit

If you plan to go on a long overseas trip and want to take your iPod with you, how do you plan on recharging your iPod while away? The solution is simple: Apple will happily sell you the World Travel Adapter Kit, which allows you to plug your iBook, PowerBook G4, or iPod into outlets in North America, Japan, China, United Kingdom, Continental Europe, Korea, Australia, and Hong Kong. It works with the white power adapter that shipped with your iPod, and supports all iPods and the iPod mini.

Cost: $39.00

www.apple.com

iPod Remote Controls

You can carry your iPod everywhere, and it is usually within easy reach. It has to be if you plan on changing volume or songs, right? Not necessarily! Welcome to the new world of iPod accessories—the remote control for iPods!

tip

The Apple World Adapter Kit also works with any Macintosh with the white brick power adapter!

If, like me, you connect your iPod to your home sound system, it can be a pain to have to get up out of your seat to switch tracks. The following products all take controlling your iPod from a distance to a new level.

ABT iJet Wireless RF Remote

How would you like to control your iPod from up to 150 feet away? That is the claim the iJet makes. You could not even see the iPod from that far; it would only be a white smudge!

The iJet ships with a keychain-sized remote control, very similar to a car alarm remote many of you have on your car keys. On the other end, the iJet itself plugs into the top of any third generation or later iPod, iPod mini, or iPod Photo. It has a headphone-out jack built-in, with an included mini-jack to RCA cable for connecting your iPod to your home stereo system. This is everything you need to use your iPod with your home stereo, all in one box.

The remote control includes a belt-clip, so you can wear the remote on your person or clip it to a lampshade on your end table if you like. The clip is removable, so you do not have to use it.

The iJet has five control buttons: play/pause, next track, previous track, and volume up and down.

Price: $59.95

www.abtech2.com

Griffin AirClick

The AirClick from Griffin is very similar to the above iJet, but it does not come with the needed RCA-to-mini-jack plug to connect it to your home stereo. It is a two-part system, consisting of the remote control and the RF receiver that plugs into the top of your iPod.

One nice feature is that the remote control has an extra hold button, similar to the one on the iPod itself. This allows you to accidentally push a button on the remote, and nothing will happen if the hold button is activated.

The AirClick is compatible with third-generation or later iPods only.

Price: $39.99

www.griffintechnology.com

DLO iDirect Wireless Remote

The DLO remote solution is also a two-piece design with both a remote and the receiver that sits atop your third-generation or later iPod. It has a mini-jack plug as well, so you can connect it to your home stereo.

The range of the DLO iDirect has been questioned in many reviews, as it needs a very clear line-of-sight to work well. The remote control has a more traditional look and feel to it and features the same five controls you would expect to find in an iPod remote control.

Price: $49.99

www.everythingipod.com

Nyko iTop Button Relocator

This is not so much a remote control as it is an add-on to the iPod. It plugs into the top of your third-generation iPod or iPod mini. Its only feature is a handy one: it puts all the iPod controls on the top of your iPod, so if you have your iPod in a belt-clip, you can still see the control buttons.

The top of the iTop features a headphone jack, two volume control buttons, a hold switch, a previous and next track button, and a play/pause button.

Each button has its own feel, so after you get used to using the iTop, you can tell which button your finger is on simply by the feel of it. This is a great solution to a problem many iPod owners never realized needed to be addressed until they use the iTop. Many users, in fact, have reported that using the iTop is much more intuitive in everyday use than the click-wheel controls of the iPod itself.

Price: $29.99

www.nyko.com

iPod Polishing Kits

So you have an older iPod and have no intention of buying a new one any time soon. Hey, who could blame you? iPods are not an inexpensive purchase. And your older iPod is still ticking along just fine—why dole out the cash just to get a new iPod?

One thing is wrong with your older iPod, though, isn't there? Yes, I can use my magical Author Psychic Power to clearly see your iPod is all scratched up. What is any self-respecting iPod owner to do? You cannot let your friends see how un-new your iPod looks! The shame and horror of letting anyone see all those little scratches on the clear plastic outer iPod case would be simply too much to bear. Is there a solution?

iCleaner Ultra Pro Kit

The iCleaner product is actually a collection of all the needs and wants of those wanting to restore the luster of their older iPod. It ships with one fluid ounce of the iCleaner, a quarter ounce of the Back and Deep Scratch Polish, and the microfiber terrycloth towel.

Sounds neat, but does it work? In a word, yes. You use the polish to basically rub away all the scratches and small gouges that accumulate over years (or days, depending on how much care you have given you iPod) of use. At least it works on the clear plastic pieces of the iPod. In many web reports, product reviewers have said they were happy with the iCleaner overall, although the product has less success with the back metal on the iPods.

Price: $35

www.ipodcleaner.com

Ice Crème

Very similar to the above iCleaner, the Ice Crème is used to remove scratches from the clear plastic of your iPod. While it works, reviewers have stated that they had better luck using the iCleaner product than the Ice Crème. It does work, seemingly whipping away years of ugly scratch marks with a single application. And like the iCleaner, it does not help much with the rear metallic base of the iPod.

Price: $24.95

www.radtech.us

iPod Stands, Docks, and Cradles

In today's age of electronic gizmos, our work desks tend to get cluttered fairly quickly. My digital camera with its dock is over there. Next to that is my iSight video camera that I use to videoconference. Then there is the spot for my Canon Digital Camcorder for when I need to import video to my computer. Of course, you cannot forget the place my high-tech speakers go. Oh, and the media card reader for the various digital cameras I review. And on and on it goes. Every few months, it seems, some new gizmo pops up that somehow finds a place on my desk. Does this sound like you?

The iPod is not an inexpensive toy—just the opposite, in fact. When you are not using your iPod, you can't simply lay it on its back on your desk. How cool would that be? So, unless you have an iPod Dock, you need to buy a stand or cradle for your iPod. Prices vary, of course, and some units look better with your computer desk layout than others. You can go for a more traditional-looking gear, high-tech, brushed metal, clear plastic, colored plastic, and many other cool stands, cradles, and docks. They all perform a similar function, so looking at price and design when making your choice might be just as important to you as features.

tip

If you move your iPod from your computer desk to, for example, your home audio cabinet, consider buying more than one stand, so that you don't have to move the stand from place to place. And if you dust as infrequently as I do, moving the stand gives away how much dust is actually on your furniture!

Habitat

The Habitat is a clear plastic stand from Bubble Design. Unlike some other stands, the Habitat, besides holding your iPod, also has a place for your earbud headphones and FireWire (or USB 2.0) wires. It is very attractive and helps with clutter. Your iPod fits into a slot standing up at a 60-degree angle or so. One drawback, however, is that because the iPod fits in a slot, this is not an ideal solution for iPod mini users, nor iPod users who use a protective carrying case.

Price: $24.99

www.BubbleDesign.com

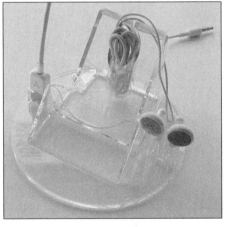

ModPod

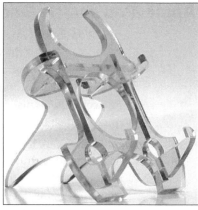

Another plastic stand, this one comes in a variety of colors besides clear. The ModPod allows easy access to the front of your iPod and to the cables, and has clips on the back of the stand to help control wire clutter. Like the Habitat, you cannot use the ModPod if your iPod is in a protective case. It works with all models of iPod, including the iPod mini, though it will not hold the thinner mini as securely.

Price: $14.95

www.MacSkinz.com

PodHolder

The PodHolder was one of the first iPod stands on the market. It is a simple "L" design with rubber bumpers to both protect your iPod from scratches, and keep it from sliding around. A clear piece of plastic, the PodHolder almost disappears when an iPod is sitting in its cradle. The simple, but effective, design makes the PodHolder a nice unit.

Price: $9.95

www.PodShop.com

PodBoard

A very unique product, the PodBoard works with all iPods, except the iPod mini or iPod shuffle. This flat piece of stainless steel has leather straps on the back, and displays your iPod on a flat panel. Think of it as a picture frame for your iPod. The iPod fits into the PodBoard almost flush, and you can also download "skins" for it. A skin is nothing more than a picture, but it gives the PodBoard the option of looking like a piece of art on your desktop. There is also a plastic wire clip on the rear of the PodBoard to help hide and organize your FireWire and headphone wires. This is a very unique product!

Price: $37.00

www.alscher.ch/podboard.html

Apple iPod shuffle Dock

The iPod shuffle Dock is Apple's own solution for docking your shuffle with your computer. Out of the box, the iPod shuffle's own USB plug is used to connect directly with your computer. Some computers with recessed USB ports, however, might not accept the iPod shuffle. Other computers have their USB ports only in the back of the computer. This is a pain if your computer is under your desk. How do you easily plug your shuffle into those ports without re-aggravating that old football back injury?

Enter the iPod shuffle Dock! It sits atop your desktop, with an attached USB cable that connects it to the computer. Simply pull off the USB cap on your shuffle and plug it into this dock. You can then recharge your shuffle as well as transfer audio content from iTunes to your iPod.

Price: $29.00

www.apple.com

Belkin USB 2.0 4-Port Hub for iPod shuffle

For about the same price as the Apple iPod shuffle Dock, and for slightly more desktop real estate, your iPod shuffle Dock can also sport a 4-port powered USB hub.

Being a powered USB hub, you do have to plug this dock into a power outlet via the included power pack.

This is a great solution for those of you who have other USB devices that you don't have room to plug into your computer. There are only three USB ports on the back, not including the port that you have to use to connect to your computer. The forth USB port, then, is on top of the dock, where the shuffle plugs in for charging and iTunes transfers.

If features are any indication, this Belkin unit is a better buy than the Apple Computer offering. It works just as the Apple unit, but gives you more bang for the buck with the three extra USB ports.

Price: $29.95

www.belkin.com

Apple iPod Dock (iPod and iPod mini)

Being able to cradle your iPod on your desktop is a wonderful way to protect it from being scratched, as well as getting rid of some loose wires on your desktop. Apple included docks with a few third-generation iPods, but now they are an optional purchase.

This dock, for either the full-size iPod or iPod mini (the only difference is the cradle size that holds your iPod in place) is a quality product, although there are cheaper third-party options out there. Still, knowing that it is an Apple product is worth some piece of mind.

You simply plug the dock into your computer via the included cable, and set your iPod into the dock for charging and audio content transfers via iTunes. Simple, elegant, and a no brainer to operate. It works perfectly.

Price: $39.00

www.apple.com

Westshore Craftworks iDockCover

Probably the best reason to own an Apple-made iPod Dock is that you can then go out and purchase the iDockCover from Westshore Craftworks. These beautiful, carved, lacquered wood covers sit over the Apple iPod dock, leaving room for all the ports and plugs the dock needs.

You can buy the original oval-shaped dock cover, but for the really eye-catching choice, check out the guitar shaped covers.

These are beautiful and elegant, and really make a statement. No, they do not bring any new technology to the table, but esthetics are important, and nothing says high quality and tastefulness than smooth lacquered wood.

Westshore Craftworks has a large variety of styles and wood choices for you to pick from. Check out its website for more information!

Price: $24.95–$34.95

www.westshorecraftworks.com

Solio Solar Charger

Want an environmentally friendly way to charge any iPod with a dock connector? The Solio is the answer for you. Using solar energy, the Solio folds out like a flower, catching sunrays and converting that energy to power and charge your iPod.

You set the Solio out in direct sunlight, allowing its internal battery to charge up. Then simply plug your iPod into the Solio, and it begins charging up your iPod.

While there are better, and more efficient, ways of charging your battery, none are as environmentally correct as the Solio.

Price: $99

www.Solio.com

iPod Cases

One of the great things about the iPod is how sexy and sleek it is. The brushed metal look is great, but it has one major problem—scratches. Apple does not like to voice the problem, but if you use an iPod without a protective case for very long, the chances of scratching your iPod are very great. Thankfully, iPod cases are the number one accessories iPod users buy, and many vendors have hundreds of cases from which you can choose. No matter what model iPod you own, you can find the perfect case for your needs. The following sections discuss just a tiny fraction of the available iPod cases.

Sheldon iPod Case

These come in a variety of colors and styles, such as Metallic Blue, Miami Geo, Pink Polish, Silver Bullet, and Checkerboard.

Price: $24.95

www.ebags.com

Speck iPod Skins

This is not so much a case as a new skin for your iPod. These protective rubber cases fit very snug, and can even give your iPod some of that iPod mini color you want so badly! They also work with the iPod Dock, so that you don't have to remove your iPod from its skin simply to plug it in to the Dock.

Price: $19.95

www.speckproducts.com

Speck iStyle

The Speck iStyle is a leather case that sports a very nice snap-over lid, as well as a plastic shield to cover the iPod's screen. It ships with a swivel belt clip.

Price: $34.95

www.speckproducts.com

Belkin Leather Flip Case

This attractive case can flip open for quick access to the front of your iPod.

Price: $29.99

www.belkin.com

MARWARE Sportsuit Convertible Case

This iPod mini case, made from 2mm neoprene outer construction, is great for those mini owners who take their iPod with them to work out. It features an interchangeable clip so that you can wear it as an armband or on your belt. You can also connect your iPod mini to your computer without taking it out of the case. It comes in a variety of colors to match your iPod mini.

Price: $34.95

www.marware.com

MARWARE SportSuit Safari

Without the picture, you probably would not believe this one. Yes, an iPod mini case looks (and feels!) like fur! Made from neoprene and faux fur, you can get these little fuzzy cases in Panther (black), Polar Bear (white), Flamingo (pink), Giraffe (brown and white), Leopard (brown, black, and white), and Zebra (black and white). What, no Smurf Blue?

Price: $19.95

MARWARE 3G SportSuit Convertible

The SportSuit Convertible is a great-looking case made from rugged neoprene. It can quickly flip open to reveal a snug and protected iPod. You can even connect your iPod to your computer without removing it from the case. And most importantly, of course, it comes in a variety of colors, including Blue, Graphite, Red, and Yellow.

Price: $39.95

www.marware.com

PodSleevz/mini Sleevz

Most iPod and mini cases either flip, fold, or leave a cutout so that you can get to the controls. After all, you have to physically run your finger over the controls to operate it. Not so with the PodSleevz—for both iPod and the mini. This superthin (less than 1mm in thickness) is a soft, yet very tough fabric that fits your iPod like a form-fitting glove! They also come in a variety of colors.

Price: $19.95 ($17.95 mini)

www.radtech.us

Gucci iPod Case

If you are a fashion maven, you know all about Gucci. This iPod case is not about protection, but fashion. And the price reflects that!

Price: $199.99

www.gucci.com

TimBuk2 iPod Case

If simplicity is more to your liking, take a look at the TimBuk2 iPod case. It attaches to a belt or a shoulder strap. Elastic side panels mean your iPod fits nice and snug. The Velcro top keeps it secure. It also comes in 12 colors!

Price: $20.00

www.timbuk2.com

Anetagenova iPod Case

Cutting-edge fashion for the iPod is found with the Anetagenova iPod case. The Anetagenova line of iPod cases come in a variety of styles and colors. Not cheap, but still not Gucci priced, these iPod cases are certain to get attention!

Price: $79.00–$129.00

www.anetagenova.com

PodPaqnappa

Made from fine nappa leather, this iPod case is as beautiful as it is sturdy. It features a removable (via sturdy metal clips) front flap.

Price: $39.95

www.booqbags.com

Apple iPod Socks

All the men will see this product and think, "It's a sock. Why would I want a sock for my iPod?" while all the women are thinking, "Now *that* is cute! I want one!" At least that was the conversation between my wife and me when I showed her the iPod Socks from Apple for the first time.

The iPod Socks are knit and come in six colors, including green, purple, grey, blue, orange, and pink. These are indeed cute and even sport the Apple logo.

Price: $29.00

www.apple.com

Bumperz for iPod shuffle

The Bumperz is a cool protective case for the iPod shuffle. Rather than wraping around the entire iPod, the Bumperz simply fit around the side of your shuffle and includes a lanyard. The rubber silicone comes in a variety of colors, and there are currently three bundles for purchase; each comes with five colors.

A neat case, well worth looking at. Works well for protecting your shuffle from nicks and dings.

Price: $19.95

www.xtrememac.com

TuffWrapz

The TuffWrapz is similar (and from the same company) as the previous Bumperz, but this case wraps all the way around the iPod shuffle while leaving the headphone jack and control wheel open.

They come in three packs, and include mist, cherry, cobalt, lime, tangerine, sky, lemon, bubblegum, and grape. They also have a lanyard for easy wearing and comfort. These are rubber, so they work well to keep your iPod dry if you get caught out in the rain.

Price: $24.95

www.xtrememac.com

Apple iPod shuffle Sports Case

Made by Apple, the Sports Case protects your iPod shuffle from the elements. It also has an integrated lanyard.

Price: $29.00

www.apple.com

Burton Shield iPod Jacket

You are probably wondering how a winter skiing jacket made it into a book about iPods and iTunes, right? Well, this is the first (and, as far as I know, only) jacket that has iPod control on the arm! The iPod is stored in the specially designed EVA molded chest pocket for protection against the elements and the stray tree branch. Burton makes both a men's and women's version. Yes, they are pricy, but this is not only a high-quality Burton ski jacket, it is also technically an iPod case as well!

Price: $379.95 (Men) $359.95 (Women)

iPod Stickers and Film

Want to change the look of your iPod quickly, cheaply, and easily? The following products do just that!

Skin EFX iPod Stickers

Want to quickly, and cheaply, dress up your iPod? The Skin EFX iPod Stickers do just that. They are applied to the front of your iPod (check their site for the iPod models supported) to cover the white with a new design. Want a gold-plated iPod for a day? How about a black and silver tiger shark look? All can be had.

These stickers are temporary only. Once used, you cannot remove it and use it again later. The company claims that they do not leave any of the adhesive glue behind, but online reports indicate otherwise, although the adhesive is easily removed from your iPod and causes no harm.

Price: Starting at $3.50 and up

www.iPod-Skins.com

HP Printable Tattoos

Ah, to be able to place any graphics you want on your iPod! The stuff dreams are made of! Well, those dreams are now a reality with the HP Printable Tattoos, a set of 10 printable stickers you can use to change the look of your iPod. (Note: these are not only compatible with the HP iPods, but the Apple-branded iPods as well.)

You can either order blank sheets of the tattoos and design and print out your own, or visit the HP website and order preprinted ones from a large gallery.

They are compatible with any color printer.

Price: $14.99

www.hp.com

Mobile Juice shuffle Art

These are simple vinyl stickers you can stick to the front of your iPod shuffle. They fit well and come in five versions, including green, monogram, Hawaiian pink, Hawaiian blue, and black.

Being a vinyl sticker, it is water resistant, and does not leave any messy residue on your shuffle after you remove it. They do hold up well while in use, so you won't have to replace it quickly.

These are attractive and nicely priced!

Price: $7.99

www.shuffle-art.com

CD-ROM Contents

On the accompanying CD-ROM disc, you will find programs for the Mac and PC that enhance your iPod and iTunes experience. Some programs are free for you to use and enjoy, whereas you have to pay for other programs should you choose to keep them. The disc contains three categories of software, which are discussed in the following sections.

Freeware

This is software made by either a company or an individual who has decided not to charge for their work. Freeware is, as the name implies, free! If you do decide to keep and use any freeware program, it is customary to at least send an email to the creator thanking them for their generosity. This shows your appreciation, and a nice email is a sure way to keep them either updating the program, or creating other worthwhile programs.

Shareware

This is software that is usually free to use for a set amount of time, after which you agree to pay the price should you choose to continue using it. Shareware is not quite commercial software, but neither is it freeware. It falls somewhere in the middle. A shareware author is usually creating software in his spare time, and allows users to download and freely use it to get a taste of how it works before committing their money.

Commercial Software

These are the big boys of the software industry. More often than not, you have to pay for these programs before using them. However, some companies freely give away their programs for one reason or another. A prime example is the Apple Computer, Inc. program iTunes. iTunes is free to download and use. Apple does not charge a dime for iTunes, for either Mac or PC users. However, iTunes is still not freeware in the pure definition of the word, but rather commercial software that is given away. In this case, Apple gives away iTunes to boost iPod sales, as well as an incentive to use the program to purchase downloadable music from the iTunes Music Store.

tip

Read the licensing agreement before installing any software to be certain you are not installing any spyware programs as well!

XPlay for Windows is another commercial program found on the CD-ROM. This program, unlike iTunes, is not free, though they do allow you to use it in Demo mode, free of charge. In this case, XPlay uses a shareware form of distribution.

If you find software you enjoy on the CD-ROM, please take a moment to follow the licensing agreement of the program in question.

Macintosh iPod Software

These are the programs for Macintosh computers found on the accompanying CD-ROM.

PodWorks

One of the antitheft options Apple uses to prevent iPod users from simply plugging their iPod
into another Mac and copying all his music
files over is its one-way transfer. In other words,
you can only copy songs to the iPod, not from
it. But what happens when your Mac dies, and
you lose all your music files? You might still have
them on the iPod, but that does you no good.
The answer is a third-party utility titled
"PodWorks" from developer Sci-Fi Hi-Fi. It copies
all the file metadata from the ID3 (Identifi-
cation Tag Studio3) stored on every song on the
iPod. It then copies that data back to the
"clean" version of iTunes on another
Macintosh.

Price: $8.00

www.scifihifi.com/podworks/

> **tip**
>
> Always run virus
> detection software on a
> PC before and after
> installing anything
> downloaded from
> the Internet.

> **tip**
>
> As with any software
> found on a CD-ROM,
> you might want to
> check to see if there
> are updated ver-
> sions of the soft-
> ware online before
> installing.

BiblePod

Want to read chapters from the King James
Version of the bible on your iPod? BiblePod for Mac and Windows lets you do just
that. BiblePod is a free program that uses the English KJV XML Bible markup language project.

biblepod.kainjow.com/

Price: Free!

Pod2Go

Pod2Go is a great application that "Takes an ordinary iPod and makes it extraordi-
nary." Using Pod2Go, you can sync news, weather information, movie listings, horo-
scopes, stock quotes, driving directions, and more. What's more, the software
autoupdates itself, helps you publish a listing of your music to a web page, and
gives you the ability to quickly and easily manage your iPod's notes. Pod2Go is a
really great program, full of features you did not even know you wanted until now!

Price: Free, but donations are welcome.

www.kainjow.com/pod2go/

PodMail

Want to transfer your email to your iPod for later viewing? PodMail is an open-source program that does just that, though you cannot use it to reply to your emails. But if you have a lot of email you would rather read later, this is a great way to take it with you.

Price: Free!

www.podmail.org/

Ejector

The Ejector is a great utility that adds an iPod icon to your Mac OS X menu bar, through which you can eject any removable disk, including an iPod, CD, DVD, or any other hardware device that shows up on your desktop.

Price: Free!

www.jeb.com.fr

iPod Launcher

The power of AppleScript is used in iPod Launcher. When you plug your iPod into your Mac via the FireWire cable, iPod Launcher launches applications for you. For instance, if you manually fire up your iSync application after connecting the iPod, iPod Launcher can automate that for you.

Price: $4.95

www.zapptek.com/

iPod It

If you use Entourage, Mail, Stickies, Address Book, or iCal, you can use iPod It to transfer your PIM (Personal Information Manager) data over to the iPod. This is a great way to carry all your contact information from those applications without having to purchase a separate Personal Digital Assistant (PDA). You can also transfer all your mail messages and events from iCal, download weather and news headlines, and much more. The iPod It is also from ZappTek software.

Price: $14.95

www.zapptek.com/ipod-it/

iSpeak It

A very underutilized feature in Mac OS X is the computer's ability to speak any text onscreen. With iSpeak It, you can take any document, be it a web page, email message, or PDF (Adobe's Portable Document File format) file, and save the spoken words to iTunes. From there, it is a simple matter of loading it onto your iPod, and you now have a vocal recording of said work anywhere you go. This is yet another great application from ZappTek Software.

Price: $12.95

www.zapptek.com/

iPodRip
The ability to move your music from your iPod to your computer is smart. Apple does not let you do it. IPodRip does, and supports iTunes song information, including ratings and play count. It can also recover songs and playlists. It provides print, HTML, and XML support, as well as an iTunes style browser. This is a nice piece of software from The Little Appfactory.

Price: $10.00

www.thelittleappfactory.com

Ollie's iPod Extractor
A simple and direct way of moving your music files from your iPod to your Macintosh, Ollie's iPod Extractor supports an easy-to-use interface, and the cost is just right!

Price: Free!

www.isophonic.net/applications/

iPod Organizer
You can use this program to store phone numbers, email addresses, flight numbers, and appointment times. The program, from proVUE Development, does not install any special or third-party software on your iPod. Instead, iPod Organizer exports the information that you input into the Mac-based software as MP3 files, allowing you to quickly find and use the information on your iPod. This is a great utility, and has received favorable comments from everyone who has reviewed it on the Mac web.

Price: $19.99

www.provue.com/ipodorganizer.html

iPod.iTunes
Using a tabbed interface for the software, iPod.iTunes does a good job of syncing the music files from your iPod to iTunes. Intelligent enough not to copy duplicates, iPod.iTunes copies the music files back from the iPod to iTunes that are missing. If, for instance, you accidentally deleted your music files from iTunes, iPod.iTunes saves your bacon! iPod.iTunes also works with not just MP3 files, but also with your protected (iTunes store purchased) AAC files, audible tracks, and even playlists! This is a great software title to add to your iPod software collection.

Price: 29.90 Euros (use PayPal for currency conversion)

www.crispsofties.com

iPod Decloak

iPod Decloak is another program that allows you to view the hidden files (MP3, ACC, and so on) on your iPod. Very similar to many other programs, it works well.

Price: $2.00

www.ipoddecloak.com/

iPod Access

The iPod Access is a tool for moving songs from your Mac to your iPod by artist/album or composer/album. Featuring an easy-to-use interface, iPod Access does a minimum task, which iTunes (free from Apple) does much more easily. Still, the program is worth taking a look at if you are having program problems with iTunes.

Price: $10.00

www.ipodaccess.com/index.html

iPod Play List Cloner

iPod Play List Cloner copies playlists from your iPod to your Mac, in a folder of your choice. Using scripts, it can then add an identical playlist to iTunes (version 3 or later), saving you the time to rebuild your playlists by hand in case you lose your iTunes playlists. This is a handy utility that could potentially save you a lot of time!

Price: Free!

homepage.mac.com/beweis/

Toggle iPod Battery Status

A nifty utility that allows you to change the battery life icon on your iPod from the battery icon to a number between 1 and 500, which represents how much voltage is remaining in your battery. This is a great little application, well worth the small fee.

Price: $2.00

homepage.mac.com/rulerk/

Rip to iPod

This nifty AppleScript only does one thing, but it does it well. It rips (copies) files seemingly directly from a CD to your iPod. In reality, it copies the files to iTunes first, then copies said files to your iPod, and finally deletes the songs from your iTunes.

Price: Free!

www.malcolmadams.com/itunes/index.php

FileMaker to iPod

If you store your vCard information in a FileMaker database, this utility allows you to transfer your contacts to your iPod. Imagine using FileMaker's powerful searching capabilities or sorting options to only copy the needed contacts to your iPod.

Price: Free!

www.bossbizapps.com/

OmniOutliner Export to iPod

For OmniOutliner users, these two AppleScipts let you export your outlines to either iPods Notes or Contacts menu.

Price: Free!

www.omnigroup.com/

Slurp

Slurp is a nice working iPod management tool that maintains a database of all the music files on your iPod. From there, you can perform search and sorts, export the data as text files, copy your music from your iPod to your hard drive, or even burn a CD directly from your iPod to your CD-RW/SuperDrive. The only drawback to Slurp is that the developer, Ambroise Confetti, has halted development on it, releasing only this working beta version.

Price: Free!

www.cellulo.info/slurp/

PodQuest

It is not always feasible to take your computer with you on a trip, but with an iPod and PodQuest, you can take both MapQuest and MapBlast driving instructions on the road. PodQuest adds a menu bar that allows you to download said directions to your iPod. The utility works well, and adds more usefulness to iPod users who are on the road often.

Price: $9.95

www.mibasoft.dk/

Lyripod

What are you missing from your iPod while listening to your music? The lyrics to your music, of course! Lyripod is a simple utility that searches the Internet (lyrics. astraweb.com) for the song you choose, and downloads it to your iPod in the Lyrics folder under Extras. This is still early in the software development stage, and does not work 100% of the time. But, it can't harm your iPod, and is worth giving a try.

Price: Free!

Windows PC iPod Software

These are the programs for Windows-based computers found on the accompanying CD-ROM.

XPlay

XPlay is a commercial software program that gives you much more flexibility with your iPod than ever before. With XPlay, you can drag and drop MP3, M4A, Audible (.aa) the popular WAVE (.wav) or AIFF (.aif, the digital format CDs use) to your iPod without the need to use Apple's iTunes software. Created long before Apple made iTunes for Windows, XPlay is also the only way for those with an older Windows OS, such as Windows 98 or Me, to be compatible with the iPod. Included on the CD-ROM is a 15-day trial demo of the software, courtesy of the Mediafour Corporation.

Price: $29.95

www.mediafour.com/products/xplay/

GoogleGet

GoogleGet is a handy utility for downloading the latest news from Google News to your iPod. This is a handy feature and shows the power of the iPod. As of this writing, GoogleGet is a free application.

Price: Free!

www.mesmerized.org/teki/extra/googleget/index.html

Weather For Me

Windows users should not feel left out, as Weather For Me downloads a 10-day forecast onto your iPod. This is a great utility if you are planning to take your iPod on vacation, and want a weather forecast for your destination. It includes foreign zip code support, auto updater, and more.

Price: Free!

www.staylazy.net/software/

Feed My Pod

Feed My Pod is a very neat software title that takes content from the iPodLounge website (a great website for all iPod owners) and puts it on your iPod. Simply put, Feed My Pod takes all the news and downloads it to your iPod, allowing you to read it at your own leisure offline.

Price: Free!

www.staylazy.net/feedmypod/

Apple iPod Plug-in for MusicMatch Jukebox

This allows you to transfer music from the MusicMatch Jukebox software to the iPod, much like Apple's own iTunes. If you are a MusicMatch user, this is the software you will want as an iPod user.

Price: Free from Apple Computer, Inc.

docs.info.apple.com/article.html?artnum=120313

PocketMac iPod Edition

If you are a Microsoft Outlook user, and store your contact information in that application, you can now use PocketMac iPod Edition to transfer Contacts, Calendar, Tasks, Notes, and even email to your iPod.

Price: $23.41

www.pocketmac.net/products/pmipodwin/demo.html

Anapod Explorer

Anapod Explorer is the first and only iPod software that allows full Windows Explorer integration with the iPod as a device in My Computer. It allows a web page interface to your iPod through its built-in web server. This gives you a powerful search and reporting capability using a Structured Query Language (SQL) database. It does not yet work with the iPod mini.

Price: $25.00

www.redchairsoftware.com

k-pod

This allows you to download all your email from your inbox to your iPod, making a new folder titled "Mail" in your "Notes" screen on the iPod. It is very simple to use!

Price: Freeware

k-deep.com/k-pod.htm

euPOD VolumeBoost

When Apple shipped the iPod to Europe, for some reason they put a restriction on how loud the volume will go. The developer of euPOD VolumeBoost wanted to crank up his music, so he wrote this small program to solve the problem. It works with all iPods, but does not work to the same extent with U.S. iPods as it does with European iPods.

Price: Free!

www.espen.se

WinniePod Updater

If you have a first or second generation Macintosh-compatible iPod and want to use it with your PC without losing all the music files, this is the application for you.

Price: Free!

www.the-midfield.com/ipod.aspx

CopyPod

This is a small program that allows you to save your iPod music to your computer. This is a nice tool if you have to send your iPod in for repair.

Price: $8.00

copypod.ouvaton.org

iPodLibrary

Ever want to read your e-Books on your iPod? iPodLibrary lets you do just that. You can import all major e-Book formats, including .LIT, .PDF, .HTML, and .TXT. It also allows you to save your last position in each book. Unfortunately, it only works with the third generation iPods.

Price: Free!

www25.brinkster.com/carmagt/ipodlibrary

MyPodPlayer

With MyPodPlayer, you can play all the music on your iPod on your computer. Simply connect the iPod, and MyPodPlayer reads all your music, allowing you to listen on your computer. You can view the music very similar to iTunes, by artist, genre, album, playlist, and so on. MyPodPlayer also allows you to copy songs from your iPod to your PC.

Price: Free!

www.ipodsoft.com/mypodplayer.aspx

iStoryCreator

Want to create your own Text Adventure games for your iPod? That is what iStoryCreator does. Do you remember the "Choose your own ending" books in which you had to turn to a certain page in the book, depending on what you wanted the character to do? This is the same premise that iStoryCreator uses to create Text Adventure games. It can be hours of fun creating and sharing your adventures with people online! To install the iStoryCreator to your computer, you must first have the ".NET Framework" installed. You can get this here:

download.microsoft.com/download/a/a/c/aac39226-8825-44ce-90e3-bf8203e74006/dotnetfx.exe

Price: Free!

www.ipodsoft.com/iCreator.aspx

In addition to iStoryCreator, 28 iStories are included for your enjoyment. Please note: The iStories found on the CD-ROM are to be viewed at your own discretion, and have not been edited by this book's publisher.

Macintosh iTunes Software

The following is software that works with the iTunes software for Macintosh computers.

NiceCast

Imagine being able to use your Macintosh as a broadcasting radio station over the Internet. Imagine no more, as NiceCast does exactly that. NiceCast broadcasts music either across the world or across you house, directly from iTunes.

With iTunes and NiceCast, you can set up a playlist for DJ-like broadcasts. All anyone else needs to listen to your music is a streaming MP3 player, the address you are broadcasting from, and you are now your own radio station.

NiceCast is a very simple-to-use application, with a level of control not found in other, similar applications. You can set the compression level so that those with slower Internet connections are also able to listen.

You will find a fully functional demo of NiceCast on the included CD-ROM. If you enjoy it, please be certain to visit NiceCast online and purchase a copy!

Price: $40.00

www.rogueamoeba.com/nicecast

RockStar

RockStar is a single- or multiperson music game that uses your very own iTunes library in a very new and innovative way. Do you remember the old game show "Name That Tune"? The concept is similar here. RockStar plays clips of your own iTunes music library, and gives you five multiple-choice answers.

The game gives you the choice of game play. You can either guess song title, artist, album, or a mixed bag of all three. During game play, you are presented with five choices, and the goal is to correctly answer in the shortest amount of time possible. During game play, a counter quickly counts down, so that when you make a correct selection, you are awarded the time left on the counter.

Multiplayer games, or "Party Games" as they are called, are a great deal of fun as well. Here, you can have up to five teams, and you rotate teams every five songs. The highest-scoring team wins. As the title suggests, this is a fun party game.

Price: $9.00

freshsqueeze.com/products/rockstar

Name That iTune!

Very similar to RockStar, it is a game that starts playing random music from your iTunes software. Your skill at answering the questions correctly, in a given time frame, reflects a good score. The questions range from naming the artists or song title. You are presented with four choices, and the longer it takes you to answer correctly, the lower your points. Not quite as much fun or polished as RockStar, but the price is better.

Price: Free!

homepage.mac.com/jonn8/as/

RadioLover

With RadioLover, you can record Internet-streaming audio as separate tracks, including iTunes Radio Tuner stations, and then save them as MP3 files for later listening. It can also record multiple streams at once, and even has a scheduling feature to record when you are away.

This is great software, and a free demo is included on the CD-ROM!

Price: $15.00

www.bitcartel.com

iTunes Publisher

Do you have a desire to publish your iTunes song list on a website? Or, do you want a printout of all your music file names? Perhaps you have a database, which you use to store all your song information. If so, iTunes Publisher is the software you have been looking for. With it, you can export in the following formats: HTML, Tabbed Text, QuickTime Streaming Server, M3U, and the general playlist formats in other audio applications, such as WinAMP.

Price: $5.00

www.trancesoftware.com

iTunes Timer

This is a fun little AppleScript studio application that calculates the total time iTunes has been playing. It can calculate on playlist, or even your entire iTunes library.

Price: Free!

webpages.charter.net/remsoftware/index.html

iTunes Library Manager

With iTunes Library Manager, you are able to make backup copies of your iTunes library and preferences. Why do you need this? If you have given your music ratings, and you lose all the preferences to iTunes (a bad crash, new version of iTunes, and so on), you have to manually go back in and change them again. Also, if you imported music in which you had to manually name the songs, album, artist, and so on, you must reenter all that information again if you changed computers. With iTunes Library Manager, this is no longer a problem.

Price: $5.00

www.malcolmadams.com/itunes/index.php

iTunes Alarm

Do you want to use your iTunes as an alarm clock? iTunes Alarm does just that by specifying a time for iTunes to play, at what volume, and even what song. This makes a great alarm clock. Simply put your Mac next to your bed, and you can wake up to the sweet sound of music or any other audio file in your iTunes library.

Price: Free!

www.johnnarun.com

iTunesCool

As you know from reading this book, you can import album artwork into iTunes. This is a tool for doing just that, without the need to copy and paste yourself. You can select multiple songs to update the artwork, as well. iTunesCool also can export artwork, delete artwork, and export iTunes library to HTML. This is a handy time-saver.

Price: $6.00

www.sandme.info

iEatBrainz

iEatBrainz is a handy, though not foolproof, method of correcting missing information tags from your MP3s. If, for some reason, a song is listed correctly, but the artist is not, this program attempts to repair it for you by using the MusicBrainz.org database.

Price: Free

homepage.mac.com/jbtule/software.html

Synergy

This is a very small application that puts three button controls on your menu bar, Previous Track, Next Track, and Play/Pause, that control iTunes. This way, whenever you need or want to either replay a song, skip to the next one, or just stop the music for a moment, you no longer have to either visit the Dock or bring iTunes to the forefront.

What's more, it also displays in various ways what is playing in iTunes. It can display floating transparent windows that show the song, album, artist, ratings, and even album art—which are all customizable! You can even set Hot Keys for systemwide control of iTunes. Even better, Synergy actually downloads album art for you. The price is cheap for everything this program does.

Price: 5 Euros

wincent.com

Track Manager

Track Manager exposes the ability to rate the playing track or copy it to other playlists without having to bring iTunes to the front and dig through the full-sized window. For convenience, most of the fundamental features of the mini iTunes window (track name, play, and volume controls) are reproduced.

Price: $10.00

www.sentientfood.com

iTunesRating

iTunesRating is a simple utility that displays the rating of the song currently playing on iTunes. It also lets you change or edit the rating with a simple click.

Price: Free!

homepage.mac.com/mhandley/

iTunesBrushKiller

Some people really dislike the brushed metal look of iTunes. Enter iTunesBrushKiller. This application keeps the metallic look, but does away with the brushed metal look.

Price: Free!

sveinbjorn.vefsyn.is/software

iTunes Screensaver Add-ons

As you know, iTunes sports a great visualizer. Sort of a screensaver, people love to watch the visualizer in action. But you don't have to be limited to the cool effects that ship free with iTunes! Many other third-party visualization animations are available for iTunes. Here are a few we have included on the CD-ROM.

Fountain Music

This animation has particles exploding to the beat of the music. You can control gravity, particle size, edges, and more—very neat!

Price: Free!

www.binaryminded.com

WhiteCap

One of the oldest, and coolest visualization plug-ins for iTunes (and other MP3 players), WhiteCap produces more than 190 effects. Truly stunning to watch, you get hours of enjoyment watching the engaging displays. It can also respond to line-in audio sources.

Price: Free!

soundspectrum.com

G-Force

G-Force features fast, antialiased effects, millions of possible effect combinations, savable and scriptable effects, video file export capabilities, and unparalleled expandability. G-Force is designed to entertain you on its own, but it can be customized and extended in many ways.

Price: $10.00

soundspectrum.com

vTunes

vTunes is a simple OpenGL iTunes visual plug-in.

Price: Free!

lorenb.com/

LED Spectrum Analyser

This visualizer displays a hi-fi style electronic display.

Price: Free!

www.maczoop.com

Hacking the iPod

Original iPod, Third Generation iPod, iPod mini, iPod shuffle.

The term *hacking* is now used many times in negative connotations. The reality is that hacking is simply a means of understanding how something works, using reverse engineering, or making something work differently than its intended use.

In this chapter, we are looking at only one type of hack; changing the iPod and iPod mini's internal battery. Sadly, there is no way to change the battery in the iPod shuffle.

Replacing Your iPod Battery

When, not if, your iPod no longer accepts a charge, it is time to replace your battery. The battery in your iPod is similar to many cell phone batteries. There are different batteries in the first second-generation iPods than the third, and the iPod mini is a different model all together. So, what do you do when your iPod decides it wants a new battery? Besides shipping it off to Apple, which sets you back up to $100, your only other option is to replace the battery yourself.

Unfortunately, replacing the iPod battery is not as simple as your cell phone. If you take a close look at your iPod, you notice that there are no screws, latches, or indentations that give you a clue on how they put the iPod together, or how you can take it apart. But fear not, we have the answers for you!

caution

Danger! Be aware that hacks could void your iPod's warranty. In other words, if you damage your iPod performing a hack, you are out of luck. Apple Computer, Inc. will not help you fix it, or if they do, the cost for the repairs will come out of your pocket. As a general rule, before hacking anything, I always ask myself a simple question: Can I afford to buy a new one if I make a mistake? If the answer is no, simply enjoy your iPod as it was intended. Otherwise, hack away!

Battery Replacement—First and Second Generation iPod

The first two generations of iPods uses a 3.7 Volts 1200 mAh battery. What does that mean? You don't really care, do you? You just want your iPod to work again. So let's skip the electrical class and go right to the point. Order the 3.7 Volt 1200 mAh batteries. Expect to pay around $30 for one.

Tools Required

The only tools you need are a small, hard plastic wedge tool. Think of it as the end of a regular flathead screwdriver, but it is plastic and not metal. Yes, you can use a regular flathead screwdriver, but you take an awful risk of scratching your iPod with the metal on metal contact. One of the nice things about an iPod is how cool it looks, so why take a chance of ruining its look?

Look around online before buying the iPod battery. Many times, the company selling you the battery will include an iPod battery tool with the sale. If not, you will want to purchase one. I have seen them for as low as six dollars online. However, any hard plastic (or nylon) sharp-edged wedge tool works.

Begin by using the wedge tool to carefully pry the case apart, starting at the top. The case is in two parts; the back metal and the front plastic. As the gap widens, work your way down the side of the iPod, and you will find case clips hidden inside the iPod. Use your tool to unclip each case clip as you find them.

After you have one side completely unclipped, you can easily swing the back metal cover off the iPod.

The old battery is actually glued in place. You can use your tool, if it is sturdy enough, to pry the battery free. Be aware, however, that the battery is connected to the iPod by small wires and a connector. Take great care not to break these.

The final task is to unclip the battery wires from the iPod itself. After this is done, install the new battery, snap the case back together, charge the new battery, and your iPod is as good as new!

Battery Replacement—Third and Fourth Generation iPod

The third generation of iPods uses a different battery than the first two. This is a 3.7 Volts 850 mAh battery. It is much smaller than the original iPod $30 range online. The forth generation iPod and the iPod photo use a 3.7 Volts 950 mAh battery. Be sure to order the correct battery for your iPod model!

Tools Required

The tools required for taking apart the iPod are a ruler with metric measurements and a plastic wedge, as described in the Tools Required section for the first two-generation iPods. You can use a small regular flathead screwdriver as well, such as the type used for eyeglass repair. However, you do run the risk of scratching your iPod, so be careful if you go that route!

The first step is to measure, using the ruler, 6cm (60MM) down either side of the iPod. This is where you start prying the plastic and metal case apart.

Insert your wedge or screwdriver, and carefully pry open the case working back and forth in the seam. This allows even pressure in the crease so that you don't run the risk of breaking any of the clips that hold the two pieces together.

After you have separated the two halves of the case, you need to work your way around the entire case to unclip each and every clip. Do this by pushing each clip inward toward the center of the iPod. After the silver case is loose, it will still be attached by a ribbon cable.

Do not pull the two pieces apart quickly. Look for the ribbon after the two halves are separated. Do not break this ribbon. Gently lay the metal half of the iPod case down, with the ribbon cable still attached. Be aware that these ribbons are very sensitive and can break or crack, and you don't want that!

Third Generation: With the front of the iPod (where the controls are) laying flat, you see the tiny hard drive surrounded by blue rubber. Remove the hard drive by lifting all the blue rubber. There is a ribbon cable connecting the hard drive to the motherboard of the iPod. You need to disconnect this ribbon from the motherboard via the tab at the end of the ribbon. Gently lift the tab and disconnect the hard drive. Set aside the hard drive. Next, you need to remove that old, dead battery. To do so, simply lift it out, being careful of the power cable running from the battery to the motherboard. You will also notice that the battery cable actually runs underneath the motherboard. Be certain to carefully pull it out, taking note of its position so that when you install the new battery, you can tuck the new power cable back out of the way in the same spot.

After the cord is out from under the motherboard, pull up on the connector to disconnect the power cord from the motherboard.

To install, simply plug in the new battery, tuck the wire back underneath the motherboard, replace the hard drive (don't forget to plug it back in as well!), and reassemble the iPod.

Charge up your battery, and you are back in the music business!

Fourth Generation and iPod Photo: With the front of the iPod lying flat, you need to disconnect the power cord from the still-hidden battery underneath the hard drive. It is easy to locate, as it has a black, white, and red cable running to it.

After the cable is disconnected, you need a torx wrench (which comes with almost all replacement iPod batteries) to remove the two screws at the end of the motherboard, at the same end that the power cord you just disconnected was located.

Your hard drive is still connected to the iPod, so you want to gently lift one end up and out of the way to access the original battery. Hold or prop up the hard drive, and then gently use a small flat head screwdriver to remove the iPod battery. It is glued down, so be careful not to damage anything while you do this!

After the old battery is out, reglue the new battery in the same spot, applying the glue that came with the new iPod battery to the glue spot on the iPod.

Reverse your steps from this point. Do not forget to put the screws back!

After your iPod is all together again, allow at least three hours to recharge your iPod.

Battery Replacement—iPod Mini

The battery replacement in an iPod mini is more involved and complex than in any of its larger brethren. The iPod mini case is one solid metal form, unlike the two-piece cases for the iPod. As such, the steps to disassemble the iPod mini are very different.

The iPod mini uses a very small Li-ion model #EC003 battery. Of all the iPod batteries, these are the most expensive, starting at around $40.

Tools Required

To disassemble the iPod mini, you need a small, regular flathead screwdriver and a small Phillips-head screwdriver. These must be small, such as the eyeglass repair type.

First, use the tip of the flathead screwdriver to carefully pry the top white plastic cover, where your headphones plug in, from the top of the mini. There is a small amount of glue holding the plastic cover, so take care not to crack or pry too hard in any one spot. Move around the edge, gently but firmly lifting the white top up and away.

When the top is removed, you see two tiny Phillips screws. Use the Phillips screwdriver to remove these two screws.

Next, use the flathead screwdriver to remove the plastic cover from the bottom of the mini. Glue is also holding this piece in place, so as in the top, take your time and gently remove the plastic. Be certain not to do any damage to the docking port on the bottom of the mini!

After the plastic cover is off, you will find a small metal clip. Using the tip of your flathead screwdriver in each corner of this metal clip, gently pry the clip free.

tip

Have an empty drinking glass handy to put your screws in so you don't lose them!

You will notice a small connector behind this bottom metal clip. Using the flathead screwdriver, you need to disconnect this clip from its socket. Don't forget to reattach this clip when you reassemble your iPod mini!

After the connector has been removed, you can gently push the guts of your iPod mini up from the bottom. The innards will slide up and out of the metal case.

The battery can now be lifted from its spot on the motherboard, unclipped, and replaced with your new battery.

Reverse the preceding steps, charge your new battery, and your iPod mini is ready to go!

iPod Shuffle

Alas, there is no way to replace the battery in an iPod shuffle. There are external AAA battery solutions and more found in the Apple Store, but after the internal battery of your iPod shuffle dies, it is time to buy a new shuffle.

Remember, however, that even when the shuffle is no longer able to hold a charge, you can still use it as a flash-memory storage solution with your Mac or PC. Think of it this way: For a few years, you have a great music player. After it dies, it is reincarnated as a removable USB Flash hard drive that can store anywhere from 512MB to 1GB or more of storage!

Index

SYMBOLS

! (Exclamation Point) problems (iPod), 76, 209

NUMBERS

3G Sportsuit Convertible (MAR-WARE), 251

A8 headphones (Bang & Olufsen), 226

A

AAC (Advanced Audio Coding) audio file format, 38, 46, 52, 58

AAC Encoder (Importing pane), 53-54

About screen (iPod)
software, viewing current version, 207
storage space, determining, 121

AC adapters (iPod), 18-19

accessories (iPod), 221
battery chargers, 249
car adapters
AirPlay (XtremeMac), 237
Car Charger (XtremeMac), 237
CPA-9C Car Cassette Adapter (Sony), 235
FireWire Car Charger (XtremeMac), 237
iCarPlay Wireless (Monster), 236
iPod Auto Kit (Belkin), 238
iTrip (Griffin), 236
PowerPod Auto Charger (Griffin), 238
TransPod FM (DLO), 239
TuneCast II Mobile FM Transmitter (Belkin), 235
TuneDok Car Holder (Belkin), 238

cases
3G Sportsuit Convertible (MARWARE), 251
Bumperz (XtremeMac), 253
Burton Shield iPod Jacket (Burton), 254
Flip Case (Belkin), 251
iPod Case (Anetagenova), 252
iPod Case (Gucci), 252
iPod Case (TimBuk2), 252
iPod shuffle Sports Case (Apple), 254
iPod Skins (Speck), 250
iPod Socks (Apple), 253
iStyle (Speck), 250
mini Sleevz (Radtech), 252
PodPaqnappa (BooqBags), 253
PodSleevz (Radtech), 252
Sheldon iPod Case (ebags), 250
Sportsuit Convertible Case (MARWARE), 251
Sportsuit Safari (MARWARE), 251
TuffWrapz (XtremeMac), 254
digital camera adapters
Digital Camera Link (Belkin), 241-242
iPod Camera Connector (Apple), 242
iPod Media Reader (Belkin), 241
docks
iDockCover (Westshore Craftworks), 249
iPod Dock (Apple), 248
iPod shuffle Dock (Apple), 248
Solar Charger (Solio), 249
USB 2.0 4-Port Hub (Belkin), 248

headphones
A8 headphones (Bang & Olufsen), 226
Apple, 222
audio splitters, 227
Bluewave Headphone headphones (Macally), 227
E2 Sound Isolating earphones (Shure), 222
E3 Sound Isolating earphones with Extended Frequency Response (Shure), 222
E5 Sound Isolating earphones (Shure), 223
i-Phono headphones (BlueTake), 227
MDR-EX71SL earphones (Sony), 224
MDR-G72LP headphones (Sony), 224
MDR-V300 headphones (Sony), 224
Nike Flight Lightweight headphones (Nike Phillips), 226
PCX250 Headphones (Sennheiser), 224
QuietComfort 2 Noise Cancellation Headphones (Bose), 223
QZ-2000 Technology Noise Reduction headphones (Koss), 225
safety, 225
SportaPro Traditional Collapsible headphones (Koss), 225
TriPort Headphones (Bose), 223
UE-10 Pro headphones (Ultimate Ears), 226
UR29 headphones (Koss), 225
polishing kits, 245

remote controls
    AirClick (Griffin), 244
    iDirect Wireless Remote (DLO), 244
    iJet Wireless RF Remote (ABT), 243
    iTop Button Relocator (Nyko), 244
speakers
    Cube Travel Speakers (Pacific Rim Technologies), 230
    Ezison personal speakers for iPod, 229
    iBoom (DLO), 233
    IceTune speakers (Macally), 232
    inMotion portable iPod speakers, 228
    iPal Portable Speaker with Tuner (Tivoli Audio), 230
    iPod Groove Bag Triplet and Tote (Dr. Bott), 229
    iSpeaker Portable (Monster), 232
    On Stage (JBL), 231
    On Tour (JBL), 231-232
    PocketParty Shuffle (PodGear), 234
    Podwave (Macally), 233
    SoundDock (Bose), 230
    SRS-T55 Folding Travel speakers (Sony), 229
stands, 246-247
stickers, 255
travel adapters, World Travel Adapter Kit (Apple), 242
voice recorders, 239-240

adapters
    AC adapters (iPod), 18-19
    car adapters, 179
        AirPlay (XtremeMac), 237
        Car Charger (XtremeMac), 237
        CPA-9C Car Cassette Adapter (Sony), 235
        FireWire Car Charger (XtremeMac), 237
        iCarPlay Wireless (Monster), 236
        iPod Auto Kit (Belkin), 238
        iTrip (Griffin), 236
        PowerPod Auto Charger (Griffin), 238
        TransPod FM (DLO), 239
        TuneCast II Mobile FM Transmitter (Belkin), 235

    TuneDok Car Holder (Belkin), 238
    cassette adapters, car stereo/iPod connections, 177
Add File to Library command (iTunes Music Library), 58
Add Folder to Library command (iTunes Music Library), 58
Add to Library command (iTunes Music Library), 58
Advanced pane (iTunes Preferences dialog)
    Browse For Folder dialog, 49
    Change Music Folder Location dialog, 49-50
    Copy files to iTunes Music Folder when adding to library option, 51
    iTunes Music folder, relocating, 47-49
    Keep iTunes music folder organized option, 51
AIFF (Audio Interchange File Format) file format, 39, 46
AirClick (Griffin), 244
AirPlay car adapter (XtremeMac), 237
Album column (Browser), 60
Album data field (iTunes Music Library), 81
albums
    artwork
        adding to songs, 92-94
        finding, 92
        viewing, 90-92
    browsing iPod music by, 145
    information, displaying (iPod Now Playing screen), 148
Anapod Explorer software (iPod), 263
Apple headphones, 222
Apple iPod Plug-in for MusicMatch Jukebox software (iPod), 263
Apple Lossless audio file format, 39-40, 46, 52
Apple Lossless Encoder (Importing pane), 53
Artist column Browser, 60
Artist data field
    iTunes Music Library, 81
    Search tool, 62

artists
    browsing iPod music by, 145
    information, displaying (iPod Now Playing screen), 148
Artwork pane (iTunes Music Library)
    adding album artwork to songs, 93-94
    viewing album artwork, 90
Attribute menu (Smart Playlists dialog), 109-110
audio CDs
    backups, 216
    copyright-protection, 37
    iTunes Music Library, 46
        batch importing to, 57-58
        import speeds, 56
        importing to, 41, 55-56
audio files
    AAC file format, 38, 46, 52, 58
    AIFF file format, 39, 46
    Apple Lossless file format, 39-40, 46, 52
    CD Audio file format
        backups, 216
        copyright-protection, 37
        importing, 41, 46, 55-58
    encoding, 36
    file size versus sound quality, 37, 52-53
    iPod, transferring to, 30-32
    iTunes Music Library
        importing to, 58
        storing in, 40
    missing song files (iTunes), troubleshooting, 216-218
    MP3 file format, 38, 46, 52, 58
    sound quality, 53
    WAV file format, 39, 46, 58
Audio Splitter (XtremeMac), 227
autos
    adapters, 179
        AirPlay (XtremeMac), 237
        Car Charger (XtremeMac), 237
        CPA-9C Car Cassette Adapter (Sony), 235
        FireWire Car Charger (XtremeMac), 237
        iCarPlay Wireless (Monster), 236
        iPod Auto Kit (Belkin), 238
        iTrip (Griffin), 236
        PowerPod Auto Charger (Griffin), 238

TransPod FM (DLO), 239
TuneCast II Mobile FM
Transmitter (Belkin), 235
TuneDok Car Holder (Belkin),
238
battery chargers
Car Charger (XtremeMac), 237
FireWire Car Charger
(XtremeMac), 237
iPod Auto Kit (Belkin), 238
PowerPod Auto Charger
(Griffin), 238
cassette adapters, 177, 235
iPod mounts, 179
iPod operation, 180
mounting kits
TransPod FM (DLO), 239
TuneDok Car Holder (Belkin),
238
stereos, iPod connections,
177-178

**Autofill tool (iPod shuffle),
136-137**

automatic updates (iTunes), 214

**Automatically Update All Songs
and Playlists synchronization
option (iPod), 123-128**

**Automatically Update Selected
Playlists Only synchronization
option (iPod), 123-124, 128-130**

B

**backlight (iPod), maximizing bat-
tery life, 201**

backups
iTunes Music Library, 216
photos in iPod, 186

**batch importing (CDs), iTunes
Music Library, 57-58**

batteries
chargers
Car Charger (XtremeMac), 237
FireWire Car Charger
(XtremeMac), 237
iPod Auto Kit (Belkin), 238
PowerPod Auto Charger
(Griffin), 238
Solar Charger (Solio), 249

iPod
charging, 19, 202-203
FM transmitters, 236
maximizing life of, 201
monitoring, 200
playing time ratings, 201, 204
replacing, 272-274
Toggle iPod Battery Status soft-
ware, 260
troubleshooting, 204-205
iPod mini, replacing in, 275-276
iPod shuffle
charging, 203
monitoring, 157, 200
playing time ratings, 204
replacing in, 276

Battery icon (iPod), 151, 200

**Battery Status button (iPod shuf-
fle), 200**

BiblePod software (iPod), 257

**Bit Rate song tags (iTunes Music
Library), 80**

**Bluewave Headphone wireless
headphones (Macally), 227**

boombox, iPod as, 176

**BPM data field (iTunes Music
Library), 81**

broadcasting iPod over FM, 175

**Browse For Folder dialog
(Advanced pane), 49**

Browser
iTunes Music Library
Album column, 60
Artist column, 60
Content pane, 60
expanding results, 60
hiding, 60
narrowing results, 60
opening/closing, 60
song tags, 82
viewing, 59
iTunes Music Store, podcasts, 68

Bumperz (XtremeMac), 253

**Burton Shield iPod Jacket (Burton),
254**

buying
iPod, 13
USB 2 cable, 18

C

cable
FireWire, iPod connections, 28
USB 2
Dock connections, 25
iPod connections, 27-28
purchasing, 18

**Camera Connector accessory
(iPod), 187-188**

cameras (digital)
adapters
Digital Camera Link (Belkin),
241-242
iPod Camera Connector
(Apple), 242
iPod Media Reader (Belkin),
241
photos, exporting to iPod,
187-189
memory cards, erasing, 189

cars
adapters, 179
AirPlay (XtremeMac), 237
Car Charger (XtremeMac), 237
CPA-9C Car Cassette Adapter
(Sony), 235
FireWire Car Charger
(XtremeMac), 237
iCarPlay Wireless (Monster),
236
iPod Auto Kit (Belkin), 238
iTrip (Griffin), 236
PowerPod Auto Charger
(Griffin), 238
TransPod FM (DLO), 239
TuneCast II Mobile FM
Transmitter (Belkin), 235
TuneDok Car Holder (Belkin),
238
battery chargers
Car Charger (XtremeMac), 237
FireWire Car Charger
(XtremeMac), 237
iPod Auto Kit (Belkin), 238
PowerPod Auto Charger
(Griffin), 238
cassette adapters, 177, 235
iPod mounts, 179
iPod operation, 180

mounting kits
- TransPod FM (DLO), 239
- TuneDok Car Holder (Belkin), 238

stereos, iPod connections, 177-178

cases (iPod)
- 3G Sportsuit Convertible (MARWARE), 251
- Bumperz (XtremeMac), 253
- Burton Shield iPod jacket (Burton), 254
- Flip Case (Belkin), 251
- iPod Case (Anetagenova), 252
- iPod Case (Gucci), 252
- iPod Case (TimBuk2), 252
- iPod shuffle Sports Case (Apple), 254
- iPod Skins (Speck), 250
- iPod Socks (Apple), 253
- iStyle (Speck), 250
- mini Sleevz (Radtech), 252
- PodPaqnappa (BooqBags), 253
- PodSleevz (Radtech), 252
- Sheldon iPod Case (ebags), 250
- Sportsuit Convertible Case (MARWARE), 251
- Sportsuit Safari (MARWARE), 251
- TuffWrapz (XtremeMac), 254

cassette adapters, car stereo/iPod connections, 177, 235

categorizing music
- iTunes Music Library data fields, 81
- song tags, 80-81

CDs
- backups, 216
- copyright-protection, 37
- iTunes Music Library, 46
  - batch importing to, 57-58
  - import speeds, 56
  - importing to, 41, 55-56

Change Music Folder Location dialog (Advanced pane), 49-50

Channels song tags (iTunes Music Library), 80

chargers (battery)
- Car Charger (XtremeMac), 237
- FireWire Car Charger (XtremeMac), 237
- iPod Auto Kit (Belkin), 238
- PowerPod Auto Charger (Griffin), 238
- Solar Charger (Solio), 249

charging batteries
- iPod, 19, 202-203
- iPod shuffle, 203

Check for iTunes Updates Automatically check box (General pane), 214

Check for new episodes drop-down list (Podcast tab), 66

Choose higher rated songs more often check box (iPod shuffle Autofill tool), 137

Choose songs randomly check box (iPod shuffle Autofill tool), 137

cleaning kits (iPod), 245

Click Wheel (iPod), Volume bar adjustments, 147

Clicker (iPod), configuring, 168

Comments data field (iTunes Music Library), 81

Composer data field (iTunes Music Library), 81

computers. See Macintosh; Windows PC

Condition dialog (Smart Playlists dialog), 109-110

Connect to Internet when needed check box (General pane), 214

Consolidate Library command (iTunes), 218

Content pane
- Browser, 60
- iTunes Music Library
  - customizing, 95-97
  - downloading podcast episodes, 74
  - Get button, 74
  - Information button, 75
  - labeling music, 87
  - Party Shuffle feature, 115-117
  - Play button, 75
  - playing podcast episodes, 75
  - Podcast Directory link, 75
  - rating songs, 89-90
  - song tags, 82-83
  - Unsubscribe button, 75
  - viewing podcast episode information, 75
- Search tool, 62

contrast (iPod screen), adjusting, 166

Convert higher bitrate songs to 128 kbps AAC for this iPod option (iPod shuffle), 135-136

Copy all photos and albums radio button (iPod Photos tab), 186

Copy files to iTunes Music Folder when adding to library option (Advanced pane), 51

Copy select albums only radio button (iPod Photos tab), 186

CopyPod software (iPod), 264

copyright-protection (CD Audio file format), 37

CPA-9C Car Cassette Adapter (Sony), 235

Create filenames with track number option (Importing pane), 54

Cube Travel Speakers (Pacific Rim Technologies), 230

customizing
- Content pane (iTunes Music Library), 95-97
- iPod appearance, 255
- music. See playlists

D

Date Modified song tags (iTunes Music Library), 80

Decrease Volume control (iPod shuffle), 156

default iPod installation location, 22

deleting
- commands from iPod Main menu, 165
- playlists
  - iPod playlists, 132
  - smart playlists, 116
- podcasts, 75-76
- songs
  - from iPod, 133
  - from iPod shuffle, 139
  - from iTunes Music Library, 64, 66
  - from playlists, 106
  - iTunes Music Store songs, 66
- standard playlists, 107

Details dialog (Importing pane), 54

Digital Camera Link (Belkin), 241-242

digital cameras
adapters
Digital Camera Link (Belkin), 241-242
iPod Camera Connector (Apple), 242
iPod Media Reader (Belkin), 241
photos, exporting to iPod, 187-189
memory cards, erasing, 189

Disc Number data field (iTunes Music Library), 81

disconnecting iPod from computer, 133-134

disk capacity (iPod), determining, 121

displaying
album artwork, 90-92
Browser (iTunes Music Library), 59
current iPod software version, 207
iTunes Music folder, 48
photos
on iPod, 189-193
on TV via iPod, 193
podcast episodes, 74-75
song tags in iTunes Music Library, 82-85

Do not disconnect messages (iPod), 32

Docks
iDockCover (Westshore Craftworks), 249
iPod connections, 25
computers with docks, 32-34
home stereo connections, 174
iPod Dock (Apple), 248
iPod shuffle Dock (Apple), 248
Solar Charger (Solio), 249
TransPod FM (DLO), 239
TuneDok Car Holder (Belkin), 238
USB 2.0 4-Port Hub (Belkin), 248

downloading
iTunes, 20
podcast episodes, 75

driving, iPod operation, 180

E

E2 Sound Isolating earphones (Shure), 222

E3 Sound Isolating earphones with Extended Frequency Response (Shure), 222

E5 Sound Isolating earphones (Shure), 223

earphones, 222
A8 earphones (Bang & Olufsen), 226
Apple, 222
audio splitters, 227
Bluewave Headphone earphones (Macally), 227
E2 Sound Isolating (Shure), 222
E3 Sound Isolating with Extended Frequency Response (Shure), 222
E5 Sound Isolating (Shure), 223
i-Phono BT420 earphones (BlueTake), 227
iPod connections, 18
iPod shuffle connections, 154
MDR-EX71SL earphones (Sony), 224
MDR-G72LP earphones (Sony), 224
MDR-V300 earphones (Sony), 224
Nike Flight Lightweight Sport earphones (Nike Phillips), 226
PCX250 Headphones (Sennheiser), 224
QuietComfort 2 Noise Cancellation Headphones (Bose), 223
QZ-2000 Technology Noise Reduction earphones (Koss), 225
safety, 225
SportaPro Traditional Collapsible earphones (Koss), 225
TriPort Headphones (Bose), 223
UE-10 Pro earphones (Ultimate Ears), 226
UR29 earphones (Koss), 225

editing
smart playlists, 114-115
song tags
multiple songs, 85
via Content pane (iTunes Music Library), 87
via Info Window (iTunes Music Library), 85

Ejector software (iPod), 258

Enable disk use option (iPod shuffle), 136

Encoded With song tags (iTunes Music Library), 81

encoders (music files), 36
AAC encoders, 53-54
Apple Lossless encoders, 53
choosing, 54
MP3 encoders, 53

episodes (podcasts)
downloading, 75
playing, 75
viewing all, 74
viewing information on, 75

Equalizer (iPod), 164, 202

Equalizer Preset option (iTunes Music Library), 88

erasing memory cards (digital cameras), 189

euPOD VolumeBoost software (iPod), 263

exclamation point (!) problems (iPod), 76, 209

exporting photos
to computer via iPod
manual exports, 196
photo management software, 195
to iPod
from computer connection, 186-187
from digital cameras, 187-189
photo management software, 184-186

Ezison personal speakers for iPod, 229

F

Fast-forward button (iPod), 146

Fast-Forward control (iPod shuffle), 155

fast-forwarding Timeline bar (iPod Now Playing screen), 148-149

Feed My Pod software (iPod), 262

file sharing (audio files), 58

FileMaker to iPod software (iPod), 261

files (audio)
AAC file format, 38, 46, 52, 58
AIFF file format, 39, 46
Apple Lossless file format, 39-40, 46, 52

CD Audio file format
  copyright-protection, 37
  importing, 41, 46, 55-58
  encoding, 36
  file size versus sound quality, 37, 52-53
  iPod, transferring to, 30-32
  iTunes Music Library
    importing to, 58
    storing in, 40
  missing song files (iTunes), troubleshooting, 216-218
  MP3 file format, 38, 46, 52, 58
  sound quality, 53
  WAV file format, 39, 46, 58

FireWire cable, iPod connections, 28

FireWire Car Charger (XtremeMac), 237

Flip Case (Belkin), 251

FM transmitters, 175
  AirPlay (XtremeMac), 237
  batteries, 236
  car stereo/iPod connections, 178
  iCarPlay Wireless (Monster), 236
  iTrip (Griffin), 236
  TransPod FM (DLO), 239
  TuneCast II Mobile (Belkin), 235

Format song tags (iTunes Music Library), 80

Fountain Music screensaver software (iTunes), 268

freeware. *See also* **shareware; software**
  defining, 256
  iPod
    Apple iPod Plug-in for MusicMatch Jukebox, 263
    BiblePod, 257
    BOllie's iPod Extractor, 259
    Ejector, 258
    euPOD VolumeBoost, 263
    Feed My Pod, 262
    FileMaker to iPod, 261
    GoogleGet, 262
    iPod Play List Cloner, 260
    iPodLibrary, 264
    iStoryCreator, 264
    k-pod, 263
    Lyricpod, 261
    MyPodPlayer, 264
    OmniOutliner Export to iPod, 261
    Pod2Go, 257
    PodMail, 258
    Rip to iPod, 260
    Slurp, 261
    Weather For Me, 262
    WinniePod Updater, 264
  iTunes
    Fountain Music, 268
    iEatBrainz, 267
    iTunes Alarm, 267
    iTunes Timer, 266
    iTunesBrushKiller, 268
    iTunesRating, 268
    LED Spectrum Analyzer, 269
    Name That iTune!, 266
    vTunes, 269
    WhiteCap, 269

full-resolution photos, 186

G – H

G-Force screensaver software (iTunes), 269

General pane (iTunes Preferences dialog)
  Check for iTunes Updates Automatically check box, 214
  Connect to Internet when needed check box, 214
  Import Songs and Eject option, 57
  Show genre when browsing option, 59

Genre data field (iTunes Music Library), 81

genres, labeling music by, 86

Get button (Content pane), downloading podcast episodes, 74

GoogleGet software (iPod), 262

Grouping data field (iTunes Music Library), 81

Habitat (Bubble Design), 246

hacks
  iPod
    battery replacement, 272-274
    warranties, 272
  iPod mini, 275-276
  iPod shuffle, 276

headphones
  A8 headphones (Bang & Olufsen), 226
  Apple, 222
  audio splitters, 227
  Bluewave Headphone wireless headphones (Macally), 227
  E2 Sound Isolating earphones (Shure), 222
  E3 Sound Isolating earphones with Extended Frequency Response (Shure), 222
  E5 Sound Isolating earphones (Shure), 223
  i-Phono BT420 wireless headphones (BlueTake), 227
  iPod earbud headphones, 18
  iPod shuffle connections, 154
  MDR-EX71SL earphones (Sony), 224
  MDR-G72LP headphones (Sony), 224
  MDR-V300 headphones (Sony), 224
  Nike Flight Lightweight Sport headphones (Nike Phillips), 226
  PCX250 headphones (Sennheiser), 224
  QuietComfort 2 Noise Cancellation headphones (Bose), 223
  QZ-2000 Technology Noise Reduction headphones (Koss), 225
  safety, 225
  SportaPro Traditional Collapsible headphones (Koss), 225
  TriPort headphones (Bose), 223
  UE-10 Pro headphones (Ultimate Ears), 226
  UR29 headphones (Koss), 225

help
  iPod
    battery, troubleshooting, 205
    help websites, 210-211
  iTunes, Check for iTunes Updates command (iTunes), 215

hiding Browser (iTunes Music Library), 60

Hold feature (iPod)
  battery life, maximizing, 201
  troubleshooting, 208

Hold mode (iPod shuffle), 157

home stereos, iPod connections, 172-175

hubs, USB 2.0 4-Port Hub (Belkin), 248

I

i-Phono BT420 wireless headphones (BlueTake), 227

iBoom speakers (DLO), 233

iCarPlay Wireless car adapter (Monster), 236

Ice Creme polishing kit (RadTech), 245

IceTune speakers (Macally), 232

iCleaner Ultra Pro Kit (iCleaner), 245

ID3 Tag song tags (iTunes Music Library), 81

iDirect Wireless Remote (DLO), 244

iDockCover (Westshore Craftworks), 249

iEatBrainz software (iTunes), 267

iJet Wireless RF Remote (ABT), 243

illegal file sharing, 58

IM3c speakers (Altec Lansing), 177

images
album artwork
adding to songs, 92-94
finding, 92
viewing, 90-92
full-resolution photos, 186
iPod
backups, 186
configuring slideshows, 191-192
exporting to computer, 195-196
importing to, 184-189
monochrome screen iPod, 184
saving in, 186
slideshows, 193
viewing on, 189-190
TV, viewing iPod slideshows on, 193

Import Songs and Eject option (General pane), 57

importing
music to iTunes Music Library
audio files, 58
CDs, 41, 55-58
format options, 52-53
Internet, 41
iTunes Music Store, 41
setting preferences, 54
sound quality, 52-53
photos to iPod
from computer connection, 186-187
from digital cameras, 187-189
photo management software, 184-186

Importing pane (iTunes Preferences dialog)
AAC Encoder, 53-54
Apple Lossless Encoder, 53
Create filenames with track number option, 54
Details dialog, 54
MP3 Encoder, 53
Play songs while importing option, 54
Use error correction when reading Audio CD option, 54

Include full-resolution photos check box (iPod Photos tab), 186

Increase Volume control (iPod shuffle), 155

Info window (iTunes Music Library)
labeling music, 85
song tags, 83-85
Summary pane, viewing song information, 84

Information button (Content pane), viewing podcast episode information, 75

information pamphlets (iPod), 18

inMotion portable iPod speakers, 228

installation CD (iPod), 18
Macintosh software installation, 23-24
Windows PC software installation
default iPod installation location, 22
installation language selection, 20
iPod registration, 21
iTunes installation, 22

installing software
licensing agreements, 256
updates, 257
virus detection, 257

InstallShield Wizard, iPod installation (Windows PC), 20

Internet
iTunes Music Library, importing music to, 41
podcasts, subscribing to, 72

iPal Portable Speaker with Tuner (Tivoli Audio), 230

iPod
About screen
determining storage space, 121
viewing current software version, 207
AC adapters, 18-19
accessories, 221
audio splitters, 227
battery chargers, 237-238, 249
car adapters, 179, 235-239
cases, 250-254
digital camera adapters, 241-242
docks, 248-249
headphones, 222-227
polishing kits, 245
remote controls, 243-244
speakers, 228-233
stands, 246-247
stickers, 255
travel adapters, World Travel Adapter Kit (Apple), 242
voice recorders, 239-240
appearance, customizing, 255
backlight, maximizing battery life, 201
batteries
charging, 19, 202-203
maximizing life of, 201-202
monitoring, 200
playing time ratings, 201, 204
Toggle iPod Battery Status software, 204
troubleshooting, 204-205
Battery icon, 151, 200
box contents, 18-19
Camera Connector accessory, 187-188
cars
mounts, 179
operating in, 180
stereo connections, 177-178

choosing, 13
Click Wheel, Volume bar adjustments, 147
Clicker, configuring, 168
components of, 8, 18-19
computer connections, 133-134
configuring, 29
digital cameras, erasing memory cards, 189
disk capacity, determining, 121
Do not disconnect messages, 32
earbud headphones, 18
Equalizer, 164, 202
exclamation point (!) problems, 209
file transfers, playing music during, 30
FireWire cable, computer connections, 28
FM transmitters, 175
functions of, 14
hacks
    battery replacement, 272-274
    warranties, 272
Hold feature
    battery life, maximizing, 201
    troubleshooting, 208
home stereo connections, 175
    direct connections, 172-173
    via Dock, 174
information pamphlets, 18
installation CD, 18
    Macintosh software installation, 23-24
    Windows PC software installation, 20-22
iPod update is complete messages, 31
iTune Music Library
    Automatically Update All Songs and Playlists synchronization option, 123-128
    Automatically Update Selected Playlists Only synchronization option, 123-124, 128-130
    Manually Manage Songs and Playlists synchronization option, 124-125, 130
    playlist updates, 125
iTunes
    compatibility, 42
    downloading, 20
    troubleshooting connections, 210

language (operational)
    resetting, 169
    selecting, 168
Macintosh connections
    Dock connections, 25
    FireWire cable, 28
    Macs with Docks, 32-34
    USB 2 cable, 27-28
Main menu
    adding/removing commands, 165
    resetting preferences, 166
    setting preferences, 165-166
model availability information website, 9
music
    browsing, 143-146
    On-The-Go playlists, 150-151
    playing entire playlists, 142
    rating, 149-150
    removing playlists, 132
    removing songs, 133
    selecting from playlists, 142
    shuffling, 160-162
    track changes, maximizing battery life, 201
    transferring files to, 30-32
    updating playlists, 131-133
Music menu, browsing music, 144-146
naming, 30
Next/Fast-forward button, 146
Now Playing screen
    album information, 148
    artist information, 148
    features of, 148
    number of song out of total selected information, 148
    song title information, 148
    Timeline bar, 148-149
OK to disconnect messages, 31
On-The-Go playlists, 150-151
Options dialog, Photos tab, 185
Pause button, maximizing battery life, 201
photo AV Cable, 193
photos
    backups, 186
    configuring slideshows, 191-192
    exporting to computer, 195-196
    importing, 184-189
    monochrome screen iPod, 184
    saving in, 186

    slideshow/TV connections, 193
    viewing, 189-190, 193
Play/Pause button, 142, 146
playlists
    On-The-Go playlists, 150-151
    removing, 132
    transferring, 32
    updating, 131-133
Playlists menu, selecting music from playlists, 142
portable stereo, iPod as, 176
Previous/Rewind button, 146
reformatting, 29
registering, 21, 30
Repeat feature, 162-163
Reset All Settings command, 169
resetting, 208
restoring, 209
screen
    adjusting contrast, 166
    monochrome screen iPod, 184
Select button, starting playlists from a specific song, 142
Shuffle feature, 160
Shuffle Songs command, 161-162
size of, 8
Sleep mode, maximizing battery life, 201
Sleep Timer, 167
Slideshow Settings menu, 191-192
software
    Macintosh format software, 257-261
    restoring, 205-207
    updating, 205-207
    Windows PC format software, 262-264
Sound Check setting, 163-164
specifications of, 10
track changes, maximizing battery life, 201
troubleshooting
    checking basics, 208
    exclamation point (!) problems, 209
    help websites, 210-211
    iTunes connections, 210
    resetting iPod, 208
    restoring iPod, 209
Updater page, 205-207
USB 2 cable, 18
    computer connections, 27-28
    Dock connections, 25
    purchasing, 18
Volume bar, adjusting, 147

Windows PC connections
Dock connections, 25
FireWire cable, 28
PCs with Docks, 32-34
USB 2 cable, 27-28
iPod Access software (iPod), 260
iPod Auto Kit (Belkin), 238
iPod Camera Connector (Apple), 242
iPod Groove Bag Triplet and Tote (Dr. Bott), 229
iPod Case (Anetagenova), 252
iPod Case (Gucci), 252
iPod Case (TimBuk2), 252
iPod Decloak software (iPod), 260
iPod Dock (Apple), 248
iPod installer, iPod software installation (Macintosh), 23
iPod It software (iPod), 258
iPod Launcher software (iPod), 258
iPod Media Reader (Belkin), 241
iPod mini. See also iPod
accessories. *See also* iPod, accessories
digital camera adapters, 241
speakers, inMotion portable iPod speakers, 228
voice recorders, 239
hacks, battery replacement, 275-276
specification of, 11
iPod Organizer software (iPod), 259
iPod Photo
backups, 186
battery replacement, 274
computer, exporting to, 195-196
configuring, 191-192
importing to, 184-189
monochrome screen iPod, 184
photos, viewing, 189-190
saving in, 186
slideshows
configuring, 191-192
viewing on TV, 193
iPod Play List Cloner software (iPod), 260
iPod Setup Assistant, transferring iTunes music files to iPod, 30-32

iPod shuffle
accessories. *See* iPod, accessories
Autofill tool
Choose higher rated songs more often check box, 137
Choose songs randomly check box, 137
music updates, 136-137
Replace all songs when Autofilling check box, 137
battery
charging, 203
monitoring, 157, 200
playing time ratings, 204
replacing, 276
Battery Status button, 200
computer connections, 137
Convert higher bitrate songs to 128 kbps AAC for this iPod option, 135-136
Decrease Volume control, 156
earbud connections, 154
Enable disk use option, 136
hacks, battery replacement, 276
headphone connections, 154
Hold mode, 157
Increase Volume control, 155
Keep this iPod in the source list option, 135
Macintosh connections, 26
manual updates, 138
music, selecting/shuffling, 155
Next/Fast-Forward control, 155
Only update checked songs option, 135
Open iTunes when this iPod is attached option, 135
Play/Pause control, 155
activating Hold mode, 157
moving to beginning of playlists, 156
playlists, moving to beginning of, 156
preferences, configuring, 134-136
Previous/Rewind control, 156
songs, removing from, 139
specifications of, 12
turning on/off, 155-156
updates, 135
USB ports, 135
Windows PC connections, 26
iPod shuffle Dock (Apple), 248
iPod shuffle Sports Case (Apple), 254
iPod Skins (Speck), 250

iPod Socks (Apple), 253
iPod U2 Special Edition, 10
iPod Update, 24, 29
iPod update is complete messages (iPod), 31
iPod.iTunes software (iPod), 259
iPodLibrary software (iPod), 264
iPodRip software (iPod), 259
iSpeak It software (iPod), 258-259
iSpeaker Portable speakers (Monster), 232
iStoryCreator software (iPod), 264
iStyle (Speck), 250
iTalk (Griffin), 240
iTop Button Relocator (Nyko), 244
iTrip (Griffin), 236
iTunes
audio files
AAC file format, 38
AIFF file format, 39
Apple Lossless file format, 39-40
CD Audio file format, 37
encoding, 36
file size versus sound quality, 37
MP3 file format, 38
storing, 40
transferring to iPod, 30-32
WAV file format, 39
Consolidate Library command, 218
functions of, 36
Help, Check for iTunes Updates command, 215
iPod
compatibility, 42
downloading to, 20
troubleshooting connections, 210
iTunes Music Store, 42
Macintosh
installing via iPod installation CD, 24
manual updates, 215
troubleshooting, support for, 218-219
Music folder
default location of, 47
organizing, setting preferences, 50-51

relating, 49
    viewing, 48
playlists, 32, 120
Preferences dialog
    Advanced pane, 47-51
    General pane, 57-59, 214
    Importing pane, 53-54
software
    iEatBrainz, 267
    iTunes Alarm, 267
    iTunes Library Manager, 266
    iTunes Publisher, 266
    iTunes Timer, 266
    iTunesBrushKiller, 268
    iTunesCool, 267
    iTunesRating, 268
    Name That iTune!, 266
    NiceCast, 265
    RadioLover, 266
    RockStar, 265
    screensaver software, 268-269
    Synergy, 267
    Track Manager, 268
troubleshooting
    Macintosh support, 218-219
    missing song files, 216-218
    Windows PC support, 218
updates
    automatic updates, 214
    manual updates, 215
Windows PC
    installing via iPod installation
        CD, 22
    manual updates, 215
    troubleshooting, support for,
        218

**iTunes Alarm software (iTunes),
267**

**iTunes Library Manager software
(iTunes), 266**

iTunes Music Library, 40, 120
    Add File to Library command, 58
    Add Folder to Library command,
        58
    Add to Library command, 58
    Album data field, 81
    Artist data field, 81
    Artwork pane
        adding album artwork to
            songs, 93-94
        viewing album artwork, 90
    backups, 216
    BPM data field, 81

Browser
    Album column, 60
    Artist column, 60
    Content pane, 60
    expanding results, 60
    hiding, 60
    narrowing results, 60
    opening/closing, 60
    song tags, 82
    viewing, 59
CDs, as music source, 46
Comments data field, 81
Composer data field, 81
Consolidate Library command,
    218
Content pane
    customizing, 95-97
    Get button, 74
    Information button, 75
    labeling music, 87
    Party Shuffle feature, 115-117
    Play button, 75
    Podcast Directory link, 75
    rating songs, 89-90
    song tags, 82-83
    Unsubscribe button, 75
Disc Number data field, 81
Equalizer Preset option, 88
Genre data field, 81
Grouping data field, 81
importing music
    audio files, 58
    CDs, 41, 55-58
    format options, 52-53
    Internet, 41
    iTunes Music Store, 41
    setting preferences, 54
    sound quality, 52-53
Info window
    configuring song options,
        88-89
    labeling music, 85
    song tags, 83-85
    Summary pane, viewing song
        information, 84
iPod synchronization
    Automatically Update All
        Songs and Playlists, 123-128
    Automatically Update Selected
        Playlists Only, 123-124,
        128-130
    Manually Manage Songs and
        Playlists, 124-125, 130
    playlists updates, 125

iTunes Music Store, as music
    source, 46
music
    configuring options, 87-89
    deleting, 64-66
    playing, 64
    rating via Content pane, 89-90
    sources of, 46
My Rating option, 88-90
Name data field, 81
Part of a Compilation data field,
    81
playlists, 41
Podcast tab
    Check for new episodes drop-
        down list, 66
    Keep drop-down list, 67
    When new episodes are avail-
        able drop-down list, 67
podcasts
    downloading episodes, 75
    playing episodes, 75
    setting preferences, 66-67
    viewing all episodes, 74
    viewing episode information,
        75
Relative Volume option, 87
Search tool, 62
Show/Hide Song Artwork button,
    90
size of, determining, 121
Smart Playlists dialog
    Attribute menu, 109-110
    Condition dialog, 109-110
    Limit to check box, 111
    Live updating check box, 112
    Match only checked songs
        check box, 112
    Operand menu, 109-110
    selected by menu, 112
song tags
    Bit Rate, 80
    Channels, 80
    Date Modified, 80
    editing, 85
    editing via Content pane, 87
    editing via Info window, 85
    Encoded With, 81
    Format, 80
    ID3 Tag, 81
    Kind, 80
    Last Played, 80
    Play Count, 80
    Profile, 80

Purchase By, Account Name, and FairPlay Version, 81
Sample Rate, 80
Size, 80
viewing, 82-85
Where, 81
songs
   configuring options, 87-89
   deleting, 64-66
   playing, 64
   rating via Content pane, 89-90
   sources for, 46
Start and Stop Time option, 88-89
Track Number data field, 81
Volume Adjustment slider, 88
Year data field, 81
iTunes Music Store, 42
   Browser, 68
   iTunes Music Library
      as music source, 46
      importing music to, 41
   music, deleting from, 66
   podcasts, subscribing to, 68-71
iTunes Publisher software (iTunes), 266
iTunes Timer software (iTunes), 266
iTunesBrushKiller software (iTunes), 268
iTunesCool software (iTunes), 267
iTunesRating software (iTunes), 268

J – K – L

k-pod software (iPod), 263
Keep drop-down list (Podcast tab), 67
Keep iTunes music folder organized option (Advanced pane), 51
Keep this iPod in the source list option (iPod shuffle), 135
Kind song tags (iTunes Music Library), 80

labeling music
   by genre, 86
   multiple songs, 85

via Content pane (iTunes Music Library), 87
via Info window (iTunes Music Library), 85
languages (iPod operational)
   choosing, 20, 168
   resetting, 169
Last Played song tags (iTunes Music Library), 80
leather flip cases (Belkin), 251
LED Spectrum Analyzer screen-saver software (iTunes), 269
Library (iTunes). *See* iTunes Music Library
licensing agreements (software), 256
Limit to check box (Smart Playlists dialog), 111
listening
   to playlists
      setting play order, 106
      smart playlists, 114
      standard playlists, 107
   to podcasts
      episodes, 75
      iTunes Music Library, 71
live updates, smart playlists, 108
Live updating check box (Smart Playlists dialog), 112
Lossless (Apple) audio file format, 39-40, 46, 52
Lyripod software (iPod), 261

M

Macintosh
   Change Music Folder Location dialog (iTunes), 49-50
   iPod
      Dock connections, 25, 32-34
      FireWire cable connections, 28
      software, 23-24, 257-261
      USB 2 cable connections, 27-28
   iPod shuffle connections, 26
   iTunes
      installation, 24
      manual updates, 215
      relocating Music folder, 47-49
      software, 265-269

troubleshooting support, 218-219
updates, 215
iTunes Music Library, Add to Library command, 58
Move to Recycle Bin, 65
Software Update window, iTunes updates, 215
Main menu (iPod)
   commands, adding to/removing from, 165
   preferences, setting, 165-166
   Shuffle Songs command, 161-162
manual updates (iTunes), 215
Manually Manage Songs and Playlists synchronization option (iPod), 124-125, 130
Match only checked songs check box (Smart Playlists dialog), 112
MDR-EX71SL earphones (Sony), 224
MDR-G72LP headphones (Sony), 224
MDR-V300 headphones (Sony), 224
media readers
   Digital Camera Link (Belkin), 241-242
   iPod Camera Connector (Apple), 242
   iPod Media Reader (Belkin), 241
mini Sleevz (Radtech), 252
missing song files (iTunes), troubleshooting, 216-218
Mobile Juice Shuffle Art stickers (Shuffle-Art), 255
ModPod (MacSkinz), 247
monochrome screen iPod, storing/viewing photos, 184
mounting kits (car)
   TransPod FM (DLO), 239
   TuneDok Car Holder (Belkin), 238
Move to Recycle Bin (Windows PC), 65
Move to Trash (Macintosh), 65
movie sound clips, 39

moving
iTunes Music folder location, 49
music from iTunes Music Library to
iPod
Automatically Update All
Songs and Playlists option,
123-128
Automatically Update Selected
Playlists Only option,
123-124, 128-130
Manually Manage Songs and
Playlists option, 124-125,
130
photos
to computer via iPod, 195-196
to iPod, 184-189

**MP3 audio file format, 38, 46, 52,
58**

MP3 Encoder (Importing pane), 53

music
album artwork
adding to songs, 92-94
finding, 92
viewing, 90-92
audio files
AAC file format, 38, 46, 52,
58
AIFF file format, 39, 46
Apple Lossless file format,
39-40, 46, 52
CD Audio file format, 37, 41,
46, 55-58
encoding, 36
file size versus sound quality,
37, 52-53
importing to iTunes Music
Library, 58
troubleshooting missing song
files (iTunes), 216-218
MP3 file format, 38, 46, 52,
58
sound quality, 53
storing in iTunes Music Library,
40
transferring to iPod, 30-32
WAV file format, 39, 46, 58
categorizing
iTunes Music Library data
fields, 81
song tags, 80-81
CDs
copyright-protection, 37
iTunes Music Library, importing
to, 41, 46, 55-58

configuring options, Info window
(iTunes Music Library), 87-89
customizing. *See* playlists
format options, 52-53
iPod
browsing, 143-146
playlists, 142
rating in, 149-150
Repeat feature, 162-163
Shuffle feature, 160
Shuffle Songs command,
161-162
Sound Check setting, 163-164
Volume bar, 147
iPod shuffle
adjusting volume, 155-156
selecting/shuffling in, 155
iTunes Music Library
adjusting volume, 87-90
configuring options in, 87-89
importing to, 52-58
labeling, 85-87
playing in, 64
rating in, 89-90
labeling
by genre, 86
multiple songs, 85
via iTunes Music Library, 85-87
On-The-Go playlists (iPod),
150-151
organizing
iTunes Music Library data
fields, 81
song tags, 80-81
playlists
iPod, 142
location of, 103
naming, 103
smart playlists, 101, 108-115
standard playlists, 100-107
uses of, 101
sound quality, 53
volume, adjusting in
iPod, 147, 163-164
iPod shuffle, 155-156
iTunes Music Library, 87-90

Music Library (iTunes). *See* **iTunes
Music Library**

Music menu (iPod)
browsing music, 144-146
Playlists menu, selecting music
from playlists, 142

Music Store (iTunes). *See* **iTunes
Music Store**

**MusicMatch Jukebox plug-in soft-
ware (iPod), 263**

**My Rating option (iTunes Music
Library), 88-90**

MyPodPlayer software (iPod), 264

N – O

**Name data field (iTunes Music
Library), 81**

**Name That iTune! software
(iTunes), 266**

naming
iPod, 30
playlists, 103
smart playlists, 113

**Next/Fast-forward button (iPod),
146**

**Next/Fast-Forward control (iPod
shuffle), 155**

NiceCast software (iTunes), 265

**Nike Flight Lightweight Sport
headphones (Nike Phillips), 226**

**Now Playing screen (iPod),
148-149**

**number of song out of total
selected information (iPod Now
Playing screen), 148**

**OK to disconnect messages (iPod),
31**

**Ollie's iPod Extractor software
(iPod), 259**

**OmniOutliner Export to iPod soft-
ware (iPod), 261**

On Stage (JBL), 231

**On Tour portable speakers (JBL),
231-232**

**On-The-Go playlists (iPod),
150-151**

**Only update checked songs option
(iPod shuffle), 135**

**Open iTunes when this iPod is
attached option (iPod shuffle),
135**

**Operand menu (Smart Playlists
dialog), 109-110**

Options dialog (iPod), Photos tab
Copy all photos and albums radio button, 186
Copy select albums only radio button, 186
Include full-resolution photos check box, 186
Synchronize photos from check box, 185

organizing
iTunes Music folder, setting preferences, 50-51
music
iTunes Music Library data fields, 81
song tags, 80-81

P

pamphlets (iPod), 18

Part of a Compilation data field (iTunes Music Library), 81

Party Shuffle feature (Content pane), 115-117

Pause button (iPod). *See* **Play/Pause button (iPod)**

Pause control (iPod shuffle). *See* **Play/Pause control (iPod shuffle)**

PC (Windows)
iPod
Dock connections, 25, 32-34
FireWire cable connections, 28
software, 20-22, 262-264
USB 2 cable connections, 27-28
iPod shuffle connections, 26
iTunes
manual updates, 215
relocating Music folder, 47-49
troubleshooting support, 218
iTunes Music Library, 58
Move to Recycle Bin, 65

PCX250 headphones (Sennheiser), 224

photo AV Cable (iPod), 193

photos
album artwork
adding to songs, 92-94
finding, 92
viewing, 90-92
full-resolution photos, 186

iPod
backups, 186
configuring slideshows, 191-192
exporting to computer, 195-196
importing to, 184-189
monochrome screen iPod, 184
saving in, 186
slideshows, 193
viewing on, 189-190
TV, viewing iPod slideshows on, 193

Photos tab (iPod Options dialog), 185-186

pictures. *See* **photos**

Play button (Content pane), podcast episodes, 75

Play Count song tags (iTunes Music Library), 80

Play songs while importing option (Importing pane), 54

Play/Pause button (iPod), 146
battery life, maximizing, 201
playlists, playing, 142

Play/Pause control (iPod shuffle), 155
Hold mode, 157
playlists, moving to beginning of, 156

playing time ratings
iPod batteries, 201, 204
iPod shuffle batteries, 204

playlists, 32, 41, 103
Automatically Update All Songs and Playlists synchronization option (iPod/iTunes Music Library), 123-128
Automatically Update Selected Playlists Only synchronization option (iPod/iTunes Music Library), 123-124, 128-130
iPod playlists
deleting, 132
iTunes Music Library synchronization, 123-130
On-The-Go playlists, 150-151
playing entire playlists, 142
selecting music from, 142
updating, 131-133
iPod shuffle playlists, moving to beginning of, 156

iTunes Music Library
backups, 216
iPod synchronization, 123-130
iTunes playlists, 120
Manually Manage Songs and Playlists synchronization option (iPod/iTunes Music Library), 124-125, 130
naming, 103
On-The-Go playlists, 150-151
smart playlists, 101
creating, 108, 110-114
default playlists, 108
deleting, 116
editing, 114-115
limiting, 111
listening to, 114
live updating, 108
naming, 113
standard playlists, 100
adding songs to, 105-106
creating empty playlists, 102
creating playlists from selected songs, 103-104
deleting, 107
listening to, 107
removing songs from, 106
setting play order, 106
updating, 125
uses of, 101

Playlists menu (iPod Music menu), 142

plug-ins, MusicMatch plug-in software (iPod), 263

PocketMac iPod Edition software (iPod), 263

PocketParty Shuffle (PodGear), 234

Pod2Go software (iPod), 257

PodBoard (Alscher), 247

Podcast Directory link (Content pane), 75

Podcast tab (iTunes Music Library)
Check for new episodes drop-down list, 66
Keep drop-down list, 67
When new episodes are available drop-down list, 67

podcasts, 46
episodes
downloading, 75
playing, 75
viewing all, 74
viewing information on, 75

exclamation point (!) icons, 76
iTunes Music Library
playing in, 71
setting preferences, 66-67
iTunes Music Store
browsing in, 68
searching in, 70
subscribing to, 68-70
removing, 75-76
subscribing to, 68-72
troubleshooting, 76
unsubscribing from, 75

PodHolder (PodShop), 247

PodMail software (iPod), 258

PodPaqnappa (BooqBags), 253

PodQuest software (iPod), 261

PodSleevz (Radtech), 252

Podwave (Macally), 233

PodWorks software (iPod), 257

polishing kits (iPod), 245

portable speakers
Cube Travel Speakers (Pacific Rim Technologies), 230
Ezison personal speakers for iPod, 229
iBoom (DLO), 233
IceTune speakers (Macally), 232
inMotion portable iPod speakers, 228
iPal Portable Speaker with Tuner (Tivoli Audio), 230
iPod Groove Bag Triplet and Tote (Dr. Bott), 229
iSpeaker Portable (Monster), 232
On Stage (JBL), 231
On Tour (JBL), 231-232
PocketParty Shuffle (PodGear), 234
Podwave (Macally), 233
SoundDock (Bose), 230
SRS-T55 Folding Travel speakers (Sony), 229

portable stereo, iPod as, 176

power (iPod). *See* **battery (iPod)**

PowerPod Auto Charger (Griffin), 238

Preferences dialog (iTunes)
Advanced pane
Copy files to iTunes Music Folder when adding to library option, 51

Keep iTunes music folder organized option, 51
locating iTunes Music folder, 47
relocating iTunes Music folder, 49
General pane
Check for iTunes Updates Automatically check box, 214
Connect to Internet when needed check box, 214
Import Songs and Eject option, 57
Show genre when browsing option, 59
Importing pane
AAC Encoder, 53-54
Apple Lossless Encoder, 53
Create filenames with track number option, 54
Details dialog, 54
MP3 Encoder, 53
Play songs while importing option, 54
Use error correction when reading CDs option, 54

Previous/Rewind button (iPod), 146

Previous/Rewind control (iPod shuffle), 156

printable tattoos (HP), 255

Profile song tags (iTunes Music Library), 80

Purchase By, Account Name, and FairPlay Version song tags (iTunes Music Library), 81

purchasing
iPod, 13
USB 2 cable, 18

Q – R

quality levels (music), 53

QuickTime, troubleshooting iTunes, 217

QuietComfort 2 Noise Cancellation headphones (Bose), 223

QZ-2000 Technology Noise Reduction headphones (Koss), 225

RadioLover software (iTunes), 266

Rating display (iPod Timeline bar), 149

rating music
in iPod, 149-150
via Content pane (iTunes Music Library), 89-90

recharging batteries
iPod, 202-203
iPod shuffle, 203

reformatting iPod, 29

registering iPod, 21, 30

Relative Volume option (iTunes Music Library), 87

relocating iTunes Music folder, 49

remote controls
Airclick (Griffin), 244
iDirect Wireless Remote (DLO), 244
iJet Wireless RF Remote (ABT), 243
iTop Button Relocator (Nyko), 244

removing
commands from iPod Main menu, 165
playlists
iPod playlists, 132
smart playlists, 116
podcasts, 75-76
songs
from iPod, 133
from iPod shuffle, 139
from iTunes Music Library, 64, 66
from playlists, 106
iTunes Music Store songs, 66
standard playlists, 107

Repeat feature (iPod), 162-163

Replace all songs when Autofilling check box (iPod shuffle Autofill tool), 137

Reset All Settings command (iPod), 169

resetting iPod, 208

restoring
iPod, 209
iPod software, 205, 207

Rewind button (iPod). *See* **Previous/Rewind button (iPod)**

Rewind control (iPod shuffle). *See* **Previous/Rewind control (iPod shuffle)**

rewinding Timeline bar (iPod Now Playing screen), 148-149

Rip to iPod software (iPod), 260

ripping. *See* importing

RockStar software (iTunes), 265

S

Sample Rate song tags (iTunes Music Library), 80

saving photos in iPod, 186

screen (iPod)
    contrast, adjusting, 166
    monochrome screen iPod, storing/viewing photos, 184

screensaver software (iTunes), 268-269

Search tool (iTunes Music Library), 62

searches
    iTunes Music Library searches, 62
    podcast searches in iTunes Music Store, 70

Select button (iPod), starting playlists from specific songs, 142

selected by menu (Smart Playlists dialog), 112

serial numbers, iPod installation (Windows PC), 21

Setup Assistant (iPod), transferring iTunes music files to iPod, 30-32

shareware, 256. *See also* freeware; software

Sheldon iPod Case (ebags), 250

Show genre when browsing option (General pane), 59

Show/Hide Song Artwork button (iTunes Music Library), 90

shuffle (iPod)
    Autofill tool, 136-137
    battery
        charging, 203
        monitoring, 157, 200
    Battery Status button, 200
    computer connections, 137
    Convert higher bitrate songs to 128 kbps AAC for this iPod option, 135-136

Decrease Volume control, 156
earbud connections, 154
Enable disk use option, 136
headphone connections, 154
Hold mode, 157
Increase Volume control, 155
Keep this iPod in the source list option, 135
manual updates, 138
music
    removing songs, 139
    selecting/shuffling, 155
Next/Fast-Forward control, 155
Only update checked songs option, 135
Open iTunes when this iPod is attached option, 135
Play/Pause control, 155
    Hold mode, 157
    moving to beginning of playlists, 156
playing time ratings, 204
playlists, moving to beginning of, 156
preferences, configuring, 134-136
Previous/Rewind control, 156
songs
    removing, 139
    selecting/shuffling, 155
turning on/off, 155-156
updates, 135
USB ports, 135

Shuffle feature (iPod), 160

Shuffle Songs command (iPod), 161-162

Size song tags (iTunes Music Library), 80

Skin EFX iPod Stickers (iPod-Skins), 255

Sleep mode (iPod), maximizing battery life, 201

Sleep Timer (iPod), 167

Slideshow Settings menu (iPod), 191-192

slideshows
    iPod
        configuring on, 191-192
        viewing on, 193
    TV, viewing on, 193

Slurp software (iPod), 261

Smart Playlist dialog (iTunes Music Library)
    Attribute menu, 109-110
    Condition dialog, 109-110
    Limit to check box, 111
    Live updating check box, 112
    Match only checked songs check box, 112
    Operand menu, 109-110
    selected by menu, 112

smart playlists, 101
    creating, 108-114
    default playlists, 108
    deleting, 116
    editing, 114-115
    limiting, 111
    listening to, 114
    live updating, 108
    naming, 113

software. *See also* freeware; shareware
    iPod software
        Macintosh format software, 257-261
        restoring, 205-207
        updating, 205-207
        viewing current version, 207
        Windows format software, 262-264
    iTunes software, 265-269
    licensing agreements, 256
    photo management software, 184-186, 195
    updates, 205-207, 257
    virus detection, 257

Software Update window (Macintosh), iTunes updates, 215

Solar Charger (Solio), 249

song tags (iTunes Music Library)
    Bit Rate, 80
    Channels, 80
    Date Modified, 80
    editing in, 85-87
    Encoded With, 81
    Format, 80
    ID3 Tag, 81
    Kind, 80
    Last Played, 80
    Play Count, 80
    Profile, 80
    Purchase By, Account Name, and FairPlay Version, 81

How can we make this index more useful? Email us at indexes@quepublishing.com

Sample Rate, 80
Size, 80
viewing in, 82-85
Where, 81

songs
album artwork
adding to songs, 92-94
finding, 92
viewing, 90-92
configuring options, Info window
(iTunes Music Library), 87-89
labeling, 85
playlists
location of, 103
naming, 103
smart playlists, 101, 108-115
standard playlists, 100-107
uses of, 101
rating via Content pane (iTunes
Music Library), 89-90
removing
from iPod, 133
from iPod shuffle, 139
*from iTunes Music Library,
64-66*
from iTunes Music Store, 66
title information, viewing (iPod
Now Playing screen), 148

**Sound Check setting (iPod),
163-164**

sound clips, 39

SoundDock (Bose), 230

**Source Information area (iTunes
window), determining iTunes
Music Library size, 121**

**Source list, determining iPod disk
capacity, 122**

speakers, 228
Cube Travel Speakers (Pacific Rim
Technologies), 230
Ezison personal speakers for iPod,
229
iBoom (DLO), 233
IceTune speakers (Macally), 232
IM3c speakers (Altec Lansing),
177
inMotion portable iPod speakers,
228
iPal Portable Speaker with Tuner
(Tivoli Audio), 230
iPod Groove Bag Triplet and Tote
(Dr. Bott), 229
iSpeaker Portable (Monster), 232

On Stage (JBL), 231
On Tour (JBL), 231-232
PocketParty Shuffle (PodGear),
234
Podwave (Macally), 233
SoundDock (Bose), 230
SRS-T55 Folding Travel speakers
(Sony), 229

splitters (audio), 227

**SportaPro Traditional Collapsible
headphones (Koss), 225**

**Sportsuit Convertible Case (MAR-
WARE), 251**

Sportsuit Safari (MARWARE), 251

**SRS-T55 Folding Travel speakers
(Sony), 229**

standard playlists, 100
adding songs to, 105-106
creating
empty playlists, 102
*playlists from selected songs,
103-104*
deleting, 107
listening to, 107
removing songs from, 106
setting play order, 106

stands (iPod), 246-247

**Start and Stop Time option (iTunes
Music Library), 88-89**

stickers (iPod), 255

storing
audio files in iTunes Music Library,
40
iPod disk storage capacity, determining, 121

subscribing to podcasts
Internet, 72
iTunes Music Store, 68-70
unsubscribing, 75

**Summary pane (Info window),
viewing song information, 84**

**Synchronize photos from check
box (iPod Photos tab), 185**

Synergy software (iTunes), 267

T

tattoos (iPod), 255

testing iPod battery, 204

**Timeline bar (iPod Now Playing
screen)**
Rating display, accessing, 149
rewinding/fast-forwarding in,
148-149

**Toggle iPod Battery Status soft-
ware (iPod), 260**

**track changes (iPod), maximizing
battery life, 201**

**Track Manager software (iTunes),
268**

**Track Number data field (iTunes
Music Library), 81**

transferring
audio files to iPod, 30-32
iTunes playlists to iPod, 32
music from iTunes Music Library to
iPod
*Automatically Update All
Songs and Playlists option,
123-128*
*Automatically Update Selected
Playlists Only option,
123-124, 128-130*
*Manually Manage Songs and
Playlists option, 124-125,
130*
photos
to computer via iPod, 195-196
to iPod, 184-189

TransPod FM (DLO), 239

**travel adapters, World Travel
Adapter Kit (Apple), 242**

TriPort headphones (Bose), 223

troubleshooting
iPod
battery, 204-205, 272-274
checking basics, 208
*exclamation point (!) problems,
209*
help websites, 210-211
iTunes connections, 210
resetting iPod, 208
restoring iPod, 209
iPod mini batteries, 275-276
iPod shuffle batteries, 276
iTunes
Macintosh support, 218-219
missing song files, 216-218
Windows PC support, 218
podcasts, 76

TuffWrapz (XtremeMac), 254

TuneCast II Mobile FM Transmitter (Belkin), 235

TuneDok Car Holder (Belkin), 238

TV
iPod slideshows, viewing on, 193
sound clips, 39

U

U2, iPod U2 Special Edition, 10

UE-10 Pro headphones (Ultimate Ears), 226

Universal Microphone Adapter (Belkin), 240

Unsubscribe button (Content pane), 75

Updater page (iPod), 205-207

updates
iPod
    playlists, 131-133
    software, 205-207
iPod shuffle
    Autofill tool, 136-137
    manual updates, 138
    removing songs, 139
    USB ports, 135
iTunes
    automatic updates, 214
    manual updates, 215
iTunes Music Library, iPod synchronization, 125
live updating (smart playlists), 108
software, 257

UR29 headphones (Koss), 225

USB 2 cable, 18
Dock connections, 25
iPod connections, 27-28
purchasing, 18

USB 2.0 4-Port Hubs (Belkin), 248

USB ports, updating iPod shuffle, 135

Use error correction when reading Audio CD option (Importing pane), 54

V

viewing
album artwork, 90-92
Browser (iTunes Music Library), 59

current iPod software version, 207
iTunes Music folder, 48
photos
    on iPod, 189-193
    on TV via iPod, 193
podcast episodes, 74-75
song tags in iTunes Music Library, 82-85

virus detection software, 257

Voice Recorder (Belkin), 239

voice recorders, 239-240

VoiceNote Voice Recorder (DLO), 240

voiding warranties (iPod hacking), 272

volume (sound)
iPod
    adjusting Volume bar, 147
    Sound Check setting, 163-164
iPod shuffle, adjusting in, 155-156
iTunes Music Library
    Equalizer Preset option, 88
    My Rating option, 88-90
    Relative Volume option, 87
    Start and Stop Time option, 88-89
    Volume Adjustment slider, 88

Volume bar (iPod), 147

vTunes screensaver software (iTunes), 269

W

warranties (iPod hacking), 272

WAV (Windows Waveform) audio file format, 39, 46, 58

Weather For Me software (iPod), 262

When new episodes are available drop-down list (Podcast tab), 67

Where song tags (iTunes Music Library), 81

WhiteCap screensaver software (iTunes), 269

Windows PC
iPod
    Dock connections, 25, 32-34
    FireWire cable connections, 28
    software, 20-22, 262-264
    USB 2 cable connections, 27-28

iPod shuffle connections, 26
iTunes
    manual updates, 215
    relocating Music folder, 47-49
    troubleshooting support, 218
iTunes Music Library, 58
Move to Recycle Bin, 65

WinniePod Updater software (iPod), 264

wireless headphones, 227

wireless remote controls (iPod)
iDirect Wireless Remote (DLO), 244
iJet Wireless RF Remote (ABT), 243

World Travel Adapter Kit (Apple), 242

X – Y – Z

XPlay software (iPod), 262

Year data field (iTunes Music Library), 81

How can we make this index more useful? Email us at indexes@quepublishing.com

What's on the CD-ROM

The companion CD-ROM contains selected utilities for the Mac and PC, such as Ejector, GNUPod, iPod Free File Sync, iPod.iTunes, LyriPod, Nicecast, Synergy, and Xplay.

Mac Installation Instructions

1. Insert the CD-ROM disc into your CD-ROM drive.
2. From the desktop, double-click on the iPod + iTunes Starter Kit icon.
3. Double-click **Start** and follow the on-screen instructions.

Windows Installation Instructions

1. Insert the CD-ROM disc into your CD-ROM drive.
2. From the Windows desktop, double-click on the My Computer icon.
3. Double-click on the icon representing your CD-ROM drive.
4. Double-click **start.exe** and follow the on-screen instructions.

note

If your version of Windows is set to hide known extensions, you may only see **start** instead of **start.exe**.

If you have the AutoPlay feature enabled, **start.exe** will be launched automatically whenever you insert the disc into your CD-ROM drive.

License Agreement

By opening this package, you are also agreeing to be bound by the following agreement:

You may not copy or redistribute the entire CD-ROM as a whole. Copying and redistribution of individual software programs on the CD-ROM is governed by terms set by individual copyright holders.

The installer and code from the author(s) are copyrighted by the publisher and the author(s). Individual programs and other items on the CD-ROM are copyrighted or are under an Open Source license by their various authors or other copyright holders.

This software is sold as-is without warranty of any kind, either expressed or implied, including but not limited to the implied warranties of merchantability and fitness for a particular purpose. Neither the publisher nor its dealers or distributors assumes any liability for any alleged or actual damages arising from the use of this program. (Some states do not allow for the exclusion of implied warranties, so the exclusion might not apply to you.)